STREETWISE®

HUMAN RESOURCES MANAGEMENT

STREETWISE®

HUMAN RESOURCES MANAGEMENT

All the Information You Need to
Manage Your Staff and Meet Your
Business Objectives

PATRICIA BUHLER, D.B.A., M.B.A.

adams media

A Streetwise® Publication.
Streetwise® is a registered trademark of F+W Publications, Inc.

Published by Adams Media, an F+W Publications Company
57 Littlefield Street, Avon, MA 02322. U.S.A.
www.adamsmedia.com

ISBN: 1-58062-699-8

Printed in the United States of America.

J I H G F E D

Library of Congress Cataloging-in-Publication Data
Buhler, Patricia M.
Streetwise human resources management / Patricia Buhler.
p.   cm.
Includes index.
ISBN 1-58062-699-8
1. Personnel management. I. Title: Human resources management. II. Title.
HF5549.B8736   2002
658.3–dc21   2002005580

Cover illustration by Eric Mueller.

This book is available at quantity discounts for bulk purchases.
For information, call 1-800-872-5627.

CONTENTS

PART I: HUMAN RESOURCES: A KEY ORGANIZATIONAL RESOURCE

PART II: STAFFING: THE RIGHT PEOPLE FOR THE RIGHT JOB

CONTENTS

PART III: MAXIMIZING EMPLOYEE PERFORMANCE

PART IV: MAINTAINING HUMAN RESOURCES

PART V: HUMAN RESOURCE TRENDS

CONTENTS

APPENDICES

Dedication

This book is dedicated to my students, colleagues, and administrators at Goldey-Beacom College. My students through the years have constantly provided the inspiration to teach others, many of my colleagues have been close friends, and the administrators have provided me support and encouragement—all of which have enabled this project to be completed. I am eternally grateful to each and every one of them.

Acknowledgments

I'd like to thank Jessica Faust of Bookends, Inc. for her continuous support in this project and Jill Alexander for the confidence she showed in me, and the guidance she provided in completing this book.

Introduction

Whether you are a human resource professional, a manager, or an individual exploring the topic of human resource management, this book is designed for you. Recognizing that the human resource management responsibilities are delegated throughout the organization–to all levels–each manager should have a more basic understanding of the functions of human resource management.

The five parts of this book each present an overview of related topics. Depending on your needs or your interest, it is possible to read *Streetwise® Human Resource Management* by selecting specific parts to read as appropriate.

Part 1 provides an overview of the context within which human resource management is performed. Read this part first if you are not familiar with the environment in which many of the human resource policies and decisions are made. Part 1 explores the role of human resources, the legal environment, and the skills that are necessary for effective human resource management.

Part 2 examines the staffing function of human resources. Getting the right people into the right jobs is certainly a tall order given today's environment. Part 2 examines the role of human resource planning and presents an overview of the recruitment, selection, and orientation process in staffing organizations.

Part 3 explores maximizing employee performance. Every organization is concerned with improving performance levels. Part 3 discusses the roles of training, motivating, and appraising the performance of developing employees. This section also examines the processes of job analysis and job design in maximizing employee performance.

Part 4 provides information on maintaining human resources. Part 4 examines the complex challenge of retaining employees in a dynamic environment and discusses the role of compensation programs in this endeavor.

Part 5 reviews human resource trends. Organizations must recognize the critical trends that are shaping the future. Some of the topics examined in Part 5 include downsizing, new organizational structures, privacy issues, and diversity.

PART I

Human Resources: A Key Organizational Resource

Human resources have become a key department for every organization. Increasing importance has been placed on the role of managing the work force today. Recognizing that it is the people who make a difference and who can be the source of the organization's competitive advantage, organizations are placing more emphasis on understanding how to manage this key resource better.

Chapter 1: Explore the environment within which human resource departments are operating.

Chapter 2: Examine the legal environment.

Chapter 3: Understand human resources' new role in response to today's environment.

Chapter 4: Discover the skills for effective human resource management.

Chapter 1

The Environment of Human Resources Today

The human resource management functions used to be performed exclusively by human resource professionals and staff personnel. Today, more of these functions have been delegated to managers and supervisors throughout the organization.

Consider the possibility that companies in the future will have human resource support positions located in each business unit. These individuals will be responsible for learning the business of that unit and advising their managers about human resource responsibilities. The ultimate responsibility for the human resource functions, however, will lie with the managers and supervisors. The human resource individual will simply be acting in a support role, which will enable the human resource function to truly support the achievement of that business unit's objectives.

> Human resources are the people (including their knowledge, skills, and abilities) within an organization who perform the actual work of the organization.

What Are Human Resources?

Human resources are the people (including their knowledge, skills, and abilities) within an organization who perform the actual work of the organization. Their efforts enable the organization to meet its objectives. The intellectual capital of each organization has been a growing focus in our highly competitive world.

Human resource management (generally referred to as HRM) is the effective use of an organization's human resources to improve its performance. This management is no small order; it takes great skill, ability, and practice.

HRM is one of the greatest challenges facing businesses today. The challenge is not just faced by human resource professionals; it is the responsibility of all managers throughout an organization. Management is the practice of getting things done through others. Only by effectively managing the firm's human resources will the goals and objectives be met.

Although all companies have access to the same technology and the same information, it is the people within each organization who make the difference in organizational performance. That is, human resources provide the foundation for the organization's competitive advantage. But the challenge remains: How can you get the most out of the work force and create a sustainable competitive advantage?

TIP

The evolution of the terminology from *personnel* to *human resources* communicates the role that people play as a crucial resource of an organization.

Each unit within every organization is responsible for addressing this challenge. Although the specific solutions may vary from organization to organization or unit to unit, the basics remain the same. A clear understanding of the basics of human resource management enables every manager to help build the company's competitive advantage through people.

A Historical Perspective

To understand and effectively manage human resources amid the challenges posed by today's environment, you must examine the history of human resource management. Today's perspective has evolved from the early approach to scientific management.

At the turn of the century (ca. 1895), Frederick Taylor conducted studies at Midvale Steel Works. Known as the father of scientific management, Taylor suggested that it was management's responsibility to develop the one best way to perform the job and then it was the employees' responsibility to perform the job in that one best way. (This approach has since been criticized because it allowed little room for the judgment or discretion of the individual worker.)

Taylor's premise was that management should systematically hire the appropriate workers for the job and then outline each detail of the job to be performed. In the case of the pig iron handlers at Midvale Steel Works, Taylor taught managers how to hire individuals best suited to the work. Then he observed the workers' performance to determine how the job could be performed most efficiently.

Workers were responsible for loading pig iron onto railway cars. Based on his observations, Taylor decided how the job should

Today's perspective has evolved from the early approach to scientific management.

Elton Mayo discovered the importance of the person in the workplace.

be performed. He determined how large the load of each man should be, the incline of the ramp to the railway car, and the length and frequency of breaks. The individual workers were allowed no discretion and no autonomy.

The shortcoming of this approach to managing people was quickly identified, and the Hawthorne Studies ushered in a new era of managing human resources. These studies, conducted at the Western Electric Hawthorne plant by Elton Mayo, ultimately brought to light the *human* element of managing human resources.

Elton Mayo discovered the importance of the person in the workplace. From 1927 to 1932, Mayo conducted research at the Western Electric plant in an effort to find solutions to the shortcomings of the scientific management era. Mayo's study highlighted the improved productivity gained by paying attention to workers (referred to as the Hawthorne effect) and the significant role social relationships played in the workplace.

TIP
The Hawthorne Studies actually included three experimental studies: an illumination experiment, a relay assembly room experiment, and a bank wiring group study. All three are collectively referred to as the Hawthorne Studies.

Mayo's work kicked off the human relations era, and since the studies' time, the human element has been considered in designing work. The contributions of scientific management cannot be disputed, but the emphasis on human relations contributed balance to the movement. Today's focus on the human element is seen in enriched jobs, increased empowerment, and participation in decision-making in the workplace.

The Challenge of Managing Human Resources in Today's Environment

Think of an organization as an open system, and its productivity as a transformation process. Inputs, or resources, are procured from the external environment. The resources go through a transformation process that results in outputs, or products. The resulting products are then absorbed into the external environment; that is, they are consumed.

For example, an automobile manufacturer procures resources: people from the local labor market and raw materials (such as steel, rubber, nuts, bolts, etc.) from suppliers. During the transformation process (in most cases, an assembly line), the resources are combined to produce the product: an automobile. For the organization to be successful, the automobiles must be absorbed into the external environment; that is, consumers must purchase them. This is an open system since the resources are acquired from the external environment, and the products are absorbed back into it.

The point, here, is that each organization must remember the impact of the external environment. In the case of human resources, the external environment becomes especially critical as organizations compete with each other for labor. Additionally, an organization's overall human resource function must be competitive to attract qualified applicants and then retain them.

Changing consumer tastes and expectations impact the output of the organization and produce a ripple effect throughout the company. Changing tastes affect the product (goods and services), which influences the choice of production methods and technology and affects the design of the jobs and the skills employees need to perform the actual work. That one small pebble will ultimately impact several human resource functions.

The world today is characterized by constant change occurring at an unprecedented pace. Nearly all companies operate in a dynamic environment. Some of the changes that characterize the world of business today include the following:

- Changing employee expectations
- Competition in a global arena
- Cultural and social diversity
- Emphasis on increased productivity
- Fall of the command-and-control manager
- Flatter organizations

> An organization's overall human resource function must be competitive to attract qualified applicants and then retain them.

- Focus on balancing work and nonwork issues
- Increasing impact of technology
- New organizational structures

Changing Employee Expectations

Today's employees (as a whole) value different things than the work force of a decade ago. Trying to manage employee expectations is further complicated by the fact that several generations are at work today, and most of them have different needs and want different things. For the most part, however, employees today expect to change jobs more frequently (every two to three years on average) and to change careers at least twice in their lifetime. Employees also expect to hold a challenging job with opportunities for growth and development.

TIP

Today's aging work force is comprised of several generations, each with a unique perspective of work and a different set of values. Veterans are those workers who entered the work force in the 1950s and early 1960s. They tend to be very loyal to their organization. The Boomers are those workers between forty and sixty years of age who are loyal to their careers. Generation Xers are between twenty-five and forty. Their concerns center around work/life issues. And those who are under twenty-five years of age are referred to as the Nexters; they place a high value on their financial success.

Human resource policies must address compensation and reward packages to meet employees' diverse and changing expectations. Even the design of jobs has become critical. As employees seek more challenges, some jobs must be redesigned to reduce monotony.

Competition in a Global Arena

Today's global economy has impacted the way all companies conduct business. Even firms operating exclusively in the domestic arena need to manage the influence of global competition. The influx of immigrants into the American work force has created marketing

> Employees today expect to change jobs more frequently (every two to three years on average) and to change careers at least twice in their lifetime.

and recruiting opportunities for firms while changing the demographics of the work force.

Companies must learn to manage diversity and to celebrate the differences among employees. Human resource management is responsible for hiring and supporting a diverse work force and needs to establish opportunities for advancement and mentoring programs.

Cultural and Social Diversity

Ever-increasing diversity is obvious in today's workplace. The white American male no longer dominates the business landscape. North American demographics have changed, and today's organization must respond to this diversity in both its work force and its client base, affecting all human resource functions.

The changing demographics of America demand that recruitment and selection policies address diversity and respond to the legal requirements. Organizations must also offer a wider variety of benefits and incentives. The key is to be flexible and avoid implementing "one size fits all" answers to everyone's needs. Different people have different needs, and companies must respond accordingly.

TIP
More companies are recognizing the need to support a diverse work force after hiring. Formal networks and support groups are in place for women and minorities, aimed at helping them learn how to climb the corporate ladder by networking with others—especially with those who have already made the climb.

> The changing demographics of America demand that recruitment and selection policies address diversity and respond to the legal requirements.

Companies must not only manage diversity but also celebrate the differences among employees. Care must be taken to hire a diverse work force and then to support that diversity by providing opportunities for advancement and by establishing mentoring programs.

Emphasis on Increased Productivity

The shrinking productivity gains of American businesses have threatened the nation's competitive standing in the global arena. Organizations in both the manufacturing and service industries have focused on how to increase productivity, which includes clearly identifying ways that human resources can produce more. The challenge is that increased productivity, or outputs, must often be accomplished with the same amount of, or even fewer, inputs—including people.

The driving force to increase productivity, however, is balanced by the need to contain costs and improve quality. That is, each organization wants its human resources to increase productivity without increasing costs or diminishing the quality of the goods or services produced. American businesses are responding to the challenge with improved human resource management. They are redesigning jobs for more efficient workflow and performance, and appraisals reflect these higher standards and expectations. Training and development programs at all levels are addressing the focus on quality as related to both performance and production.

Fall of the Command-and-Control Manager

With the demise of the command-and-control manager, supervisors use a different set of skills to get things done through others. Managers can no longer "direct" people to get things done. Now, strongly developed interpersonal skills have become critical. The legitimate, or literal, power inherent in any position within the organizational hierarchy is no longer of paramount importance.

With fewer management positions available in some organizations, new career paths have to be created. Training and development options must also consider the new skill sets that are necessary for employees' professional development. It takes more than just time and experience to be successful in these new environments.

> With fewer management positions available in some organizations, new career paths have to be created.

Flatter Organizations

With flatter organizations, people are asked to produce more using fewer resources. Employees are asked to fulfill a variety of ever-changing roles, taking on new responsibilities on a regular basis. The recent decade's layoffs have affected both management and blue-collar positions. No one seems exempt from corporate cuts.

Frequent reorganizations impact an organization's human resources in multiple ways. First, human resources and corporate leaders must develop and implement standard policies to address lay-offs. These policies need to set standards for everything from communicating the termination to the employee and other staff, to security issues and severance packages.

Second, those being laid off must be let go with dignity. Fair severance agreements may include transitional training, outplacement services, or extended benefits. Although layoffs may be the result of financial considerations—and these severance policies will cost money—such efforts will preserve the organization's reputation within the local community and maintain goodwill among both current and former employees.

Finally, care must be taken to address the survivors, those remaining with the organization after the downsizing. Loyalty and security are emotional factors that cannot be easily addressed with spreadsheets and memos. Through effective human resource management, an organization should be able to keep its staff positive and productive through difficult transitions.

Focus on Balancing Work and Nonwork Issues

Today's employees are demanding more time to balance all facets of their lives. With dual career couples in the workplace, more people need time away from the job to take care of family issues. Younger employees today also value time off to pursue other interests.

Employers of choice are meeting this challenge by being creative in the work alternatives they offer employees. Progressive organizations are providing opportunities for job sharing, telecommuting, and flexible scheduling. Incorporating floating holidays into the corporate calendar also enables employees to pick and choose which secondary holidays they will work in return for an alternate day off. Such flexibility provides an option for paid time off that almost everyone needs at some time or another.

Increasing Impact of Technology

Advanced technology and communications have altered workflow and productivity in all organizations. Even more important, technology

Through effective human resource management, an organization should be able to keep its staff positive and productive through difficult transitions.

has reshaped the way that people communicate with one another. This technology has also provided new alternative work arrangements.

Technology's greatest impact in the area of human resources has been on training and development. Companies today invest millions of dollars updating their employees' skills to keep pace with changing technology. Technological advancements have also influenced the recruitment and selection processes. Companies must hire a more skilled work force and redesign jobs to take advantage of this new technology.

Even the options for where the work is being performed are changing. People can become members of virtual teams and collaborate with others across the globe. In many cases, given today's telecommuting options, employees can choose to work from home or from a satellite office.

> Changing organizational structures are the direct result of a rapidly changing external environment and the global economy.

New Organizational Structures

Changing organizational structures are the direct result of a rapidly changing external environment and the global economy. More organizations are recognizing the importance of "sticking to the knitting" in the words of Thomas J. Peters and Robert H. Waterman Jr., authors of *In Search of Excellence* (Warner Books, 1988). That is, they identify their core competence—what they do bigger, better, faster than the competition—and then focus their efforts and resources on that one thing. These organizations can outsource all nonessential functions by developing strategic alliances with other firms to provide this support.

Outsourcing has changed the human resource landscape in many organizations. Some employees have been leased to other firms, some have become contract employees, and some have been laid off altogether as their functions are outsourced.

How Do Human Resources Assist the Organization?

Human resources are the organization's source of knowledge and information. In an information age, the knowledge that resides in the minds of an organization's work force has become critical. As employees leave one organization for a competitor, their knowledge goes with them, benefiting the new organization and handicapping the former.

People are indeed the cornerstone of every organization. Their ability to be responsive and flexible in a rapidly changing world impacts the success (or failure) of the entire organization. Only fluid, flexible organizations will survive in the twenty-first century. Without their *human* resources, organizations could not be successful. And without the knowledge of these people, organizations could not thrive in this information age in which knowledge has become king.

As organizations change, the traditional approaches to human resource management are being replaced by new approaches. Organizations must concentrate on building their employees' commitment and creating an environment that encourages cooperation among employees.

The need for flexible organizations reflects the increased empowerment of the work force. Employees closest to the work must be allowed to make decisions. The team approach to work is replacing the individualistic approach. Products arrive in the marketplace much faster as companies employ cross-functional teams in which employees from different functional areas work together, rather than in a linear fashion.

Human resource policies and programs will influence an organization's ability to create a competitive advantage. Effective human resource management provides a win/win situation: As employee satisfaction levels improve, an organization's performance levels increase. And high-performing organizations will continue to draw high-performing employees.

An organization can reap long-term rewards, including increased productivity, as a result of effectively managing its human resources. People are an investment. People who are given opportunities to grow and use their skills contribute to the success of their organization. The self-fulfilling investment becomes a critical spiral to success: As the organization enables its employees to meet their individual needs, the organization in turn will meet its goals. And so the cycle

> As organizations change, the traditional approaches to human resource management are being replaced by new approaches.

continues with employee satisfaction levels increasing and organizational performance improving.

Building High-Performance Organizations

More organizations are striving to become high-performance organizations, or HPOs. Such progressive organizations place a great deal of value on their human resources and provide opportunities for their employees to achieve their full potential. In this way, the organization benefits with superior performance and a sustainable competitive advantage.

People are truly indispensable in HPOs. High-performance organizations are comprised of five key components:

- Employee involvement
- Empowered work teams
- Integrated technology
- Organizational learning
- Total quality management

Power to the People

In an HPO, employees are highly involved in the decision-making process, especially when the decisions influence their own work. Employee participation improves both their satisfaction levels and their performance on the job. Similarly, empowered work teams (also known as self-directed work teams) are a critical component of high-performance organizations. Just as involvement improves satisfaction and performance on the individual level, empowerment encourages creativity and effective production with teams. Increased levels of autonomy in either scenario also increase employees' commitment.

The Learning Curve

Ongoing development and learning is just as important for an organization as it is for its individuals. The learning organization has

> Employee participation improves both their satisfaction levels and their performance on the job.

received a great deal of publicity as an example of how to adapt to changing environments. This kind of organization gathers information and then uses it to make appropriate internal changes in order to quickly and adeptly respond to changes in the marketplace.

Total quality management focuses on continuous improvement. Successful organizations have learned that they cannot continue to do things the same way they were done in the past just because the approach was successful. Beyond learning and adapting to a changing environment, HPOs must aggressively optimize their learning. Products need to remain innovative; training and development needs to focus on quality management at a corporate level; and employees throughout the organization must be responsible for the quality of their work.

High-performance organizations integrate technology across the organization. Technology is available to employees, providing them with current (and efficient) work tools to perform their jobs. HPOs must also offer appropriate training and support for new technology.

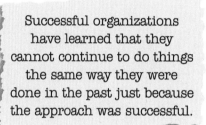

Successful organizations have learned that they cannot continue to do things the same way they were done in the past just because the approach was successful.

The Functions of Human Resources

To ensure that human resources are effectively managed while creating high-performance organizations, specific functions must be addressed. The primary functions of human resource management are the following:

- Recruitment and selection
- Human resource development
- Compensation and benefits
- Safety and health

Although the functions may seem independent, their alignment is critical for the effective performance of the organization. That is, all of the human resource functions must support one another and be sufficiently developed to ensure that the organization meets its overall corporate objectives.

> In order to make effective contributions to an organization, a talented individual must continuously update his or her skills.

Recruitment and Selection

The recruitment and selection of new employees is critical in building a high-performance organization. Only by identifying a qualified labor pool and then hiring the most qualified individuals can an organization meet its objectives. Without talented and knowledgeable individuals, no organization can achieve levels of high performance.

Human Resource Development

Hiring talented individuals is not enough. The benefits of hiring qualified people can be short-lived in today's constantly changing world. In order to make effective contributions to an organization, a talented individual must continuously update his or her skills. Without renewed and refreshed skills, the talented individual can become obsolete. Just as any other resource of the organization becomes obsolete without proper maintenance, so, too, do human resources.

There are two by-products of well-crafted employee development programs. First, employees tend to remain longer at organizations that provide opportunities for them to update their skills. Second, as employees' skills are updated, the organization is acquiring skills in-house to position itself for future challenges.

Compensation and Benefits

An effective compensation and benefits plan ensures that employees are rewarded appropriately for their contributions to an organization. Competitive compensation provides the incentive for continued good performance. Benefits plans today provide organizations with the opportunity to allow employees to select from a menu of benefits that best fit their needs. A flexible benefits plan responds to the challenges of supporting a diverse work force with varied needs.

Organizations should also use their compensation plans as a tool for recruiting talented individuals. Employees may remain with the organization for longer periods as the organization is recognized as an employer of choice.

Safety and Health

Organizations are responsible for creating a safe and healthful work environment. Many organizations, however, go beyond the letter of the law to ensure that their employees are more productive. Progressive companies have created wellness programs that focus on the prevention of illness. Many safety programs likewise emphasize the prevention of accidents with state-of-the-art facilities and equipment and advanced safety training.

Summary

Human resource management is challenged to meet the demands of today's dynamic environment. This environment has changed significantly with the impact of the global arena, changing demographics, technological developments, and legislation. Human resources can be the very source of an organization's competitive advantage if they are effectively managed. Human resource management has evolved from scientific management through the human relations movement in which people are truly valued. The move to high-performance organizations reflects today's increased emphasis on human resources as an indispensable asset that is also viewed as a long-term investment.

> Progressive companies have created wellness programs that focus on the prevention of illness.

For more information on this topic, visit our Web site at www.businesstown.com

The Legal Environment

I gnoring the legal aspect of human resources can result in substantial costs, through either financial losses or subtle yet real damage to a firm's reputation. Lawsuit settlements topping $14 million have been awarded in some cases. Today, individuals also run the risk of personal liability if they underestimate the power of the policies and procedures established in accordance with employment law.

Society in general has changed in its attitudes toward discrimination. Greater public awareness has brought less tolerance for the unfair treatment of employees, whether it's overt harassment or compensation disparities. In the 1960s, social movements started to address the progress of equality in the workplace. Although blatant discrimination has been curbed, the more subtle forms of discrimination continue to need attention.

> EEO impacts everyone, as proved by the large amount of legislation addressing EEO and the resulting litigation.

Encouraging Work Force Diversity

Equal employment opportunity (EEO) has been the focus of more attention in human resources during the past four decades than any other topic. EEO impacts everyone, as proved by the large amount of legislation addressing EEO and the resulting litigation.

Changing demographics in the American work force spurred this attention. As the work force ages, as more women enter the labor market, and as more diverse groups are represented, organizations are asked to ensure that equal employment opportunities exist for everyone. Meeting this ideal, however, has become an increasingly complex task.

Employers have responded with carefully crafted policies that address the appropriate points of major legislation, executive orders, fair employment practice laws, and the key rulings of court cases. The intent, of course, is to try to end discrimination and harassment in the workplace. (See Appendix A, page 305, for a sample corporate EEO policy.)

Major Legislation Impacting Human Resources

Every employee should be aware of the major legislation that impacts human resources. First, this knowledge will help the employee better understand the workplace; and second, on some level, the individual is responsible for his or her role and actions within the company. Employers, however, don't have the luxury of *should.* They must be aware of the laws that they are legislated to uphold.

TIP
Management's responsibility is to become educated in the law. Should violations occur, ignorance of the law is no excuse. The manager and the organization may still be held liable.

The Equal Pay Act of 1963

The Equal Pay Act of 1963 prohibits discrimination in compensation, benefits, and pensions based on gender bias. Males and females must be paid at equal rates for jobs that require the same levels of skill and effort. Exceptions can be made based on seniority but not based on gender. (Excerpts from the act appear in Appendix B, page 322)

Once inequalities are identified, the law is specific about the way remedies are to be made. If one gender is paid less than the other gender, the compensation of the lower-paid workers must be raised to the level of the higher-paid workers. For example, if female assembly line workers are paid less than their male counterparts, the pay of the male workers cannot be lowered to the level of the female workers. Instead, according to the Equal Pay Act of 1963, the wages of the females must be raised to the level of the male assembly line workers.

> Males and females must be paid at equal rates for jobs that require the same levels of skill and effort.

Title VII of the Civil Rights Act of 1964

Title VII of the Civil Rights Act of 1964 has provided the foundation for many of the human resource policies in organizations today. This legislation prohibits discrimination in employment on the basis of race, color, religion, sex, or national origin. Note that *employment* has been defined broadly to include more than simply hiring practices. Discrimination is prohibited in all phases of employment: promotion, training opportunities, termination, compensation, and benefits. (See Appendix B, page 323, for excerpts from the act.)

The Civil Rights Act also created the Equal Employment Opportunity Commission (EEOC) as its enforcement arm. The commission processes and investigates discrimination claims. The EEOC is an advocate of fairness, not only to the individual but to all employers subject to EEOC jurisdiction.

Limited exceptions to the act are permitted with a bona fide occupational qualification (BFOQ). A BFOQ enables a firm to discriminate when there are proven, reasonable necessities for the performance of the job that only certain candidates can meet. For example, an employer may refuse to hire a female as a male lead in a play. The employer, however, is responsible for demonstrating that the discriminatory practice (hiring a male) is a business necessity.

> The Age Discrimination in Employment Act (ADEA) prohibits discrimination based on age.

The Age Discrimination in Employment Act of 1967

Complaints of age discrimination account for nearly one-fifth of all discrimination charges now filed, which is understandable given the growing numbers of older workers in the labor market. There are now more than 75 million baby boomers in the United States, increasing the number of workers who are subject to age discrimination.

The Age Discrimination in Employment Act (ADEA) prohibits discrimination based on age. This legislation makes it illegal to discriminate against people forty years of age and older in any employment practice. (See Appendix B, page 315, for excerpts from the act.)

The Equal Employment Opportunity Act of 1972

The Equal Employment Opportunity Act of 1972 amended the Civil Rights Act as passed in 1964. This act broadened the enforcement capabilities of the Equal Employment Opportunity Commission. The legislation was also applied to a broader group of employers (including certain governments and educational institutions).

The Pregnancy Discrimination Act of 1978

The Pregnancy Discrimination Act of 1978 amended the Civil Rights Act of 1964 to include pregnancy. It is against the law to discriminate against a pregnant woman in any employment practice, including hiring, promotions, or terminations. An actress recently won a pregnancy discrimination suit when she was written out of her television show role after she became pregnant.

The Americans with Disabilities Act of 1990

The Americans with Disabilities Act of 1990 (ADA) delivered a real victory to people with disabilities in the work force. The law prohibits discrimination against individuals with either mental or physical disabilities and also protects individuals who are chronically ill. (See Appendix B, page 316, for excerpts from this act.)

The ADA specifically defines a disability as

> . . . a physical or mental impairment that substantially limits one or more of the major life activities, a record of such impairment, or being regarded as having such an impairment.

Unfortunately, this still leaves room for both interpretation and ambiguity. For example, there is a continuing debate about certain personality disorders.

The ADA requires employers to provide reasonable accommodations for the employment of people with disabilities; in other words, these accommodations should not cause undue hardship for the employer. Research has indicated that most reasonable accommodations cost less than $100 and might include minor adjustments such as allowing flexible work hours (to accommodate public transportation schedules), raising the level of a workstation, or widening doorways to accommodate a wheelchair.

> The law prohibits discrimination against individuals with either mental or physical disabilities and also protects individuals who are chronically ill.

The Civil Rights Act of 1991

The Civil Rights Act of 1991, an additional amendment to Title VII of the Civil Rights Act of 1964, addresses the damages that can be awarded in discrimination suits. The new legislation substantially relaxed limits on both compensatory and punitive damages that can be awarded to victims of intentional discrimination or harassment. The 1991 amendment also extended protection to employees of

United States–based companies when they are working abroad. (See Appendix B, page 321, for excerpts from the act.)

This act also established the Glass Ceiling Commission, which focuses on opportunities for advancement for women and minorities. The Glass Ceiling Commission addresses the under-representation of women and minorities in top management positions. The commission examines not only the opportunities available for women and minorities, but also the preparation they receive to be qualified for these positions.

This commission has highlighted some very important information, including one widespread misconception that women were leaving certain companies to start families. Only too late did many employers realize that their female employees left for positions with competitors who offered more advancement opportunities for women.

> The Glass Ceiling Commission addresses the under-representation of women and minorities in top management positions.

The Uniformed Services Employment and Reemployment Rights Act of 1994

The Uniformed Services Employment and Reemployment Rights Act passed in 1994 protects individuals who serve in the military for short periods. The legislation requires employers to allow these individuals to return to their jobs with the same seniority and benefits they previously enjoyed. The Veteran's Employment and Training Service, which falls under the Department of Labor, enforces this law.

TIP

Excerpts from the major legislation administered by the Equal Employment Opportunity Commission can be found in Appendix B. Managers must be familiar with the language and flavor of these laws.

State Fair Employment Practice Laws

Most states have enacted discrimination statutes. Employers must be aware of these laws as well; they are also referred to as *fair employment practices*. State laws can be more stringent than some federal legislation. Organizations should check with their state departments of labor to ensure that they are compliant with their state's fair employment practice laws.

Discrimination and Harassment

Discrimination and harassment refer to the unfair treatment of people in the work force. It is illegal for an organization (or its employees) to discriminate against individuals of a protected class in any phase of the employment process. It is also illegal for an organization (or its employees) to allow harassment of individual employees who are members of protected classes.

Discrimination

Discrimination is the process by which people are treated differently based solely on their differences. It is, however, illegal to discriminate against people in employment situations based on their race, color, religion, sex, or national origin. To successfully prove a charge of discrimination, an individual must demonstrate adverse impact or disparate impact.

Adverse Impact

Adverse impact occurs when, in employment practices, a protected class experiences a higher rejection rate than an unprotected class. This discrimination is alleged to be unintentional. Even though unintentional, it is still illegal and prohibited by law.

Disparate Impact

Disparate impact, on the other hand, is intentional discrimination. That is, the employer purposely discriminates against a protected class.

The Four-Fifths Rule

Adverse impact is demonstrated by employing the four-fifths rule. Here is how to determine adverse impact by the four-fifths rule:

1. Calculate the selection rate for the protected and unprotected classes. To calculate this rate, divide the total number of individuals selected from each class by the total number of applicants from each of those classes.
2. Determine the class with the highest selection rate.

> Discrimination is the process by which people are treated differently based solely on their differences.

3. Compare the selection rate for each of the other classes with the highest selection rate (identified in step 2). To find the comparison, divide the rate of selection for each class by the highest selection rate.
4. Finally, determine if the rate of selection for a class is 80 percent or less than the rate of selection for the highest class. If the selection rate for a protected class is less than 80 percent (or four-fifths) of an unprotected class, you've proved adverse impact.

For example:

	Caucasians	African-Americans
Applicants	200	100
Hires	50	10
Selection Rate	25%	10%

The selection rate of Caucasians is the highest. When the selection rate of African-Americans (10 percent) is divided by the selection rate of Caucasians (25 percent), adverse impact is proved since 10/25 is two-fifths or 40 percent. This is significantly below the 80 percent mark of the four-fifths rule.

Harassment

There are two types of sexual harassment. Known as *quid pro quo*, the first type usually involves unwelcome advances of a sexual nature, or requests for sexual favors, in exchange for employment. For example, if a male manager suggests that a female subordinate can receive a desired promotion if she dates him, the male manager is guilty of sexual harassment. This is generally what most people think of when they hear the term *sexual harassment*.

The creation of a hostile work environment is the second type of sexual harassment. In such instances, conduct of a sexual nature interferes with another's ability to perform his or her job. A hostile environment is just as serious as *quid pro quo* and is actually more prevalent in the workplace, yet it is not always easily

Quid pro quo usually involves unwelcome advances of a sexual nature, or requests for sexual favors, in exchange for employment.

recognized. Organizations, then, have a responsibility to communicate their policy on all forms of sexual harassment to their employees. Failure to communicate, and enforce, such policies can leave the company vulnerable to legal action.

Creating a sexual harassment policy is one of the most effective steps an organization can take to protect itself. To create a more effective policy, consider the following:

- Create a policy that is comprehensive, then communicate it to all organizational members—managers and employees alike. Ensure that the policy is written.

- Conduct regular training on sexual harassment to ensure that all employees understand how they can help create a work environment that is free of sexual harassment. Training should include clear examples of inappropriate behavior that is considered sexual harassment to help employees distinguish between appropriate and inappropriate behavior.

- Put a complaint procedure in place. Each employee must understand how to file a complaint and how charges will be investigated. The complaint procedures must be widely distributed throughout the organization. Review complaint procedures (for any type of discrimination or harassment) during the new employee orientation process.

- Handle investigations immediately, and conduct them with sensitivity and objectivity. Timely investigations communicate the severity of the offense. Handle the complaint with confidentiality to convey the sensitive nature of the topic. Maintaining confidentiality also ensures the protection of those who are bringing the charges.

- Apply immediate, consistent discipline for infractions. Discipline employees across all organizational levels in the same way. There can be no favoritism shown in the administration of this policy.

See Appendix A, page 306, for a sample sexual harassment policy

> Creating a sexual harassment policy is one of the most effective steps an organization can take to protect itself.

The Equal Employment Opportunity Commission: Enforcement

The EEOC is responsible for ensuring that employers comply with the Civil Rights Act. In addition to issuing guidelines, the EEOC is the administrative agency that investigates charges of discrimination. The complaint procedure is as follows:

- The complaint must be filed within 180 days of the discriminatory incident. (This may be accomplished with a state agency or the EEOC.)

- If grounds are found after an initial interview, a charge is filed. The employer must be notified within ten days.

- An information-gathering conference is held with the employer and the complainant. The complainant receives a right-to-sue letter or a suit is filed in federal district court.

TIP

State and local agencies addressing EEO through fair employment practice laws take precedence over the EEOC when filing complaints. That is, complaints begin with the local or state agency and then may be moved to the federal level with the EEOC.

> The EEOC is responsible for ensuring that employers comply with the Civil Rights Act.

Affirmative Action: A Remedy for Past Discrimination

Affirmative action is an opportunity for organizations to remedy past discrimination. By analyzing the composition of their work force, employers may develop action plans to create a more balanced work force that reflects the local labor market.

Affirmative action plans can be either mandated or voluntary. A company may be required to implement an affirmative action plan if it is found guilty of discrimination. Some companies may analyze the labor market and determine that they need to implement their own action plan to "correct" the composition of their work force.

The need for affirmative action is a subject of debate throughout the United States. Proponents of affirmative action suggest that the programs have not achieved everything that they needed to, meaning that discrimination and injustices still exist. Interestingly, opponents argue the same point: affirmative action plans have not abolished discrimination. In addition, the ultimate goal of affirmative action—to assimilate protected classes into organizations—has not been achieved.

Beyond the theoretical debate, there are issues that arise from the individuals directly affected by affirmative action. Individuals in protected classes have been perceived as undeserving of their positions, and individuals in unprotected classes may feel the effects of reverse discrimination. Two people may be equally qualified, yet the unprotected individual can be passed over in favor of a member of a protected class.

The Rights of Employees

The issue of employee rights is being heavily debated today. There are basic rights that each employer must protect for every employee. The laws and courts have clarified some rights, but the extent of others is still under discussion.

Clearly Defined Rights

Employment-at-will allows either an employer *or* an employee to terminate the employment relationship without providing either notice or reason. Remember, this is both the employer's *and* the employee's right. Employment-at-will, however, does not allow an employer to discriminate or to wrongfully discharge an employee.

The Workers' Adjustment Retraining and Notification Act, known as the WARN Act, gives employees (and their communities) *the right to be notified of plant closings.* Organizations that employ more than 100 people must give their workers sixty days' notice.

> Two people may be equally qualified, yet the unprotected individual can be passed over in favor of a member of a protected class.

> Explicitly stating the rights of employees and the rights of the company can improve the company's legal position if charges are brought against the firm.

Employees also have *the right to see their personnel files*. The degree of access to the file will vary by state. Employees are also granted *the right to due process*. That is, each employee has the right to be heard if he or she is involved in a disciplinary process. When accused of an infraction of the organization's rules, the employee has the right to present his or her side of the issue. In most companies, this is accomplished through a process of appeal outlined in the employee handbook.

TIP

Organizations should address employee rights in the employee handbook. Explicitly stating the rights of employees and the rights of the company can improve the company's legal position if charges are brought against the firm.

. . . and the Not-so-Clear

In the workplace, emphasis has been placed on privacy rights; the balance has shifted in favor of the workers. Employees are guaranteed fair treatment from their employers and have the right to communication within the organization.

Employers walk a fine line in protecting the rights of their employees. Companies are required to provide a safe and healthful workplace for everyone, but doing so may infringe on the privacy rights of some employees. The need to conduct drug tests to ensure a safe workplace has been questioned, and state legislation is addressing the issue nationwide—without any successful resolution.

Privacy rights are not as clear when it comes to defining what other things employees are entitled to. Every day, the individual's autonomy in the American workplace is challenged. Employees' work performance and movements are monitored; their bodies and workstations are searched; and they are frequently tested for drugs. How much surveillance should be conducted, and where should it be done?

Businesses have conducted employee surveillances to protect against costly theft. Searches of employee work areas may reduce internal theft. When there is probable cause, employees are required to comply with the search. To ensure that employee rights are not violated during searches, employers should consider the following:

- Develop and distribute a policy on searches. Outline probable causes and clearly define the consequences for failure to comply with a search.

- Implement the policy throughout the organization. Treat all organizational levels the same. Consistent treatment is critical for the legal protection of the firm.

- Obtain the employee's consent before the search and conduct the search discreetly and in private to avoid unnecessary embarrassment.

More progressive employers grant additional rights to their employees. These include the right to know what is expected of them on the job, the right to fair management, and the right to progressive and objective discipline.

Employers Have Rights, Too

Employers have the right to monitor their employees' e-mail and voice mail. Although many employees are fighting this issue, the employers' need to know is winning the battle. E-mail messages are copied and stored (even when employees think they have deleted them). Should an employee choose to take legal action over this issue, the employer's right to monitor e-mail and voice mail will be supported if a clear corporate policy has been consistently distributed to all employees. E-mail and voice mail policies should address the following points:

- The method of monitoring the voice mail and e-mail, and who will do it. Be clear that employees do not have privacy rights in these messages.

- The "proper" use of e-mail and voice mail for business purposes. Communicate clearly the extent of personal use

> Obtain the employee's consent before the search and conduct the search discreetly and in private to avoid unnecessary embarrassment.

allowed, if any. Most companies make an explicit statement that all e-mails are the property of the company.

- The consequences of violating the policy. The company must abide by its policy and address violations in a timely and consistent manner.

The purpose of having these kinds of policies is to ensure that employees and employers alike are aware of the same ground rules. Only by clearly defining what is acceptable (or unacceptable) can an employer protect itself and its assets, including other staff, from employee violations or legal repercussions.

> Only by clearly defining what is acceptable (or unacceptable) can an employer protect itself and its assets, including other staff, from employee violations or legal repercussions.

Responsibilities of Organizations Today

Ignorance of the law is no excuse. Therefore, companies are responsible for obeying appropriate legislation and for communicating these laws to their employees. If a manager violates a law, the organization is responsible for that manager's action.

Our society increasingly expects organizations to be socially responsible. In other words, they are expected to be proactive, to anticipate and prevent potential legal infractions and violations. They are responsible for ensuring that their employees uphold the ethical standards of the organization, the industry, and even of society itself.

Organizations are also responsible for preventing disciplinary problems and for taking corrective action when necessary. In accordance with due process, implementing corrective action requires careful and thorough documentation of inappropriate behavior, and all efforts to correct it.

Formal disciplinary action, however, requires that organizations have set and communicated fair rules for their employees. If corporate policies and positions are clearly, publicly, and frequently communicated, employees should know what is expected of them and what the consequences of violating those rules are.

To ensure the effectiveness of setting rules, consider the following:

- Communicate the rules to all employees, preferably in writing. Obtain a signed receipt from each employee, indicating his or her acknowledgement and understanding of the particular document. If possible, provide justification for and the reasoning behind the rules. It may be easier for employees to adhere to corporate positions if they understand the reasons behind them.

- Review and revise rules and policies regularly to ensure their relevance. Keeping out-of-date and irrelevant rules on the books can be de-motivating and demoralizing. In addition, it can diminish the importance of adhering to other, more appropriate rules.

- Keep rules business related, not whimsical. Policies, guidelines, and rules should be based on sound business practices that address productivity, safety, ethics, and performance.

Organizations are responsible for treating their employees with dignity and respect. Courtesy may get lost in the day-to-day shuffle. Managers and supervisors should be reminded that employees are not replaceable commodities. Rather, they are a valued resource that enables the organization to meet its strategic objectives.

> Policies, guidelines, and rules should be based on sound business practices that address productivity, safety, ethics, and performance.

TIP

Ensure that each employee signs a receipt for the employee manual. Place the signed receipt in the employee's personnel file. If the appropriate policies are explicitly stated in the handbook and the signed receipts are on file, the company has protected itself to a large extent, legally speaking. Without proof of an employee's knowledge of policies, the company has a more difficult time defending itself in legal battles..

Summary

It is no longer enough for just the human resource department to understand the legal environment within which all businesses operate. Now, managers throughout an organization must have a solid understanding of the legislation that impacts employment practices. Organizations *and* their representatives (such as managers) may be held accountable for illegal acts committed in the workplace, even if the individuals were ignorant of the law. The human resource department has to ensure that all managers are appropriately educated about legal requirements.

> Managers throughout an organization must have a solid understanding of the legislation that impacts employment practices.

Streetwise Advice

- **Age discrimination has also grown increasingly expensive for organizations**. Settlements for age discrimination cases are among the highest awards of all discrimination cases.

- **More progressive organizations are actively recruiting older workers, especially those who have already retired.** Several proactive fast-food giants have sought out retired individuals to return to the work force. These companies are seeking new talent pools to fill entry-level positions.

- **Try *www.llr.cornell.edu/library/e-archie/gov-reports/ glassceiling***. This Web site gives additional information on the glass ceiling. The Glass Ceiling Commission reports are posted, along with discussions concerning invisible barriers and recommendations for managing them.

- The Americans with Disabilities Act was passed to help combat discrimination that denied employment opportunities to more than 12 million people with disabilities in the work force. **These workers represented an untapped labor pool of talented individuals.**

- Some conditions not defined as a disability by the Americans with Disabilities Act include obesity, substance abuse, alcoholism, and depression.

- Many conditions that fall within the aegis of discrimination are still being debated. **For example, although AIDS is considered a disability under the ADA, you cannot withdraw an employment offer if a medical examination reveals the applicant has AIDS.**

- Although women file the majority of sexual harassment cases, the number of claims by men is now increasing. **Some of these claims involve same-sex harassment, a growing area of litigation.**

- Ensuring compliance with employment legislation is an ongoing task, especially given the evolving legal environment. **It is a good idea to consult with your firm's attorney and review procedures regularly. Also consider engaging an outside law firm to review your policies and procedures for compliance. An outside consult, or legal audit, will provide an objective and current assessment of your human resource policies in light of the legal environment.**

> Although women file the majority of sexual harassment cases, the number of claims by men is now increasing.

For more information on this topic, visit our Web site at www.businesstown.com

The New Role of Human Resources

A human resource department must be responsive to both internal organizational changes and external changes in the industry or marketplace. In an effort to build and maintain a fast, agile company, the department must also be prepared to shift gears at a moment's notice. By partnering with line managers, the human resource department can also help develop policies and procedures that support the company's business objectives.

The strategic transformation of an organization begins with the transformation of the human resource department and its role within the organization. Today's human resource department must coordinate hiring, training, and maintaining the firm's intellectual capital while meeting the challenges of a changing business environment.

Know Your Roots

To understanding any transition, you must have some sense of history. The evolution of human resource management (HRM) is no different. The human story is one of struggle and change. Over time, people's desires and needs change. Technological innovations, developed in response to these changing needs, impact industry and the climate in which business is conducted. It only makes sense, then, that human resource management has had to remain flexible to bridge the gap between the employee and the company.

From There to Here

From the craft system, to scientific management, to the human relations movement, human resource management has evolved to its current function. During the seventeenth and eighteenth centuries, the craft system thrived on customized work performed by craftsmen. An apprentice would work with a craftsman to learn a particular skill or trade. There was no need for an elaborate system of managing human resources for this small-scale business (usually comprised of one or two workers).

With the Industrial Revolution, the factory became the popular means of producing goods. With a focus on increasing productivity, the scientific management movement was developed to respond to a

> Today's human resource department must coordinate hiring, training, and maintaining the firm's intellectual capital while meeting the challenges of a changing business environment.

larger, more centralized work force. Industrial engineers conducted time and motion studies to identify the one best way to work. Workers were expected (with virtually no input) to perform the job in that one best way.

In response to this lack of consideration for the human element, the human relations movement emerged. The Hawthorne Studies (see Chapter 1) impressed upon managers the need to take into account the individual in the workplace. The effects of the work environment and the managerial approach on productivity proved that workers produce more when they are treated well.

Through the years, organizations have responded to, and been shaped by, the changes in their external environment. Changes in technology, globalization, increasing diversity, and advanced communication have brought human resource departments to where they are today. It's a giant leap from the early years, when human resource departments were known as personnel departments, and the emphasis was on record keeping.

Once again in response to changes in the external environment, today's organizations use the human resource function for more than simple record-keeping functions. Most executives believe that effective use of human resources will result in gains in productivity that will lead to improved performance of the company as a whole.

A Changing Environment

Human resources may be the one area in every organization that has experienced the greatest change in the past twenty years. This evolution has been driven by the globalization of business, changing demographics, a trend toward cost containment, integration of advanced technology, increased legislation, and the need to align the HRM with the firm's strategic objectives.

Today, the worldwide nature of business impacts virtually all organizations. Competing in new markets brings growing challenges in managing the human resources needed to support international operations. The human resource department must consider laws and cultures of other countries, compensation of expatriate managers (U.S. citizens who work abroad), work practices abroad, and training

> Changes in technology, globalization, increasing diversity, and advanced communication have brought human resource departments to where they are today.

programs. Due to increasing competition, organizations have been pressured to cut costs and improve productivity. Labor costs are often an organization's greatest costs, so the most popular cost-cutting strategy has been to downsize. This strategy presents a real challenge for human resource departments to manage. The most critical elements include severance packages, outplacement programs, reassignment or retraining, and motivation of the remaining employees.

Changing demographics have created a more diverse work force than ever before. A variety of legislation has been passed to protect the equal employment opportunities of many groups, and organizations must develop policies and procedures to comply with these laws. The challenge of managing a diverse work force, however, also presents opportunities for competitive advantages in the marketplace.

> By leveraging its work force diversity, a company can gain valuable insight into other markets.

TIP

By leveraging its work force diversity, a company can gain valuable insight into other markets. For example, employees representing diverse populations understand the best ways to market products and services to these groups, and can provide insight into more effective advertising campaigns to reach these markets.

Not only has technology changed the way that work is performed, it has also enabled human resource departments to become more efficient. Computers facilitate human resource planning, database management, and development of sophisticated information systems. Administrative functions such as payroll and benefits are computerized, and even the hiring process uses technology to streamline operations. Training, whether in the form of computer skills training or computer-based training, has reaped the benefits of technology's impact on business groups.

Legislation has also influenced nearly every aspect of the employment relationship. Several major court cases have impacted employment with regard to EEO, wages, health benefits, training, and immigration. To ensure compliance with the law, the human resource department must continue to monitor any legal cases that provide interpretation of relevant legislation.

The human resource department–like all other functional areas–must be closely aligned with corporate strategic objectives. This alignment is crucial if the HRM is to be instrumental in helping the firm achieve its overall objectives.

The Strategic Approach to Human Resource Management

Progressive organizations today are adopting a more strategic approach to HRM. The strategic approach has long been the norm in several other functional business areas, but only recently have large numbers of firms started using it in their human resource departments. On the surface, strategic HRM may seem no different than the traditional approach, but in reality there are significant differences.

The traditional approach to human resources focused on record-keeping and administrative tasks. The department was the area that maintained employee records, including data on pay, benefits, and the jobs performed. In many cases, the department was not perceived as adding value to the firm. This perception kept human resources isolated from the actual business of the organization. In many cases, the department had little knowledge of the firm's day-to-day business.

Human Resources as a Business Group

The strategic approach to human resource management encourages the department to interact with the company's other functional areas. This new department plays a major role in helping the organization meet its strategic objectives by trying to determine how human resources can be used more effectively to improve the company's competitive position.

All human resource functions must complement one another. To achieve this goal, department practices must be consistent and they must be aligned with the corporate business strategy. Since the human resource department provides internal services to line managers throughout the company, it must look at all programs in the context of the "big picture."

> The traditional approach to human resources focused on record-keeping and administrative tasks.

For example, if a firm is committed to hiring large numbers of entry-level employees (with lower skill levels) for the information technology area, the training function must be in place to support the recruitment function. Similarly, if a company is in the process of downsizing, the compensation and benefits functions need to have both outplacement options for terminated employees and retention programs to keep those still on staff.

A human resource department has a critical partnership with line managers in the strategic approach. The partnership ensures that a given division or business function is in line with broader corporate goals and has the support it needs to help achieve them. Even more important, the partnership ensures that human resource professionals know and understand the business of the organization and can contribute to its operation.

> A human resource department has a critical partnership with line managers in the strategic approach.

TIP

More organizations are relocating human resource staff to the business unit they support. Location within the unit enables these staff to be perceived as partners of the line managers (and of the other members of the business unit). A human resource presence in a business group shows a united corporate front, expedites assistance (a logistical benefit), and facilitates the human resource professionals' understanding of the business unit they support.

Keeping Score

Under the new model, the human resource department must measure human resource contributions and emphasize its contributions to the corporation's bottom line. The department is held accountable, as are all other functional areas, which helps bolster its credibility. Human resource functions are critical to the operation of the business, and the department must be willing and able to prove it. The strategic approach to human resources takes into account the external environment, including the competition and the labor market. If the human resource department concentrates solely on the internal environment and fails to track trends in the marketplace, it will leave the firm in a vulnerable position. By monitoring external factors, the human resource department will be able to identify threats as well as opportunities.

The competition and the labor market are two external elements that the strategic approach monitors. Competitors' actions will impact what the organization should be doing. Some industries are characterized by moves and countermoves as organizations respond to each other's strategies. The labor market also provides valuable information concerning who will be available, including what skill sets these individuals are likely to possess.

Strategic human resource management takes a long-term approach. The planning horizon should extend at least five to ten years. Planning just one year out is no longer sufficient, because the strategic approach requires focusing on the future and preparing for it.

TIP

The suggested planning horizons have changed with the rapidly changing environments. The short term is now considered about one year. Depending on the industry, it may be somewhat longer. The intermediate term extends from one to five years (at a minimum). And the long term ranges from five to twenty-five years. The length of these planning horizons really depends on the industry and the time required to develop products for market.

The strategic approach to human resource management also takes into account all employees of the organization. Gone are the days of the traditional approach when the personnel department focused primarily on the hourly employees and their paperwork.

The Transition to Strategic Human Resource Management

The strategic transformation of a corporation begins with its employees and their skills. It is important to identify the skills that will be needed throughout the organization in order to effect this transformation. Human resource professionals can act as critical change

> Strategic human resource management takes a long-term approach. The planning horizon should extend at least five to ten years.

agents in this process, but they will need new skills in order to implement the strategic approach in their department.

The transition may require a restructuring of the human resource department. A centralized team approach for cost efficiencies is valuable, especially in compensation and human resource information systems (HRIS). Business units, however, should be decentralized. The key is to know what to centralize and what to decentralize; both must be balanced to meet the strategic goals of the firm.

Transforming the human resource department to a strategic approach requires a renewed focus on communication. Information must be shared throughout the organization, especially to ensure the alignment of strategies and objectives. Part of this communication involves speaking the language of the business, not just the language and terminology of human resources. This ability to communicate demonstrates that human resource professionals are knowledgeable about the business of the firm.

The department must also focus on both the present and the future. That is, human resource professionals must use strategic thinking, which includes focusing on the customer. They must recognize and respond both to internal customers, such as line managers, and to corporate customers. The department's transition to a strategic approach is only possible if the staff is creative. They must rethink everything the department does and the way it is done, and they must adopt new methods of accomplishing their goals. The future should not be an extension of the past; it should be a radically new place. This approach must take into account the firm's internal environment as well as the external environment within which it operates.

Human resource professionals must also be efficient administrators, acting as role models for the rest of the firm. Improving their efficiency will open up more time for the human resource staff to engage in other strategic activities.

Corporate-, Business-, and Functional-Level Strategies

Strategies are found on three levels within the organization. The corporate-level strategy is the firm's overall strategy. It is supported

> Transforming the human resource department to a strategic approach requires a renewed focus on communication.

by the business-level strategies. Finally, each functional area develops its own strategy to support the other two.

In smaller organizations, there may only be a corporate-level strategy and the functional-level strategies. If the organization has only one product or service line and operates in only one industry, a business-level strategy is the same as the corporate-level strategy. The two strategies, however, still must be aligned to achieve optimum performance levels.

Corporate-Level Strategy

There are three corporate-level strategies:

- Growth
- Retrenchment
- Stability

Growth is the most popular of the three since it is generally associated with success. A growth strategy, which results in the firm's expansion, can be achieved in a number of ways. For example, growth can be achieved through concentration or diversification. Concentric growth is when the firm expands by adding related products and services. The Limited Stores employed concentric growth by acquiring Lane Bryant and Victoria's Secret and by developing Limited, Too. Concentric growth enables a firm to expand on existing synergies or core competencies. In the case of the Limited, the core competency was specialty retailing. The human resource strategy focused on hiring and training individuals to build on this competitive advantage.

Diversified growth is when the firm expands by adding products and services that are unrelated to its current offerings. Diversification is often used to grow the firm by spreading risk. It does, however, require hiring employees to support several different types of businesses. The 3M Company is a conglomerate that has grown through diversification.

As more organizations consider value chain analysis, they are using backward and forward integration to achieve growth by examining individual activities and their linkages. That is, these companies are moving into the businesses of suppliers that provided them

> Diversified growth is when the firm expands by adding products and services that are unrelated to its current offerings.

upstream or downstream services or products. For example, McDonald's has engaged in backward integration in some foreign nations to ensure that supplies essential to its operation are available. McDonald's has purchased potato farms to ensure that enough potatoes are available to make French fries.

Some apparel firms have used backward integration as a growth strategy as well. While still primarily engaging in the manufacture and sale of apparel to specialty or department stores, more firms are moving into retail and outlet operations to sell their own goods. Once again, however, human resources must make sure that the appropriate talent is available to support this growth in whichever direction it's headed.

Retrenchment has also become a popular strategy for organizations in the past few decades. Also know as *turnaround*, this strategy is used when the firm needs to reassess its operations, especially when its performance has been lackluster. Often a change is needed to correct the company's efficiency and effectiveness.

Retrenchment strategies include downsizing, liquidation, or bankruptcy. Downsizing is used to cut back on operations, focusing especially on containing costs. Liquidation and bankruptcy tend to be more extreme strategies.

> Downsizing is used to cut back on operations, focusing especially on containing costs.

TIP

Some top-level executives are specialists in implementing specific corporate-level strategies. These executives move from organization to organization, selling their skills to the highest bidder in the hopes of repeating past successes. Chainsaw Al Dunlap was a well-known turnaround specialist. The Scott Paper Company was one of his more publicized strategic endeavors.

Stability is a temporary strategy. It is a decision to maintain the status quo. With the world constantly changing, an organization cannot remain in a holding position for long; or it will fall quickly behind. This strategy is used after exceptional growth or perhaps after downsizing. The organization is able to regroup by keeping things as they are while planning the next strategy.

Stability is also used when events are changing rapidly in the external environment. Rather than committing to a strategy, the organization may decide to simply wait to see what happens. This temporary holding strategy puts the firm in a better position to craft an effective approach once external impacts are better understood.

Business-Level Strategy

The business-level strategy is found at the business-unit level. The plan focuses on achieving an improved competitive position for the unit's products or services. The four major business-level strategies include:

- Cost leadership
- Differentiation
- Cost focus
- Differentiation focus

Business units that target the mass market with low prices use the *cost leadership* strategy. Costs are reduced within the firm in order to offer low prices to the consumer. These cost reductions may be the result of gathering experience in the market, controlling overhead expenses, containing costs in the sales force, or buying less advertising, to name just a few. Wal-Mart has successfully employed a cost leadership strategy in its stores.

Differentiation also targets the mass market (trying to appeal to the majority of the market). Instead of offering low prices, however, organizations create a unique brand or image for their product, which customers are willing to pay a premium for. Walt Disney and Mercedes-Benz have implemented successful differentiation strategies.

The *cost focus* strategy positions the organization to compete based on low cost, but it targets a specific market niche rather than the mass market. A regional food store competing on lowest cost (perhaps through the use of self-service check-out) is an example of this strategy.

In a similar manner, the *differentiation focus* strategy targets only a part of the market. This strategy, however, uses differentiation rather than cost to compete in this smaller niche market. The firm

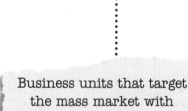

Business units that target the mass market with low prices use the *cost leadership* strategy.

targets a niche market and creates a unique image or brand to appeal to that market's needs. The health food section and brand names in your local grocery store chain are examples of regional retailers using a differentiation focus strategy.

Functional-Level Strategy

Functional-level strategies are put into place to make sure that a proper alignment exists between the firm's functional areas and the corporate and business levels. These strategies ensure that organizational resources, such as properly trained employees or finances and physical resources, are available to implement the overall corporate strategy. The primary concern here is to maximize the productivity of the resources. The common functions of most organizations include marketing, human resources, finance, and operations. Some organizations may have additional functional areas such as research and development (depending on their business).

Marketing strategies focus on the prices of products and services, the sale of these products and services, and how they will be distributed. These strategies may use market development to capture a bigger market share. Product development strategies center on developing new produces for existing markets or for new markets. Charging more for a product when it's new and unique or selling it at a lower price to jump-start market penetration are examples of pricing strategies.

Financial functional strategies focus on getting the needed funds to support the firm's operations. These strategies determine how capital will be raised for the firm, taking into account the balance of current and long-term investments. For public companies, the distribution of dividends is also part of the strategy.

The operations strategies identify how to create or develop the firm's product or service. In the case of products, many manufacturing decisions, such as developing the process and identifying the location of factories, must be made.

Aligning the Strategies

For maximum effectiveness, the corporate-, business-, and functional-level strategies must be closely aligned; this is often referred to

> Marketing strategies focus on the prices of products and services, the sale of these products and services, and how they will be distributed.

as the *hierarchy of strategy*. As you would imagine, the corporate-level strategy acts as the umbrella strategy for the entire firm.

Strategy may be crafted from the bottom-up or from the top-down. In other words, the corporate-level strategy may drive the business- and functional-level strategies, or vice versa. For example, many organizations still like to use an executive-level strategic planning forum to develop corporate-level strategy. This strategy then drives the development of the business-level strategy and the functional-level strategy after that.

Integrating All Functions of Human Resources

Once the human resource strategy is aligned with the corporate- and business-level strategies, then all of the department's functions must be integrated as well. A firm's human resources must be carefully integrated into its strategic decision-making. A strategy can only be implemented if the appropriate human resources are available to support it. For instance, if a firm formulates a strategy to grow through diversification into printing, qualified employees must be available (or the human resource department must be able to acquire that talent) to successfully implement the strategy.

The department's functions include hiring, training, compensation, safety, and administration. All of these functions must be integrated before they can be aligned with business- and corporate-level strategies. That is, each function must support the achievements of the others.

Hiring includes the recruitment, selection, and orientation of new employees. This is a critical function to align with other human resource functions. The firm's compensation package must be aligned with recruitment efforts so that competitive wages can be paid to attract the talented people the firm needs.

Training must then be provided to the new hires. The training needs are determined by the skills of the people hired, the skills required for the new position, and the overall corporate strategy. For example, a firm that is expanding into a new business must plan to provide training in new skill areas to compete in that market.

> Once the human resource strategy is aligned with the corporate- and business-level strategies, then all of the department's functions must be integrated as well.

Human resource departments must develop compensation policies, conduct surveys of rates, and keep adjustments up-to-date. The compensation package must appropriately reward employees for their work; it is a motivational tool to encourage high performance levels. The total compensation package (including benefits) also helps retain employees.

Each human resource department is also responsible for the development of safety and health policies and procedures. These policies and procedures help the organization comply with the law and provide a safe work environment that is conducive to successful performance.

The human resource department is also responsible for administration, including the record-keeping function that traditionally characterized the old approach to HRM. Even though the department's functions have expanded, administration is still a critical responsibility. And as the requirements for record-keeping continue to increase due to legislative changes, administrative responsibilities follow suit.

> Each human resource department is also responsible for the development of safety and health policies and procedures.

Career Opportunities in the Human Resource Department

A number of opportunities are available for individuals interested in a career in human resources. They can choose to become generalists or specialists in a particular function. Of course the size of the organization as a whole will dictate whether breadth or depth of knowledge is more effective.

Smaller organizations usually require a human resource generalist because one individual needs to wear several hats and perform a variety of functions. In larger organizations, the human resource manager is a generalist who oversees several human resource functions. Still larger companies have human resource managers who coordinate and supervise the programs of all the specialists in a certain area, such as recruitment, in all the company's locations. These generalists usually have experience in several functions.

A human resource specialist focuses on one specific function within a human resource department. Larger organizations tend to have larger human resource departments and are more likely to hire specialists. Specialist positions are entry-level and include the following:

- Recruiters
- Compensation analysts
- Benefits administrators
- Job analysts
- Trainer/development specialists
- Human resource information specialists

Larger organizations are likely to offer a career path in these specialized areas. For example, a human resource employee may start out as a compensation analyst for hourly workers, then move to a position as senior compensation analyst for hourly workers, then become a compensation specialist for professionals and executives, and end up as a compensation manager (overseeing all compensation specialists working in the department). In a smaller organization, one compensation specialist may perform all of these functions for both salaried and hourly workers.

Finally, human resource executives oversee all human resource functions with the strategic objectives of the firm in mind. This executive, a member of the dominant coalition, is involved in making decisions at the corporate level.

Summary

An increased focus on creating fast, responsive organizations has charged human resource departments with the tasks of recruiting, training, and retaining talented employees with the skills necessary to carry out the firm's strategic objectives. The traditional approach to human resources has been replaced with a more strategic approach in which the human resource department and its professionals are perceived as full business partners with line managers throughout the organization. The human resource department is no longer an isolated business unit. It is now an integral participant contributing to a firm's overall performance.

> Human resource executives oversee all human resource functions with the strategic objectives of the firm in mind.

Streetwise Advice

- **The American work force has shifted to "knowledge" work.** As jobs require more advanced skills, the work force has eliminated "touch labor" and replaced it with more advanced skill-level knowledge work.

- **More jobs in the human resource field do not require a college degree in human resource management (or a related field of study such as industrial organizational psychology).** Liberal arts managers with broad-based skills are being hired and given technical training.

  Professional certifications are growing in importance in the human resource field.

- **Two human resource certifications offered by the Human Resource Certification Institute test a mastery of human resource knowledge: the Professional in Human Resources (PHR) and the Senior Professional in Human Resources (SPHR).** The PHR requires four years of experience, two years of experience and a college degree, or one year of experience and a graduate degree. The SPHR requires eight years of experience, six years of experience and a college degree, or five years of experience and a graduate degree.

- **Strategy formulation can be evolutionary in nature.** Organizations must take into account changes as they occur, so true strategy formulation is never really "finished." Try implementing flexible planning, which enables the organization to put a plan in place but still constantly monitor the external environment for any changes that must be considered.

- **An important part of formulating strategy is to know what strategies to avoid.** Strategy formulation is a complex process that takes into account a firm's unique strengths and weaknesses. Don't just follow the leader. Adopting an industry leader's strategy is ineffective at best since it does not reflect the unique position of your organization.

Two human resource certifications offered by the Human Resource Certification Institute test a mastery of human resource knowledge: the Professional in Human Resources (PHR) and the Senior Professional in Human Resources (SPHR).

- Strategy formulation is an ongoing process. **Implementing strategic management and scanning the external environment can help you better manage environmental uncertainty. However, this process does require that you constantly have your "ear to the ground" to pick up any signals.**

- **Part of the strategic approach is seeing the "big picture."** Most organizations are incorporating a strategic approach to management at all levels and in nearly all jobs. Seeing the "big picture" is the key to this approach. The firm is viewed as an integrated whole, with individual employees and units recognizing the interconnectedness of everything they do.

> The firm is viewed as an integrated whole, with individual employees and units recognizing the interconnectedness of everything they do.

For more information on this topic, visit our Web site at www.businesstown.com

Chapter 4

Skills for Effective Human Resource Management

As more human resource management functions are delegated to managers throughout an organization, the skills necessary to support these functions must be developed. Both human resource professionals and business unit managers must be aware of the variety of skills required to effectively manage human resources today.

Today's astute organizations are attempting to achieve high-performance levels while providing the work force an opportunity to contribute to their fullest extent. High-performance organizations walk a very fine line because they are equally concerned with employee satisfaction.

These organizations must pay particular attention to the skills that are necessary for success, including the skills required of human resource managers, line managers, and employees throughout the organization. Only by ensuring that all organizational members possess the right mix of skills can the firm be ensured of continued success.

> Only by ensuring that all organizational members possess the right mix of skills can the firm be ensured of continued success.

Managerial Roles

Henry Mintzberg, *The Nature of Managerial Work* (Harper & Row, 1973), conducted a classic research study that has been highly publicized. He observed the work of corporate managers and identified ten key managerial roles that they fulfill regardless of the type of organization or industry.

These managerial roles are as follows:

- Disseminator
- Disturbance handler
- Entrepreneur
- Figurehead
- Leader
- Liaison
- Monitor
- Negotiator
- Resource allocator
- Spokesperson

These ten roles have been grouped into three categories: interpersonal, decisional, and informational. Figurehead, leader, and liaison are interpersonal roles. Entrepreneur, disturbance handler, resource allocator, and negotiator are considered decisional roles. Informational roles include monitor, disseminator, and spokesperson.

Interpersonal Roles

Interpersonal roles focus on specific interactions with others. In managing human resources, managers often act as figureheads. The manager, who may be the head of a department, unit, or team, represents the people within that unit. The figurehead role is used, for example, when the team leader makes a presentation to top management soliciting more funds for the team's work. Or, the head of a business unit may petition top management representing his or her employees who seek postponement of a projected layoff.

The leader role may be filled formally or informally. Although a manager may be assigned the formal role of leader of a unit, other employees often emerge informally as leaders. Depending on the focus of the unit, these informal leaders may change over time. For example, Joseph may be the formally designated leader of a team. However, when the company purchases a new software package and doesn't provide training for the team members, Sarah may emerge as the informal team leader because she is the only one who has had experience with the software.

> Although a manager may be assigned the formal role of leader of a unit, other employees often emerge informally as leaders.

TIP
The role of informal leaders has taken on added importance as the importance of position power in organizations diminishes. Today's organizations care less about legitimate authority and more about informal leadership and personal power, such as expert power.

Since every organization is a collection of interrelated parts, coordination is essential. The liaison role, in which people often serve as "go-betweens," provides this coordination by helping one unit of the firm better understand what another unit is doing. And most important, the units come to understand how they impact each other.

Decisional Roles

The decisional role of entrepreneur has increased in importance over the past several years. Each organizational member needs to begin to think as an entrepreneur. For example, he or she may seek out opportunities for the firm, such as new markets or new ways of conducting business.

TIP

Changing terminology confirms the growing importance of entrepreneurship in organizations. Companies now focus on *intrapreneurship*. Thinking creatively no longer has only an external focus; now it helps position the organization for success and to take advantage of new market opportunities.

> Resources within an organization are limited, whether they are financial, human, or physical.

Resources within an organization are limited, whether they are financial, human, or physical. Each manager is responsible for effectively allocating these resources; that is, dividing them to ensure that they are used in the most efficient way possible. Most managers spend a fair amount of time in the role of disturbance handler. As conflicts arise among employees, the manager is responsible for settling them, usually with the assistance of the human resource department. Managers can be called in on conflicts as petty as who gets the vacant window cubicle.

The role of negotiator is closely related to that of disturbance handler. Managers must be master negotiators, demonstrating and teaching the art of compromise. It takes both practice and skill to craft a win/win situation, which is often required in the role of negotiator.

Informational Roles

Managers must monitor conditions both inside and outside the organization so they are not blind-sided by change. Organizations are responsible for communicating with their employees and with their customers and vendors. This function is generally accomplished through the role of disseminator. Managers must carefully fill this role and take it seriously. The communication also involves listening to ensure it is two-way.

The manager must also act as spokesperson. The management role often involves acting in a more formal capacity—as the representative of the firm (or perhaps the unit)—providing information about the organization to those outside the firm (or outside the unit).

The Functions of Management

The functions of management were identified by Henri Fayol, a French engineer and author of the 1916 book *General and Industrial Management*. These functions, which are performed universally, include planning, controlling, organizing, and leading. Each function is especially critical in the management of human resources.

Planning is a critical function that prepares an organization for the future by anticipating its needs and developing action plans to ensure that the organization reaches its goals.

TIP

A strategic human resource plan enables an organization to anticipate its staffing needs for the future. Recognizing the skill sets required for the future helps the organization develop a plan for how best to actually achieve its goals.

Without careful planning, an organization cannot meet its objectives. Developing a plan for the future, and then communicating that plan, provides an opportunity for human resource departments and managers throughout the organization to ensure that the appropriate people are hired and/or trained to implement those plans.

The controlling function involves measuring actual performance and then comparing it to the expected (or planned) performance. This function, then, provides an opportunity for the organization to take corrective action, which may very well involve human resources in a variety of ways.

The performance appraisal system used by the human resource department and the line managers measures employee performance. The employee's actual work performance is measured or compared against the standards of performance developed for that specific

> Planning is a critical function that prepares an organization for the future by anticipating its needs and developing action plans to ensure that the organization reaches its goals.

employee in that specific job. Improving performance (when gaps are identified in the standards of performance and the actual performance) may mean training employees, transferring employees, hiring more talented applicants, changing the design of jobs, or perhaps, in extreme cases, terminating employees.

The organizing function focuses on the structure of the work and the work group. How a firm's work will be organized—even how tasks and responsibilities will be blended into a job—fall under the purview of this function. For example, an organizing decision may be to group jobs into a team rather than have individual employees responsible for separate pieces of a project.

The leading function is especially critical. With the demise of the command-and-control manager, the ability to lead has become essential in managing human resources. The importance of this function is even reflected in the terminology of many job titles today. For example, some of the more progressive organizations are replacing "manager" with "leader" or "coach." Being a leader in the twenty-first century requires a different set of skills to meet the challenges of today's work force. Leading now is more closely related to coaching and mentoring than to commanding. Managers today have less legitimate authority (with the accompanying power) and must rely more on their personal power to effectively lead human resources. Leading is really a better response to a work force that wants more freedom and autonomy.

> With the demise of the command-and-control manager, the ability to lead has become essential in managing human resources.

The Role of Conceptual, Technical, and Human Skills

Robert Katz, a researcher working in the 1970s, has suggested that managers at all organizational levels must possess conceptual, technical, and human skills. The key, however, is recognizing that the relative mix of these three skills should change as the worker progresses up the organizational hierarchy. That is, the mix of skills should be slightly different for top-level managers than for middle-level and lower-level managers. The skills remain the same; it is simply the percentages of each skill in the mix that change as different management levels are explored.

Conceptual Skills

Conceptual skills, or the ability to see the big picture, are required to see beyond the immediate functional area in order to understand how it fits into the larger overall organization. Too often in today's companies, workers cannot see beyond their own functional level. Marketers see the company through their marketing lens, and accountants see it through their accounting lens. This is commonly referred to as the *silo mentality*. Rather than gaining an understanding of the inter-relatedness of all the parts of the organization, some individuals see only their own piece of the company. They fail to understand that any actions taken in their functional area will have consequences in other areas of the firm.

TIP

The need for conceptual skills is especially important in strategic thinking. As organizational managers are called on to engage in strategic management, the need for conceptual skills will increase.

> A change of equipment in the operational area may mean that the human resource department must provide training for the new equipment, conduct a job analysis to generate a new job description and job requirements, and perhaps hire new people with different skills.

For example, a decision to change the equipment used on an assembly line will have consequences for other functional areas of the organization. A change of equipment in the operational area may mean that the human resource department must provide training for the new equipment, conduct a job analysis to generate a new job description and job requirements, and perhaps hire new people with different skills.

People with conceptual skills understand the bigger picture and the inter-related nature of the parts of the organization. They are also able to take into account the impact of the external environment on their company.

Technical Skills

Technical skills are required to perform more specialized tasks. These skills include using technology, equipment, education, and experience to perform a job. The advanced technology available today has provided an opportunity for employees to become more proficient. Acquiring these technical skills enables a worker to take advantage of this technology. For example, managers who have advanced technical skills are able to use available equipment and technology to perform more routine tasks. As a result, they can take on more advanced and challenging responsibilities. Acquiring technical skills provides these workers with more opportunities for advancement.

Human Skills

Human skills are the skills used to interact with others. These skills are a crucial component of success today, especially with the demise of the command-and-control manager. The need for human skills has been further underscored by the trend toward a lateral organizational structure that involves interaction with peers.

At lower management levels, Katz has suggested that about 30 percent of the skill mix should be human skills, about 50 percent technical skills, and about 20 percent conceptual skills. At middle management levels, the skills mix shifts to include slightly more emphasis on conceptual skills and slightly less on technical skills. This shift continues into top management positions, with the resulting mix being about 30 percent human skills, about 50 percent conceptual skills, and about 20 percent technical skills.

Note that Katz's suggested percentage of human skills in the mix remains relatively constant across management levels. The ability to interact effectively with others is critical at all organizational levels. Technical skills become less important as the manager moves further away from the operational people (those who are actually performing the work of the company). Conceptual skills become more important as the manager moves up the organizational hierarchy. At higher levels, it becomes more essential to see the bigger picture more clearly.

All managers should work to cultivate these skills. Then as they move up in the organization, they can adjust the mix of conceptual, technical, and human skills as necessary.

The need for human skills has been further underscored by the trend toward a lateral organizational structure that involves interaction with peers.

Human Resource Manager Competencies

Today's human resource managers must be competent in business, have a thorough knowledge of human resource information, be able to manage change, and be trustworthy. These competencies are also valuable for all managers in all functional areas of an organization, especially in light of the strategic approach we discussed in Chapter 3.

First, because their role is so closely aligned with the actual business of the organization and with its strategic objectives, human resource managers must understand the business inside and out. Part of this business expertise is internal and part is external.

Only by understanding the company's business can managers design human resource policies and procedures to support that business. Understanding how the company conducts its business also helps managers design better compensation systems that will reward appropriate performance.

Human resource managers must also understand the customer. They must explore changing consumer expectations and changing trends in the industry's environment. For example, managers need to monitor technological changes in the industry to ensure that their department is hiring people with the appropriate skills to meet these technological advances and is providing the necessary training.

Second, human resource managers must have a strong foundation in human resource knowledge—and this is no small order with the changing environment. These managers must develop a method of staying current with human resource practices and procedures. In other words, they must stay on top of changes and watch for the latest developments in the areas of staffing, performance evaluation, compensation, and communication. It often means developing a system of benchmarking the best practices of other companies.

Third, human resource managers must be able to manage change. A constantly changing business environment must be reflected within the organization, and this can only be accomplished by effectively managing the change process. For example, managers must align compensation systems to support these change efforts.

> Managers need to monitor technological changes in the industry to ensure that their department is hiring people with the appropriate skills to meet these technological advances and is providing the necessary training.

> Employees across the company must be comfortable with problem-solving techniques, including creative problem-solving.

TIP

Understanding the resistance to change is a critical component of change management. The manager must be able to successfully identify where the resistance is centered. Typically, the resistance will be to the change itself, to the strategy being employed to implement the change, or to the change agent. Sometimes, employees resist the change because they don't like it or don't understand it. Sometimes they may agree with the change itself but take exception to the method of implementation. Finally, employees may simply resist the change because they don't like the person who is leading the change effort.

In addition, managers must ensure that others in the organization are trained in the change process. Employees across the company must be comfortable with problem-solving techniques, including creative problem-solving.

Finally, the effectiveness of human resource managers depends on their ability to establish credibility and trustworthiness with their business counterparts—both inside and outside the organization. Every important relationship is built on trust. Without it, human resource mangers cannot achieve much.

The Basic Responsibilities of Human Resource Managers

Human resource managers have several basic responsibilities. These responsibilities include acting as a counselor, providing services, formulating policies, and serving as the advocate for employees.

With their knowledge of human resource functions and their understanding of business in general, human resource managers are valuable sources of information for line managers. Their expertise can help line managers integrate business goals with human resource functions. For example, line managers moving to a team approach may ask human resource managers how to align the performance appraisal system to support the change. The human resource department also provides support services such as recruiting, testing, training, and counseling employees. Policy formulation, is another key responsibility. In this area, human resource managers revise existing policies to better meet the changing environment and legislative mandates.

Finally, human resource managers walk a fine line as they fill the role of advocate for employees; that is, they listen to employees and represent their position to line managers. The human resource managers serve as the support system for employees within the firm.

Ethics Still Counts

Ethics transcends the law. Ethics is more than compliance with legislation. Ethics reflects personal beliefs about what is right or wrong. Society places increasing pressure on businesses and their employees to do the "right thing"—regardless of legal requirements.

Organizations are expected to behave ethically. If business do not conduct their operations in an ethical manner and are not socially responsible, legislation is usually enacted to force legal compliance. Organizational members, then, want to ensure that they go beyond legal compliance and address the ethical issues.

Human resource departments have often taken the lead in responding to societal expectations of ethical behavior. A corporate code of conduct or code of ethics stipulates what behavior is appropriate for organizational members and what behavior is not appropriate. The code also addresses consequences for violation.

The Society for Human Resource Management (as well as most other professional associations) has a code of ethics to guide members' behaviors and decision-making processes. This code explicitly states what behaviors are expected of its members.

> If business do not conduct their operations in an ethical manner and are not socially responsible, legislation is usually enacted to force legal compliance.

TIP
The iron law of responsibility suggests that if businesses do not police themselves, the government will step in to legislate them. Over the years, as businesses have failed to live up to their ethical responsibilities, the government has enacted legislation to ensure that business responds with the appropriate course of action.

> Ethics should be included in training programs as well. Ideally, it should be integrated across all training rather than presented as a separate topic.

Human resource managers can also encourage ethical behavior in new employee orientation programs, training programs, and the disciplinary system. These methods must be explicit in communicating the expected behaviors. To clarify the organization's expectations, it often helps to provide examples of what is considered inappropriate or unacceptable behavior.

During orientation programs for new employees, ethical conduct should be stressed and discussed. Any review of organizational policies should include a careful examination of the code of ethics. This examination reinforces values important to the organization. Giving examples of how the code guides behavior can also be used to reinforce ethics.

Ethics should be included in training programs as well. Ideally, it should be integrated across all training rather than presented as a separate topic. For example, ethics in advertising and marketing should be included in a discussion of marketing. Trainees would certainly benefit from a review of likely scenarios and appropriate responses. Employees should also be encouraged to talk about ethics in the training sessions. And, perhaps most important, top management must model the ethical behavior discussed in training.

The firm must respond to violations. The consequences must be significant and the firm must stand by them. This ethical behavior must also be modeled by the top management of the firm, and there must be penalties for violations. Looking the other way sends a contradictory message. The consequences must, however, be fair, be communicated clearly in advance, and include a system of due process. Any violations must be addressed promptly.

As organizations are being held to higher standards, the human resource department must take the lead in encouraging and rewarding ethical behavior. The department's own policies and procedures must set the stage for ethical behavior throughout the organization.

Summary

As the workplace continues to evolve, increasing emphasis is placed on new skill sets. The very heart of an organization's competitive advantage lies in ensuring that all of its employees have the right skills, which means planning for future skill sets and constantly assessing the changes impacting the organization's human resources. Only by anticipating future change and by taking a proactive stance can an organization be positioned for success.

Streetwise Advice

Here are the most important skills for success in managing human resources:

- Change management
- Communication skills
- Continuous learning
- Creativity
- Delegation skills
- Flexibility
- Strategic thinking
- Team orientation

Change Management

With the unprecedented pace of change, organizational members must be able to manage change effectively. More than just being able to accept change, today's change management requires that individuals be able to generate and design some of these change efforts.

The old change philosophy was "if it ain't broke, don't fix it." Reactive in nature, this style of management waited for a change and then responded to it. Today's philosophy reflects a more proactive stance: "If it ain't broke, fix it anyway." Change requires breaking with the old way of doing things.

Process re-engineering focuses on the radical redesign of the work process. It requires starting over by critically assessing every process and asking if this is the best way to do it—or even if it has to be done at all.

As most organizations move to a team orientation, all employees must be team players. Managers must also be skilled in building teams.

> With the unprecedented pace of change, organizational members must be able to manage change effectively.

Communication Skills

Effective communication is essential to the successful management of human resources. Without effective verbal and written communication skills, good ideas can be lost forever.

Part of an effective communication policy is to have an open door, so employees feel comfortable approaching managers. Employees are closer now to the work and the customer; it is important that they share information and ideas with managers about improvements.

Continuous Learning

In a constantly changing world, everyone must be willing to learn. The need for a learning organization has been well publicized for over a decade. The same is true for individuals within these organizations. To stop learning means to fall behind.

A constant updating of skills positions an individual to grow and to take advantage of opportunities. Continuous improvement for the organization begins with the continuous improvement—through learning—of every member.

> Managers and the human resource department are responsible for identifying individual training and development needs.

Managers and the human resource department are responsible for identifying individual training and development needs. Both on-the-job and off-the job training should be offered to employees once these needs are assessed. Coaching and mentoring can also be used in this process. It is the responsibility of each manager to become a lifelong learner and a role model for employees to do the same.

Creativity

Creativity is sorely needed in all organizations. Business as usual is not a philosophy that will respond to a changing environment. Organizations must develop new ways to address their challenges.

Delegation Skills

Effective managers delegate. In doing so, they empower their employees, enabling them to build confidence while they build their skills, knowledge, and abilities. Failing to delegate means getting less done.

Flexibility

Flexibility is essential in managing human resources today. With a diverse work force, "fair" does not necessarily mean the same thing to all people. Sometimes "fair" just means thinking flexibly and creatively.

Strategic Thinking

Thinking strategically means having a long-term focus and being goal oriented. Managers today must have a clear idea of where they are going before they can lead others. They must be able to explain what that vision is and how their employees can help meet the goal.

Team Orientation

Effective management of human resources means having a positive attitude. A negative attitude will hinder your interaction with others and adversely impact performance levels.

> Thinking strategically means having a long-term focus and being goal oriented.

For more information on this topic, visit our Web site at www.businesstown.com

Staffing: The Right People for the Right Job

Finding the right people for the right job—and at the right time—is a multi-faceted challenge in any organization. The hiring process begins by identifying the human resource needs of the firm, then moving through the processes of recruitment and selection, and finally orienting new employees to the organization.

Chapter 5: Explore the role of strategic human resource planning.

Chapter 6: Consider external and internal options for recruiting job applicants.

Chapter 7: Examine the selection process beginning with the initial screening of applicants through the final decision to hire.

Chapter 8: Review orientation's role in acclimating employees to your organization's culture.

Chapter 5

Human Resource Planning

H uman resource planning is a key initial step in getting the right people in the right place at the right time. Without accurate planning, the organization may not be positioned to compete effectively in the marketplace. This proactive process anticipates future staffing needs by forecasting the supply and demand of the firm's human resources.

Effective human resource planning will save the organization considerable money. The organization cannot afford to be overstaffed or understaffed because it will incur additional costs. If the company is overstaffed, it is paying for workers who are not being challenged to their fullest capacity. If it is understaffed, productivity and quality may suffer because not enough people are available to perform the work effectively.

Those organizations that fail to engage in human resource planning also impact the career development of their employees. Employees who have no knowledge of their firm's staffing plans may seek employment elsewhere to further their careers. Companies incur significant costs when employees are unhappy with their career development and leave the organization to work for the competition.

> Employees who have no knowledge of their firm's staffing plans may seek employment elsewhere to further their careers.

The Role of Strategic Human Resource Planning

The planning function of human resources (traditionally referred to as *manpower planning)* drives all the other functions. Staffing needs must be identified before other functions can be addressed. Once the staffing plans are completed, then the remaining human resource functions can be integrated into a cohesive plan. The strategic human resource planning process drives the other human resource management functions, from recruitment to training and development.

Human resource planning is the organizational process used to determine how people will be hired and used in the firm. To be the most effective, this process should be ongoing, and it requires foresight. The planning process is concerned with all aspects of the employment function: recruitment, selection, compensation, training, job design, and advancement. These functions in turn support organizational performance.

Human resource planning assists the organization in meeting its strategic objectives. By projecting the firm's human resource needs, the appropriate people can be identified, hired, promoted, transferred, and/or trained. As a result, the right people will be in the right job at the right time.

Effective human resource planning builds in flexibility and enables the organization to change in response to the environment. The plan should not to be so rigid that adjustments cannot be made as environmental changes occur. A certain amount of flexibility is needed to take advantage of opportunities as they become available or known to the organization.

The firm's overall strategy provides the framework and the destination for this human resource plan. The human resource plan will provide answers to questions such as the following:

- How many people will be needed for the organization to meet its objectives?
- What jobs will these people need to fill?
- What knowledge, skills, and abilities will new hires be required to have?
- What new skills will be required of the current work force?
- Can these new workers be transferred or promoted from within the firm or do they need to be hired from outside?
- What type of training is required for workers to acquire the knowledge, skills, and abilities that are needed?
- What type of compensation plan is required to support this talent?
- How will this process alter the career plans of existing employees or potential candidates?

There is a two-way relationship between human resource planning and strategic planning. That is, the plans influence and support each other. In most organizations today, the processes of human resource planning and strategic planning have become closely integrated. Human resource planning helps the organization craft a feasible strategy that makes sure people are available with the appropriate skills to pursue the strategic objectives. Human resource planning

> Effective human resource planning builds in flexibility and enables the organization to change in response to the environment.

again plays a major role when the strategy is implemented to ensure the firm's human resources are appropriately allocated to effectively implement the strategy as designed. Human resource policies must reinforce the firm's strategic objectives and must be closely aligned with one another.

The Impact of the External Environment: The Local Labor Market and More

Human resource planning involves forecasting the supply and demand of appropriate human resources for the organization. To produce this forecast, planners must understand the external business environment and the trends that occur within it.

The external environment impacts the human resource plan of every organization. The employment market and economic policy play a major role in the development of these plans. If the external environment cannot provide the necessary supply of key workers, the human resource plan may need to be altered. In some cases, the overall strategic plan must be re-evaluated as well. If the resources for staffing are not available, a new strategy may have to be formulated.

The U.S. Department of Labor influences these plans by encouraging training in specific skill areas and training of targeted groups in the labor force. Businesses are often asked to participate in these efforts and offer additional training. Firms can also take advantage of training that is provided by the government to recruit skilled workers in these areas.

> If the external environment cannot provide the necessary supply of key workers, the human resource plan may need to be altered.

TIP

Work force needs may vary from region to region. Businesses must monitor the migration of workers in specific fields in order to identify pockets of skill concentrations. Rather than attempting to bring the workers with the appropriate skill sets to you, it may make more sense to locate the work where the workers are. To make the best strategic corporate decisions, therefore, it is important to monitor the availability of specific skill sets across the nation.

Changes in administration will bring revisions in national economic and human resource policies. Each presidential administration tends to focus on different skill areas and different groups within the labor pool. For example, one administration focused its efforts on retraining veterans. Many such programs are focused on training disadvantaged groups.

The U.S. Job Corps establishes regional offices that provide training to local youth. The programs offered vary from location to location. The Job Corps establishes an industry council to provide insight into the local labor market and identify where likely job opportunities may be found. Training is then focused on these areas. For example, one regional office offers a large culinary training program. These programs reflect the needs of the local employers—in this case, in the hotel and food industry.

In recent years much of the national human resource policy has been decentralized as more responsibilities have been shifted to the state and local levels. In this way, states can respond more effectively to their local and regional needs.

There are several sources of reliable information concerning the external environment:

- Educational institutions' enrollment statistics by major
- Demographic trends
- Regional population shifts

The enrollment statistics for colleges and universities are a good indicator of the number of new graduates by major. These enrollment statistics can also be used for high schools and vocational or trade schools to provide forecasts for the expected number of individuals who will graduate trained in a specific field.

Regional population shifts will change the size of the general labor pool. As more people in the United States moved to the South, the size of the labor markets in other regions decreased while the size of the market in the South increased. The movement of workers worldwide has likewise created shifts in the size of labor markets around the globe. There has been increased emigration to the developed countries from less developed countries.

> In recent years much of the national human resource policy has been decentralized as more responsibilities have been shifted to the state and local levels.

Political trends (including legislative changes), social trends, and demographic trends affecting the composition of the work force will also impact human resource planning.

TIP
Some less developed countries have been concerned with what they refer to as "brain drain." In some cases, educated people leave to seek out more challenging jobs; in other cases, young people leave to be educated in more developed nations and then never return to their country. Such emigration leaves the country with a larger number of less skilled workers. This also means that there is less opportunity for the country to attract businesses that require more advanced skill sets in their work force.

The external environment is ripe with both opportunities and challenges. All of the competitive trends must be monitored. Innovations and technological advances should also be closely followed. These technological changes may result in changes in skill sets, jobs performed, and job openings. Political trends (including legislative changes), social trends, and demographic trends affecting the composition of the work force will also impact human resource planning. By monitoring these trends, the organization will be positioned to make the appropriate changes when needed.

Changes in Skill Requirements

The need for highly skilled workers has increased as advanced technology has been integrated into more jobs. The work force needs higher skill levels than ever before, and as these changes continue, training and retraining of employees must keep pace. When training lags behind demand, shortages result in lost productivity, lower performance, and poorer quality products or services. Workers today need the following higher-level skills:

- Ability to think critically
- Ability to solve problems
- Computer proficiency
- Flexibility and adaptability

Employees at all organizational levels must be able to *think critically*. With more advanced technology available, a larger number of less challenging, routine jobs have been replaced with jobs that require employees to critically assess their work and the way in which it is being performed. Organizations are implementing process re-engineering, in which each employee is asked to assess his or her work processes and determine if there is a better way to accomplish the task. With a more creative approach to business, employees must think critically to invent that better mousetrap and to challenge the status quo.

Problem-solving has also become more complicated today. In the past, it was sufficient to be a skilled, rational problem-solver. Today's rapidly changing environment requires that employees also be creative problem-solvers. The very nature of today's problems requires workers to develop a new perspective (and a new solution) to replace timeworn solutions that are no longer working. They must constantly think outside the box.

Very few workers today can escape the need for some level of *computer proficiency.* Those workers who fail to develop computer skills fall behind in their ability to communicate. Advanced computer technology is used extensively to provide access to the vital information that employees need to do their jobs and to communicate with one another and with customers and suppliers. In a constantly changing world, people must be *adaptable*. There is no time to prepare to make changes. Those who remain wed to the past will quickly find themselves left behind in a world that moves at warp speed on a daily basis. There is no doubt that the skills required to perform in this information age will continue to evolve and organizations must continue to monitor them.

TIP

The new educational paradigm suggests that students should be learning *how* to think rather than *what* to think. It is impossible to teach all the "right" answers when the questions keep changing. Consider the hungry man: Give him a fish, and he'll eat for today; teach him to fish, and he can eat for a lifetime. Teaching students how to *think* means concentrating on critical thinking and problem-solving skills.

> Advanced computer technology is used extensively to provide access to the vital information that employees need to do their jobs and to communicate with one another and with customers and suppliers.

Throw It on the Curve

The simple rules of economics also apply to the supply and demand of human resources. The best-case scenario is a balanced relationship, in which there are enough people to fill the organization's staffing needs. Unfortunately, this is not the most likely scenario.

Back to Strategy

Overall corporate strategy impacts the demand for human resources. When a company is growing, it needs more people and will put into effect a plan to increase its work force. A company that is following a stability strategy, on the other hand, usually has a relatively stable demand for human resources and its strategic plan will reflect that. Finally, a company employing a retrenchment strategy usually has a decreased demand for human resources and will make plans to reduce its work force.

Although supply and demand can be equal on an organizational level, that may not be the case on a unit level. That is, there may be the right number of employees in the organization, but one department may have too many workers while another may not have enough or may not have workers who have the right skill sets.

Forecasting Techniques

Forecasting is both an art and a science, but it is not exact. Organizations use both quantitative and qualitative forecasting techniques, often to complement each other.

Trend analysis is a popular quantitative forecasting technique, in which an index is used to project current trends into the future. For example, many retailing companies use sales as the index. If sales are expected to increase by a specific percentage, this increase can be used to predict staffing needs, assuming that the trend continues. The index (sales) is plotted against human resource needs (represented by the number of employees). This historical data is used to calculate the ratio of sales to employees. Then both this sales factor and the human resource needs can be projected.

> Although supply and demand can be equal on an organizational level, that may not be the case on a unit level.

There are also software programs that use more complicated mathematical models. They often use multiple factors in these calculations. Using trend analysis, however, they still project the future based on the extension of a historical trend, regardless of the number of factors considered.

A popular qualitative approach is to use management forecasts, in which knowledgeable managers give their opinion on future staffing needs. These managers may also be subject area experts drawn from outside the organization.

TIP

The Delphi technique, like management forecasting, is a popular qualitative forecasting approach. Experts take part in round robin–type decision-making sessions until they arrive at a consensus for the organization's human resource needs. The consensus then serves as the forecast for the corporate strategic human resource plan.

Both qualitative and quantitative techniques should be used to strengthen the effectiveness of the planning process. This approach capitalizes on the strengths of both methods, combining art and science.

Markov Analysis

Although there are a number of methods for forecasting corporate human resource needs, staffing tables and Markov analysis are two of the more popular methods used today. Staffing tables are a graphical depiction of the jobs within the organization. These tables show the number of employees currently employed in each job. The future staffing requirements for each job are included as well to provide a simplistic picture of staffing across the organization. At a glance, analysts can see where the majority of the people are employed and what future projections are likely to be.

Markov analysis provides a more detailed look. In addition to showing the information reflected in staffing tables, Markov analysis includes the movement of people into and out of these jobs. That is, this analysis captures the number of employees who are being promoted, being demoted, making lateral moves out of or into the job,

> Both qualitative and quantitative techniques should be used to strengthen the effectiveness of the planning process.

and leaving the organization. For this reason, it is sometimes referred to as a *transition matrix*.

Both staffing tables and Markov analysis focus on the number of people occupying specific jobs. More organizations today are moving toward skill inventories in order to address their changing needs. Instead of listing the number of people in specific jobs, a talent inventory captures information on each employee's knowledge, skills, abilities, education, experience, and compensation history. These inventories enable the human resource department to know at a glance, then, if talent must be found outside the organization to fill labor shortages that occur.

> The human resource department must determine the future skill requirements of workers in each occupation within the organization.

A General Model for Human Resource Planning

The human resource department must determine the future skill requirements of workers in each occupation within the organization. To accomplish this objective, the human resource plan must include several distinct steps:

- Determine the organizational objectives
- Determine the human resource objectives
- Forecast shortages or surpluses
- Determine the objectives for each employment function
- Identify future skill sets
- Review job designs

Determine the Organizational Objectives

The overall human resource plan is driven by the company's strategic plan. Plans are established for three different time horizons: short-term, intermediate-term, and long-term. A short-term plan traditionally covers about one year. The intermediate-term plan ranges from about two to five years. Depending on the industry within which the firm operates, the long-range plan can cover from five to twenty-five years. The shorter the time horizon is, the more specific the details of the plan are. Longer time frames tend to be somewhat more general.

Determine the Human Resource Objectives

Once the organizational objectives are identified, it is time to develop the human resource objectives. These objectives must be aligned with the organizational objectives to ensure that the overall corporate goals are met.

For example, an organization may develop a growth strategy by moving into related businesses. The human resource objectives must then be geared toward growth; that is, hiring, training, and promoting individuals to support this new related business.

By contrast, a firm forced to engage in a retrenchment strategy will craft a very different set of human resource objectives. Here, the focus will be on layoffs. As a result, the plan may include the development of a policy to determine who will be laid off, the creation of severance packages, and an examination of retraining for employees.

Forecast Shortages and Surpluses

A shortage or surplus must be determined for each job in the organization. Then it is time to develop specific action plans to respond to the finding. If surpluses are anticipated, the organization must plan to redirect extra employees. If shortages are forecast, individuals must either be trained or recruited to acquire the needed skills. These action plans must consider the general labor market. If shortages for the job category are also being forecast for the general labor market, the firm may have to revise its compensation and benefits packages, revise its recruitment strategies, and/or revise career development opportunities to attract this limited talent.

The simplest method of determining surpluses and shortages is the transition matrix, which depicts the movement of employees through the organization. The matrix helps identify trends by tracking the transition of people over time. (Numerous software programs are available to help companies with all of these tasks.)

Generally, organizations use historical information to project the likely supply or availability of human resources (those with the required skill sets) within the organization. With some adjustments, mathematical trend models can project past data. Firms can also examine their voluntary and involuntary turnover and the number of

> The simplest method of determining surpluses and shortages is the transition matrix, which depicts the movement of employees through the organization.

retirements for jobs or job categories. These trends are then extended into the future to calculate the forecast.

A simple calculation of shortages and surpluses begins with the number of people currently in the job categories being examined. The number of employees who are expected to leave these jobs during the planning time frame is then subtracted from this total number. (This number may include people who are retiring during this period, expected promotions, and general attrition data from historical information for voluntary and involuntary terminations.)

The number of people who are likely to be promoted into the job category and the number of replacement people are then added in. Next, the predicted demand is compared to the predicted supply to determine if there is a surplus or shortage. Unless the company makes major internal changes, shortages must be filled from the general labor pool.

Retaining employees is a critical component in this projection. The firm's ability to retain employees impacts the internal supply of human resources.

> The firm's ability to retain employees impacts the internal supply of human resources.

Determine the Objectives for Each Employment Function

Once the shortages and surpluses are identified, the human resource plan needs to determine specific objectives for each employment function within human resources. Specific objectives are then created for recruitment, selection, training, compensation, performance appraisals, promotions, retirement (including early retirement incentives), terminations, and layoffs. Programs within each of these functions are developed to support the human resource objectives, which in turn support the overall corporate strategy.

Identify Future Skill Sets

As jobs evolve, the skill sets that are required to successfully perform those jobs will also change. Effective human resource planning anticipates the skill sets that will be required. Examining job designs throughout the organization often leads to the identification of future skill sets.

It is too late to wait until the skills are needed to train or hire individuals. The key is to be prepared and to anticipate what skills will be required. Many of the professional associations and trade journals provide forecasts and future outlooks to assist organizations in anticipating what skill sets will be required in the future.

The skills inventory is a valuable organizational tool that can help track the skill sets of the current work force. The inventory enables employees to be tapped for future jobs as the skill sets change. By accessing the skills inventory once the future skill sets are projected, the human resource department can identify those employees who either possess the required skills or are in a position to be trained in these skills.

Review Job Designs

The design of current jobs is not stable over time. Instead, job designs are dynamic; they constantly incorporate available new technology. Changing job designs, in turn, impact the way job categories are configured. The ensuing ripple effect is felt through all the human resource functions.

For example, changing from a manual accounting system for accounts receivable to a computerized system requires a redesign of the job. The skills required to perform the job will change as well. Either a new person must be hired or the current employee must be retrained to support the new technology. This need for an employee with higher skill levels will also require an examination of the compensation and benefits offered for that position. In addition, the need to learn the new technology will require training, thus creating a need to re-examine the employee's career path.

> The need to learn the new technology will require training, thus creating a need to re-examine the employee's career path.

A Special Challenge: Management Succession Planning

Management succession planning, or executive succession, has become a critical component of human resource planning. In what can be a multiyear process, replacement candidates must be systematically identified for middle and top management levels. Unlike general human resource planning where the focus is on entry-level positions and general numbers, management succession planning tends to focus more on specific individuals.

The grooming of a cadre of talented managers takes years. As a result, organizations must plan well into the future to ensure that sufficient talent is in the pipeline. A formal succession plan is a more systematic, logical approach to human resource development; it builds depth in the organization's management talent.

> Human resource departments must identify employees with high potential and then address their development.

TIP

The lack of potential executive management talent has reached critical levels. With about 33 percent turnover expected in the next five years in top management positions and a price tag of $750,000 for each executive position, most companies are increasingly concerned with management succession.

Human resource departments must identify employees with high potential and then address their development. Management talent is too critical to leave to chance or whim. Early identification enables the organization to provide cross-functional training to better prepare top managers. This development may include formal training and planned job assignments (often through a series of lateral moves).

Succession planning is not necessarily succession by position. Leadership profiles are developed in a broad-based approach, which uses broad management categories instead of specific jobs and broad competencies instead of specific skills. This approach matches these core management competencies to core business competencies and to more than one specific job. The key emphasis is to identify pools of candidates and then develop the competencies needed. This process is constantly evolving.

Some organizations use the terminology *growing leaders* to reflect what is actually happening in their succession planning. The very term implies the ongoing nature of the process and the shared ownership.

Summary

The critical nature of engaging in human resource planning cannot be overemphasized. Failure to plan for future needs can be devastating and can possibly leave the organization with a shortage of talented individuals with the right skill sets. Only by forecasting future needs can an organization take action today to meet tomorrow's needs.

Streetwise Advice

- **Human resource planning is a continuous process.** Planning requires constant monitoring to ensure that human resource objectives are aligned with corporate objectives. As the environment changes, corporate objectives and human resource objectives must be revised and realigned.

- Firms operating in a dynamic environment might find it beneficial to identify competitive competencies for use in human resource planning rather than use specific skill sets. **Since human resource plans should be flexible enough to enable the organization to make the appropriate changes and respond to the environment, specific skill sets (which can be more rigid) should be abandoned in favor of more flexible, broader competencies.**

- Many succession-planning systems today use committees to identify management candidates.

- **Human resource planning can be top-down or bottom-up.** Whether the forecasting process is initiated at top management levels or in the units (i.e., bottom-up), the forecast should always include input from line managers.

- The forecasting of human resources can be very informal. **Your firm doesn't have to have a complex, sophisticated system. An informal forecasting system may be just as effective. The value of planning lies as much in the exercise as in the plan itself.**

> Firms operating in a dynamic environment might find it beneficial to identify competitive competencies for use in human resource planning rather than use specific skill sets.

The planning process requires the firm to think about the future of the business and to identify trends.

- Avoid being unduly influenced by current job responsibilities. **The responsibilities today for a given job are not generally those that will be required in the future. You must break with the old way of thinking to envision future job responsibilities.**

- **The Delphi technique uses experts to predict needs and develop likely scenarios for specific industries. Trade publications provide many of these scenarios.**

- **During the next decade, forecasts indicate that there will be almost 1.5 million high-tech job openings.** Without effective human resource planning, your firm may be unable to fill some of these positions.

The Delphi technique uses experts to predict needs and develop likely scenarios for specific industries.

For more information on this topic, visit our Web site at www.businesstown.com

Recruitment

Recruitment and selection are critical to every organization. A firm is only as good as the people it recruits. If it is unable to attract talented individuals, the organization may very well fail to meet its corporate objectives. The company's performance, then, depends on its ability to attract a qualified work force through effective recruitment strategies.

As the labor market contracts (or as certain components of the market tighten up), the competition for the best candidates increases. Then it becomes an even bigger challenge for firms to attract talented applicants as well as retain valued employees whom competitors are attempting to lure away.

The increasing diversity of the labor market also presents greater challenges for recruitment. Recruiters must think more creatively when attempting to attract a diverse work force. There are numerous options available to recruit employees. The key is to use those methods that are most effective given the position, the industry, and the company's needs.

> Recruiters must think more creatively when attempting to attract a diverse work force.

Advances in technology present new opportunities for recruitment as well. Companies that fail to take advantage of new technology—such as Web recruiting, online applications, and the use of computers to screen applicants—may miss out on talented applicants. Recruitment has changed drastically in the past few years. To find the best candidates and hire them, organizations and their recruiters need to change as well.

Attracting Internal and External Applicants

Each organization should develop a recruiting strategy that is communicated to and understood by all its recruiters and managers. The first step is to identify the recruiting options that the firm will use. The next step is to create a timetable to make sure the position is filled when needed. Generally, the manager selects a hire date and then the human resource department can determine a recruiting schedule.

Recruiters can either use internal or external methods to fill openings in the organization. Each option has its advantages and disadvantages. Most organizations use a combination of the two methods to gain the advantages of each.

Internal Recruitment

Advantages

The internal recruitment method has the following advantages:

- It generally costs less.
- It hires employees already acclimated to the organization.
- It improves employee morale.
- It keeps knowledge within the company.
- It has potential for a better success rate since the track record of the employee is known.

Hiring internally means that the candidates already know the organization and its culture and their transition into another position will be easier than for a new hire. Hiring from within keeps proprietary and industry knowledge inside the firm. In addition, the company is already familiar with the candidates' performance. It is also less expensive to recruit applicants internally. Finally, recruiting internally improves the morale of all employees as they recognize future opportunities for advancement.

Disadvantages

Internal recruitment does have some disadvantages:

- It creates a ripple effect; more job openings occur as employees are moved about.
- It lowers the morale of those employees not selected for the position.
- It may result in stagnation since new outlooks and ways of doing things are not being brought into the firm.
- It creates negative internal competition for the position.

There are some drawbacks to internal recruitment. Since there are limited opportunities for advancement, there is often negative competition among employees for openings. Then those who are not selected may feel demoralized. Not bringing in fresh ideas to the firms can result in stagnation; this is often referred to as inbreeding

> Hiring internally means that the candidates already know the organization and its culture and their transition into another position will be easier than for a new hire.

or the cloning of employees. Finally, as openings are filled internally, new openings are created, causing a ripple effect and more hiring.

Methods of Recruiting

The most common method of internal recruiting is *job posting*, which notifies employees about current openings so they can apply when appropriate. The manner in which jobs are posted is changing with advances in technology. The posting can be accomplished in print via bulletin boards, memorandums distributed to employees, company newsletters, or the company intranet. Some companies may routinely post openings on a cafeteria bulletin board or in other high-traffic areas. Today it is common practice to notify employees of job openings by e-mail.

Some firms have even used advanced technology to combine a skills inventory with an electronic job posting system. With this system, the human resource department reviews the skills that are required and matches them to the skills their employees have. Those workers with the appropriate skills are notified of the position to determine their interest.

Job bidding is used in union environments. Qualified employees learn about the openings and then bid on the jobs. The most senior qualified individual or, if they are tested, the highest scoring individual is awarded the position. This system is perceived as quite objective with measurable criteria.

Skills inventories, or *skills banks*, have also become popular as a recruiting method in recent years. These inventories contain data on all employees, including qualifications, skills, knowledge, ability, education, experience, and special training. When positions open up, the inventory data bank can be searched for the appropriate candidates. Computerized databases make it easier to locate good applicants within the organization.

Some organizations also use *supervisor recommendations*. When openings occur, other managers are often in a position to recommend employees who have the appropriate skills and would be a good match for the position.

More companies today depend on *job referrals*—and pay substantial incentives to employees for recommending good

> The most common method of internal recruiting is *job posting*, which notifies employees about current openings so they can apply when appropriate.

applicants who are later hired. These rewards are both financial and material. Although cash bonuses are common, companies are also using creative nonfinancial options to inspire employees. Some of these rewards include trips, vacation days, points to "buy" goods from select catalogs, and gift certificates to local restaurants. The most important aspect to remember about a rewards program is to offer a variety of incentives so that there is something for everyone.

The referrals are usually of high quality since employees are not likely to refer poor applicants for jobs. The current employee's reputation is on the line. In fact, referrals are one of the more reliable methods of recruiting today.

TIP

Research has shown that employees who offer referrals generally stay with the firm for longer periods. It is worthwhile for the organization to invest in referral programs since they win in two ways: with improved retention rates and with better-qualified applicants.

External Recruitment

Advantages

External recruitment has the following advantages:

- New blood/ideas are infused into the organization, producing a revitalizing effect.
- It brings an opportunity to acquire new skills not found in the organization.
- It enables the firm to hire people who have knowledge of competitors' secrets.

There are numerous benefits to external recruitment. Hires from outside the organization bring new ideas and new knowledge that can enhance creativity. Hiring employees from competitors has become a popular means of legitimately conducting competitive intelligence gathering.

> It is worthwhile for the organization to invest in referral programs since they win in two ways: with improved retention rates and with better-qualified applicants.

Disadvantages

External recruitment also has some disadvantages:

- The applicant doesn't fit into the organizational culture.
- It costs more than internal recruiting.
- Knowing that positions are filled from outside the organization may adversely impact employees' commitment levels.
- New hires will take a longer time to become acclimated to the organization and its culture.

External recruitment has several drawbacks. The candidate may fit the position but not the culture of the organization. In addition, it takes a significantly longer time for the individual to become fully acclimated to the corporate culture. There is often decreased morale among employees when they know that positions are filled externally, leaving fewer opportunities for them. Finally, external recruiting methods generally are more expensive than internal methods.

Sometimes internal recruiting methods are not appropriate, and the company must recruit from outside the organization, especially for entry-level positions. As employees are promoted from within the organization, there is a ripple effect as other openings are created.

Methods of Recruitment

Colleges and universities can be especially good sources for management talent. Some organizations have even developed close relationships with regional colleges and universities to hire graduates in specific fields. Local community colleges and high schools may also be sources of good younger candidates.

Some organizations have developed *internship programs* to provide work opportunities for college students. These programs give students experience and enable the company to begin training and testing future applicants. A good relationship with the campus placement office helps companies gain an edge with the good students.

Advertising is one of the most popular external recruiting methods. The biggest drawback to advertising, however, is the large number of unqualified and marginally qualified applicants who must be screened out. More effective advertising is often targeted to a specific industry using a trade journal.

TIP

Many good jobs are not advertised in regular newspapers. More often, companies use their professional network to aid them in hiring. For instance, the Institute of Management Accountants maintains an active member bulletin board for hiring. They even focus on job openings at their annual conference. The Society for Human Resource Managers (SHRM) uses their own publications to advertise job openings in the human resource field. The advantage to using these sources is that the people who attend these meetings or read these publications are already working in the field and have experience.

For example, a university could advertise a job opening for a business professor in a local city newspaper or in the *Chronicle of Higher Education*. The newspaper ad would probably result in a higher number of unqualified applicants because everyone reads the newspaper. *The Chronicle of Higher Education* is the trade journal for education and would likely result in fewer unqualified applicants.

Radio ads, television, or billboards are other possibilities. Firms may contact professional organizations to place ads in their internal newsletters or to announce job openings at their regional meetings. Whatever the advertising medium, the effectiveness of the method is increased by ensuring that the ad communicates the essentials of the position as accurately as possible and is targeted at the people who should be applying for the position.

Organizations often hire *public or private employment agencies* to recruit talent. Public agencies, administered by the state, focus more on blue-collar positions. These agencies use national job banks that companies may also access.

Private employment agencies generally charge a fee (usually in the range of 25 to 30 percent) based upon the position's salary. They often perform the initial screening for the firm as well. Many employment agencies specialize in an occupational field. For instance, one well-known firm specializes in accounting professionals nationwide.

> Whatever the advertising medium, the effectiveness of the method is increased by ensuring that the ad communicates the essentials of the position as accurately as possible and is targeted at the people who should be applying for the position.

Those private employment agencies that focus on executive-level positions are referred to as executive search firms or headhunters. Although executive search firms can be expensive (since the company is responsible for the fee, even if a suitable candidate is not located), they can be very effective in recruiting specialized talent.

> Although executive search firms can be expensive (since the company is responsible for the fee, even if a suitable candidate is not located), they can be very effective in recruiting specialized talent.

TIP

While organizations cannot always contact executives employed at competitor firms, headhunters routinely undertake this task. Headhunters often make calls under the guise of asking if the executive knows of anyone else who is interested in a specific position. In this way, they can determine if the person is interested or is considering a move. Although it may be construed as unethical for the competitor to make the call, it is perfectly acceptable for the headhunter to make that same call.

Unsolicited resumes and applications provide yet another source of external recruiting. Applicants simply walk in to apply for a position even though they are not responding to a specific advertisement—and in fact, there may not be any openings. These direct applicants generally yield a small percentage of the candidates eventually accepted for employment. This is, however, a public relations opportunity for the company and the company must treat these applicants well.

Job fairs can be another good source for applicants. A local chamber of commerce or a consortium of businesses may hold a regional job fair. These fairs are usually held at local hotels and are well publicized.

If there are a large number of openings, the organization may decide to hold an *open house* and invite local applicants. Open houses may be held at a company facility or in a large local hotel. It is best to hold them after business hours or on weekends to permit attendance by those who are currently employed.

Organizations are cautioned to use a healthy mix of both internal and external recruiting methods. The advantages of both are then enjoyed. An over-reliance on one or the other puts the organization at a disadvantage.

Writing an Effective Advertisement

Advertising a position is only as effective as the advertisement itself. Only a well-written ad will attract the best candidates. The key is quality as well as quantity. The ad must effectively communicate the necessary qualifications so that some unqualified applicants will screen themselves out. The ad should generate high numbers of applicants, but only those of high quality; that is, those who actually possess the skill set being sought.

The advertisement should include the following information:

- **Job title:** The job title should effectively communicate where in the organization the job is—for example, junior accountant, senior accountant, assistant vice-president. Clear titles can help unqualified applicants screen themselves out before they even apply.

- **General job responsibilities:** The advertisement should include a brief summary of the essential job responsibilities and highlight any specialized skills. The idea is not to re-create the entire job description but to provide the reader with a concise overview of the tasks regularly being performed in this job.

- **Company name and business:** The company name can be a marketing tool if the organization has a good reputation. Some organizations choose to run blind ads to avoid identifying themselves. For example, if a firm has recently had public relations difficulties, it may choose not to reveal its identity, believing that it can sell itself to the applicant at a later time. Companies that are not easily recognized should include a brief statement identifying the industry within which they operate. Some firms may even choose to include their mission statement.

- **Required education and experience:** Required education and required experience should always be included. Without this essential information, prospective candidates cannot determine if they have the necessary skills.

> The advertisement should include a brief summary of the essential job responsibilities and highlight any specialized skills.

However, to comply with legislation, only job-related experience and education can be included.

- **Contact information:** Applicants must know how to submit their application or resume. More firms today are encouraging applicants to submit resumes electronically. Therefore, the contact information should also include the name and position of the contact person. The applicants will then be able to address their cover letters directly to this individual, and on the other end, the applications and resumes will get to the right person in the organization.

Online Options to Augment the Traditional Approaches

The Internet has provided a number of opportunities and challenges for recruiters. Web-based recruiting has grown significantly in the past few years. And it has proved to be substantially less expensive than print advertisements. Some sources suggest that using Web-based recruiting saves almost $2,900 per applicant.

Online recruiting enables the firm to reach a broad range of applicants rather quickly. In addition, the applicants are apt to have at least basic computer skills—since they searched the Web for a job.

There is, however, one major drawback. Since Web-based recruiting is relatively easy to respond to, the organization is likely to receive a large number of unqualified or marginally qualified responses that must be screened out.

Here are some of the more popular Web sites:

> The Career Builder Network: *www.careerbuilder.com*
> CareerMosaic: *www.careermosaic.com*
> Hot Jobs.com: *www.hotjobs.com*
> JobTrak: *www.jobtrak.com*
> Monster.com: *www.monster.com*
> Online Career Center: *www.occ.com*
> America's Job Bank: *www.ajb.dnl.us*

> Online recruiting enables the firm to reach a broad range of applicants rather quickly.

Companies can post openings and job seekers can post resumes on these sites. As the sites become more popular, more firms use them to effectively locate talented applicants. These sites can be especially helpful when the firm is tapping into the national labor market.

A company's own Web site is a public relations tool that also can be used as a recruiting tool. Many organizations post their current job openings on their Web site. In addition, some continually accept applications and provide a link for applicants to submit resumes electronically.

Alternatives to Hiring

There are a number of alternatives to hiring full-time employees. For example, firms can lease employees, hire part-time workers, outsource, or use temporary employees.

Employee leasing came about in the early 1980s. A company terminates an employee and then a leasing company, or professional employment organization (PEO), hires that employee. The PEO pays the employee's salary and benefits, and then leases the employee back to the original firm. The employee leasing industry has grown as organizations outsource more of their nonessential functions.

Part-time employees alleviate the need to hire more full-time employees. In some cases, companies prefer to use part-time workers to provide more flexibility during the peaks and valleys of the business cycle. The selection process for part-time employees is generally not as rigorous as for full-time positions. The company can, however, find some real gems who may eventually move into full-time positions.

The trend toward outsourcing has helped organizations "stick to the knitting" in the words of management gurus Peters and Waterman. That is, organizations have focused on their core competencies and outsourced nonessential functions, those functions that are not central to their core business.

With outsourcing, an outside vendor performs a service for the firm. As a result, the organization does not have to staff this function. For example, instead of hiring a new department to provide support to a new region of operation, the firm may choose to outsource

> The PEO pays the employee's salary and benefits, and then leases the employee back to the original firm.

and forgo any need for staffing. The hiring is left to the outside vendor providing the service.

TIP

The most popular area for outsourcing is information technology. The "test" for outsourcing is how essential the function is to the operations of the organization. Essential functions should not be outsourced. The company should consider outsourcing only those functions that are considered nonessential. And this may vary from organization to organization. What is essential to one company may be nonessential to another.

When the need for additional help is for a finite period, the firm can use temporary employees. Using the services of temporary help agencies is an increasingly popular alternative to hiring full-time permanent employees. Companies often find that temporary employees provide a short-term solution to unfilled openings and then provide a long-term solution as they are hired into full-time permanent positions.

If the position is not needed for the long term, one option may be to offer the current employees overtime. This is only a short-term solution, however. This alternative is used during temporary upswings in business. It also avoids costly layoffs at the end of the upswing.

International Recruitment: A Special Challenge in a Global Arena

As organizations expand into the international arena, they need to hire employees to work in overseas assignments. This situation has come with a higher price tag in recent years. The cost of a failed overseas management assignment now ranges from $500,000 to nearly $2 million. Organizations can no longer afford to make hiring mistakes. The firm's ability to compete globally is also at stake if there are no managers with international experience at the helm.

There are three major international recruitment options. Firms can hire an expatriate manager, a host-country national, or a third-country national. Each option has advantages and disadvantages.

An expatriate manager is from the home country. That is, if a multinational firm is based in the United States and has an opening in its operations in Thailand, an expatriate manager would be a manager from the home country, the United States. The major advantage of hiring an expatriate manager is his or her experience with the firm. A host-country national is a candidate from the country in which the facility is located. In this example, it could be a person from Thailand. The advantages of hiring a host-country national include fewer costs for the firm and less adjustment to the country's culture. Companies pay compensation premiums for overseas assignments taken by home-country nationals. A host-country national is not paid this premium, thus reducing the cost. A home-country national must be trained extensively in the host-country culture. Obviously, the host-country national forgoes this training since he or she is already familiar with the culture. Local governments sometimes look more favorably on the hiring of host-country nationals.

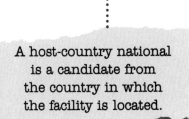

A host-country national is a candidate from the country in which the facility is located.

The final option is to hire a third-country national. This individual can be from any other country. In this example, he or she would be a candidate from a country other than the United States (the home country) or Thailand (the host country).

Generally, as organizations begin to move into the international arena, they tend to use home-country nationals. As the firm gains more global experience, it hires more host-country nationals.

Cost Benefit Analysis: Remember to Measure

All aspects of companies today are measured. Recruitment is no exception. Without measuring, there is no way to determine the effectiveness of the process; that is, if it accomplished what it needed to do. Yield ratios and costs of recruitment help measure the effectiveness of the process.

Yield ratios help determine which recruiting methods produce the most qualified applicants. The idea is to spend the money on those methods generating the highest yield of qualified applicants. To determine this ratio, the percentages of applicants from each recruiting source are calculated and then compared.

For example, if the Acme Company used advertisement and college recruiting to fill a position, yield ratios would be calculated for each method. If the advertisement generated 200 applications and 10 qualified for an interview while the college recruiting generated 50 applications and 10 qualified for an interview, the yield ratios would be 5 percent for the advertisement and 20 percent for college recruiting. (Note: $10/200$ = 5 percent for the advertisement and $10/50$ = 20 percent for college recruiting.) Therefore, in the example, the college recruiting provided the best yield ratio.

The yield ratio doesn't take into account the cost involved in recruiting applicants. This is captured in the following calculation:

> The average source cost per hire is calculated by adding the total advertising costs, the costs for all the agencies, the incentives paid to employees for referrals, and then dividing that total by the number of new hires brought on during the period in question.

For example, during the month of January, 100 employees were hired. The following costs were incurred in recruiting these 100 employees.

- $32,000 for advertisements
- $18,500 for employment agency fees
- $5,500 for employee referral incentives

The average source cost per hire is then $56,000/100 or $560.

> Effective recruitment ensures that the organization will indeed attract the most qualified applicants.

Summary

Effective recruitment ensures that the organization will indeed attract the most qualified applicants. Only through attracting talented individuals can the organization create a sustainable competitive advantage. In today's dynamic environment, firms must take advantage of both internal and external recruitment alternatives.

Employee referral programs continue to grow in popularity as the competition for talent in the marketplace heats up. Progressive organizations are also taking advantage of technological advances to recruit from a broader labor market. The globalization of business has added to the complexity of recruitment as organizations seek to fill overseas assignments as well. In keeping with the trend across the majority of functional units, human resources must pay particular attention to cost benefit analysis to ensure they are getting the biggest bang for their recruiting buck.

> The globalization of business has added to the complexity of recruitment as organizations seek to fill overseas assignments as well.

Streetwise Advice

- **Recruitment generally requires a balance of internal and external strategies.** When you hire from within the organization, you provide opportunities to improve employee morale and career growth. You must balance this internal recruiting with recruiting from outside, however, to bring new blood into the organization and enhance creativity.

- **Advanced technology is an important element in recruiting today.** While new technology should be used in the recruitment process, use it as a complement to the more traditional methods. You want to use your Web site and other Internet sites, but certainly not to the exclusion of the traditional recruiting methods.

- **Job referrals can be a source of excellent employees, but make sure that this practice is not discriminatory.** Providing incentives to employees for referring successful applicants is a growing practice that has been quite effective in yielding high-quality employees. A side benefit has been the longer retention rate of those employees participating in referral programs. There is, however, a drawback. If past discrimination has resulted in an underutilized work force, referrals can perpetuate that discrimination as the current employees tend to refer employees who are likewise from unprotected classes.

- **More creative options for external recruitment are available today.** These options include relocation consultants, welcome wagons, and outplacement firms. Relocation consultants help spouses find employment. Welcome wagons provide names of new people in the area and outplacement firms provide names of those who have been laid off because of downsizing by other organizations.

- **The Association of Executive Search Consultants has a code of ethics that provides guidelines for the ethical recruitment of executives.**

- **Focus college-recruiting efforts on a smaller number of institutions with a more intensive effort.** You might choose colleges based on your past experience with their graduates, the degree programs offered, the demographics of the student population, and the reputation of the graduates.

- **The human resource department must attract talent to the organization through its recruitment efforts.** The goal is to attract a larger number of talented individuals than there are positions for. This is how the organization is able to be more selective. Attracting four people for four openings does not leave any room for the organization to be selective.

- **Direct applicants may be good recruitment sources in some industries.** Walk-in applicants (also referred to as *direct applicants)* can be good sources for entry-level positions for retail operations. However, organizations must develop methods for retaining these applications and following up with the candidates.

- **Public employment agencies can be effective sources of applicants for some companies.** These agencies do not charge and often maintain a file of job applicants that can be called for specific positions. America's Job Bank can assist with national recruitment from public employment agencies.

The Association of Executive Search Consultants has a code of ethics that provides guidelines for the ethical recruitment of executives.

- **Firms often use blind ads in publications.** To avoid revealing its identity, a firm may choose to use a post office box instead of its address. If you are changing strategies and don't want your competitors to know what your human resource needs are, you may decide to run a blind ad. However, the company name is often a big attraction and response rates are lower for blind ads.

- **Use both internal and external methods of recruiting for maximum effectiveness.** One survey suggested that employee referrals are the most effective method of recruiting, followed by college recruiting and executive search firms. Public employment agencies and unions were found to be the least effective overall methods.

> Use both internal and external methods of recruiting for maximum effectiveness.

For more information on this topic, visit our Web site at www.businesstown.com

Chapter 7

Selection: The Steps to the Decision to Hire

T he quality of its employees makes a strategic difference in how a firm competes in the marketplace. Therefore, the selection process is a critical component of success. The responsibility for the effective selection of employees lies in a partnership between human resource professionals and the operating or line managers.

The recruitment process enables the organization to attract a talented pool of candidates that is large enough to satisfy the company's needs. Then through the selection process the most qualified of these applicants are chosen.

In most companies, the human resource department takes the initial responsibility for selecting candidates. Generally this department also administers the selection devices. However, the line or operating manager usually makes the final decision. If an organization has an ineffective hiring process, it opens itself up to two risks. One is the risk of hiring employees who aren't up to the job. Taking into account the legal difficulties that can ensue by terminating an employee, a poor hiring decision can be very expensive for the organization. Therefore, it makes more sense to spend time ensuring good decisions are made in hiring rather than dealing with poor hires after the fact.

The second risk of poor selection is losing good candidates to the competition. Missing out on talent can mean losing a competitive advantage. The selection process generally involves the following steps: screening applications and resumes, conducting testing of the applicants, interviewing, performing background investigations, and deciding whether to hire.

> In most companies, the human resource department takes the initial responsibility for selecting candidates.

Applications and Resumes

The employment application is the most commonly used selection tool. This form is the firm's opportunity to solicit basic selection criteria, which includes, but is not limited to, information about the applicant's education and experience. The application helps the organization gather the same basic information for all applicants.

The trend today is toward placing more emphasis on education. With more advanced skills required in more positions, organizations are increasingly interested in the educational levels of their applicants.

The other basic selection criterion is experience, which is the amount of time an applicant has spent working in a specific field. This criterion provides insight into the candidate's level of competency.

Standard Application

Any questions asked on the application must be job-related. The following issues are not considered job-related:

- Age
- Gender
- Marital status
- Number of children
- Religion

These types of questions are prohibited by law; asking them can lead to legal difficulties.

Even when candidates submit resumes, most organizations still ask applicants to fill out a company application. This form solicits the information that the company wants and in the format that it prefers. Most companies see it as a good exercise to have candidates transcribe information from the resume to the application form since resumes often contain exaggerated information.

These application forms are also important because they contain a statement of accuracy. This last paragraph states that the information on the application form is true and requires a signature from the applicant. If any of the information is later found to be untrue, there are grounds for termination.

Alternative Applications

More companies today use a weighted application blank (WAB). This method recognizes that some information obtained from applicants is more important in predicting job success. For example, if most successful performers on the job have had a college degree in accounting, this criterion could be used as a predictor of job success and would be weighted heavier than other items, such as experience.

> Most companies see it as a good exercise to have candidates transcribe information from the resume to the application form since resumes often contain exaggerated information.

Weights are assigned to various pieces of information. During the screening process, the human resource staff is able to develop a numerical profile, which reflects the total of these categories, for each applicant.

More organizations are also beginning to use biographical information blanks (BIBs), or *biodata applications*. BIBs are used instead of applications—or sometimes in combination with regular application forms—to gather information about an applicant's personal history. For example, BIBS may solicit information about hobbies or childhood interests. Questions such as the following may be used if they are valid predictors of job success:

> Which college courses did you enjoy the most?
> How old were you when you left home?
> Did you play team sports growing up?
> Why did you pick your college major?

Human resource staffs develop questions such as these to predict job performance and success. In formulating these questions, staff members look for those items that differentiate a good performer from a poor one. For example, the sports the candidate played or the kind of town he or she grew up in are factors that shape that person's behavior and provide insight into job performance.

> Organizations must carefully design their application forms to ensure legal compliance.

Walking the Legal Line

Organizations must carefully design their application forms to ensure legal compliance. The form should focus on soliciting information about the applicant's education and experience.

The key is to acquire information in a legal manner to avoid charges of discrimination. Some information cannot be solicited at all, and other information must be solicited very carefully.

Information concerning education is essential in making hiring decisions. However, questions about the dates of attendance are illegal. These dates can provide information concerning the approximate age of the applicant and can potentially be used for discriminatory purposes.

While applications can ask candidates about criminal convictions, questions concerning arrests are not legal. An organization can ask if the applicant is in any way prevented from working in the United States but cannot ask the applicant's country of citizenship.

....

TIP
Before using any employment forms (especially an application), the human resource staff should ask the firm's legal counsel to review them to ensure their compliance with federal, state, and local laws.

....

Screening Applicants

The human resource staff screen applicants with information obtained from the application, resume, or biographical information blank. They review these documents to determine which applicants possess the competencies and experience required for the position. This stage of the selection process is all about evaluating the qualifications of the applicants.

The recruitment process itself determines how much screening must be performed. If the recruitment process targeted a large pool of qualified applicants, the screening process may be somewhat easier. If, however, the recruitment process did not target as many qualified applicants, the screening process becomes more difficult because a larger percentage of unqualified and marginally qualified candidates must be screened out.

> The human resource staff screen applicants with information obtained from the application, resume, or biographical information blank.

The Human Resource Department's Role

In larger organizations, staff members from the human resource department screen the applicants initially. Once the department creates a pool of qualified applicants, the operating or line managers enter the process to conduct interviews.

The human resource department screens the applicants with general questions to ensure that they meet the basic job qualifications and to verify the information submitted on the application form. Line managers generally provide a more in-depth interview.

They tend to examine the fit of the candidates with the specific job responsibilities and fine-tune the qualifications screening.

TIP

Human resource professionals must have a clear understanding of the company's business in order to conduct effective screening interviews.

> The job specification lists the competencies, knowledge, skills, and abilities necessary to successfully perform the job.

The heart of the screening process lies in the documents generated by the job analysis, which identified the requisite competencies and responsibilities. These documents are the job description and the job specification. The job description details those responsibilities and the tasks expected to be performed. The job specification lists the competencies, knowledge, skills, and abilities necessary to successfully perform the job. Using these two documents to screen the applicants also increases the probability that the screening process will stay job-related, thus avoiding some of the legal pitfalls.

Some more progressive organizations use electronic screening. With the right capabilities, the firm can scan electronically submitted resumes into a database and then determine whether the minimum qualifications have been met.

Testing in the Employment Process

Employment testing is being used more extensively today to assist in the selection process. Some estimates suggest that almost three-fourths of all organizations use some type of testing. Given the increased costs of making hiring mistakes, many firms find it more cost effective to invest in testing applicants in an attempt to improve the selection process. The tests range from personality and aptitude tests to integrity tests. Although testing complements the selection process, the courts have been putting increasing pressure on organizations to ensure that any tests used are job-related.

The employer is responsible for ensuring that any selection devices reflect criteria that are essential for successful performance on the job. For example, a typing test may not be administered to

screen out applicants for a job driving a forklift if no typing is actually performed on the job. All testing used in the selection process
must follow guidelines for proving that it is job-related.

Ability and Aptitude Tests

Organizations are interested in what the applicants are able
to do and what they have the potential to do. To capture this data,
employers administer both ability and aptitude tests.

Ability, or *achievement,* tests provide organizations with insight
into what the applicant can do or what knowledge the applicant currently possesses. This information is especially important in some
positions. Job knowledge tests and work sample tests can determine
how the candidate performs the actual work that is performed on
the job. Work sample tests, also referred to as *work simulations,* give
the applicant sample job tasks to complete.

Specific cognitive ability tests measure applicants' mental skills
or knowledge. This information becomes increasingly important as
organizations compete on the basis of the knowledge possessed by
their work force. Aptitude tests measure the candidate's capacity to
acquire new skills. They tend to more predictive in nature. For example, the SAT and GMAT are predictive aptitude tests that students
take to help colleges and universities determine how well they will
perform in an institution of higher education.

Intelligence tests are increasingly being used as aptitude tests.
A general intelligence test can predict an applicant's general job success. Emotional intelligence testing is also on the rise. Inspired by
the work of Daniel Goleman, a psychologist and an international
business consultant, firms use emotional intelligence as another
predictor of future job performance.

> Job knowledge tests and
> work sample tests can
> determine how the
> candidate performs the
> actual work that is
> performed on the job.

Polygraphs and Honesty Tests

Federal legislation prohibits administering polygraph tests
in most industries. The few exceptions cover sensitive jobs in
industries such as pharmaceuticals, security, and the government.
(However, polygraph tests can be administered to employees under
certain conditions.)

Some companies still measure the honesty of applicants, but they do so by giving pencil-and-paper integrity tests. Despite having received considerable criticism, these tests have been especially popular in the retail industry where internal theft can cost an organization a considerable amount of money. Although these tests are certainly not foolproof, many retailers continue to administer them in an effort to gain an insight into the applicants' beliefs about theft and the pattern of consistency in their responses.

> Some companies still measure the honesty of applicants, but they do so by giving pencil-and-paper integrity tests.

TIP

If there is a reasonable cause to suspect an employee of internal theft, a polygraph test may be administered to current employees. Organizations should, however, still exercise extreme caution when using lie detector tests.

Personality Tests

The use of personality tests has increased dramatically over the past decade. Personality is relatively stable over time and can be a predictor of job performance. Although these tests have been used at the management level for some years, they are now being used across all organizational levels.

This increased usage has occurred for two reasons. First, companies have realized the importance of the person-job-organization fit. That is, it is no longer enough to consider the match between the person and the job; the fit with the organization and its culture is also essential. Personality tests help obtain a better fit between the individual and the firm, thereby improving the ability to make better hiring decisions.

Second, companies are increasingly using a team approach to conduct business. An insight into the personality of new team members can be helpful when building these teams.

To validate the use of personality tests, organizations should consider the following guidelines:

- The instrument must be validated.
- The test must measure a job-related issue.

- The personality test should not be the only selection device.
- The consent of the candidate must be obtained before administering the test.

As with all other selection devices, the personality test must be related to performance to use it in making decisions about selection. Personality tests cannot be used as the only selection device.

Instead of administering costly personality tests, companies may use handwriting analysis, or graphology. Although used extensively in Europe, graphology is still not used in most U.S. firms. Many firms do, however, believe that an analysis of an applicant's handwriting can provide insight into their performance on the job through added information about their personality. According to proponents of graphology, the slant of the letters or the pressure of the writing instrument on the paper can provide information about a person's intelligence or energy level. Once again, however, the personality dimensions being measured must be job-related.

Drug Testing and Medical Examinations

Some jobs require a medical examination to ensure that the applicant can meet the physical requirements of the position. For example, firefighters and police officers are generally required to submit to a medical examination. To avoid legal difficulties, the organization must ensure that the medical examinations are job-related and that they do not discriminate. In addition, the timing of examinations is critical. They should be administered at the end of the process.

TIP

Employees in more organizations are subject to random drug testing. This issue is still being debated in the courts in terms of the employee's right to privacy.

> Some jobs require a medical examination to ensure that the applicant can meet the physical requirements of the position.

In order to create a drug-free workplace, organizations are including drug testing as part of the selection process. The urine test remains the most common form of testing. Hair sample tests are more common when administering drug tests to employees or when retesting an employee.

The Interview: Navigating Land Mines

In most organizations, the interview is the cornerstone of the selection process. Ironically, it is the least reliable method of selecting applicants. This sad fact can usually be laid at the door of the interviewer who is often untrained, lacks objectivity, and makes large numbers of errors. Organizations can, however, take steps to improve the validity of the interview. For example, they can train interviewers in terms of the questions to ask, where to hold the actual meeting, and how to structure the interview. Appendix A provides tips for conducting successful employment interviews (see page 311).

Determine an Approach

The framework of the interview may be either structured or nondirective. The validity of the interview is improved with the structured method, in which questions are prepared in advance and used with all applicants for the same job. By using the same questions, the interviewer can compare answers (and therefore, applicants) across similar measures.

The nondirective method enables the applicant to take more responsibility in defining the direction of the interview. This method is unstructured, and there are no prepared questions. The applicant is free to decide what to discuss. The interviewer may ask open-ended questions but does not control the direction of the interview. This method is not as valid as the structured interview, because it is almost impossible to compare applicants across interviews. In some cases, a panel interview may be used. In this format, a single candidate is interviewed by up to five or six people who take turns asking questions. Some firms believe that these interviews provide greater insight into the candidate's ability to handle stressful situations. There is also an opportunity for several interviewers to reach a consensus based on hearing the same information versus several separate interviews at different times.

> The framework of the interview may be either structured or nondirective.

Interviews may also be situational or behavioral. The situational interview solicits information from the applicant about how she would respond in specific hypothetical incidents. The behavioral description interview asks for descriptions about real work situations that the applicant has experienced. For example, a candidate might be asked to share how he resolved an actual conflict between two employees.

The Objective Elements

Because an interview is a personal experience for both parties, as many objective elements as possible must be established beforehand. Preparation is the key to effective interviews. The place to conduct the interview must be carefully selected to afford the necessary privacy and to avoid interruptions. Before the actual meeting, the interviewer should review the candidate's resume and/or application, prepare and review the interview questions, and reread the job description and job specifications. The skills and competencies required for the job, as well as the applicant's skills and competencies, should be fresh in the interviewer's mind when the meeting begins.

TIP

Regardless of the structure of the interview, always use a realistic job preview, which is an objective overview of the position and its responsibilities. Giving the applicant an overview of only the positive aspects of the job can lead to rapid turnover in the position. It is critical to present a *realistic* picture of the job—including both the positive and negative aspects—to ensure that the appropriate person is hired.

> Before the actual meeting, the interviewer should review the candidate's resume and/or application, prepare and review the interview questions, and reread the job description and job specifications.

The interviewer should also be aware of any errors that could cloud his or her objectivity in the process. Personal biases can result in an unfavorable reaction to an applicant. Contrast errors can cause an interviewer to be unduly influenced by the last person interviewed. For example, if the last applicant was an exceptionally good candidate and the current applicant is average, the interviewer will most likely be influenced by the exceptional candidate and not rate the current applicant as highly (or as objectively).

First impressions cause errors in judgment as well. Interviewers generally make their decision within the first thirty seconds of the meeting. They then spend the rest of the interview confirming their first impression and screening out any contradictory information that might disprove their first impression.

Technology is also being used more extensively in the interviewing process. Applicants answer multiple-choice questions online and then a profile is developed to rank the applicants based on their responses.

Legal Pitfalls and Questions to Avoid

> Interviewers must be carefully trained to avoid bringing up any illegal questions and issues.

The interview is filled with potential legal pitfalls. Interviewers must be carefully trained to avoid bringing up any illegal questions and issues. (See Appendix A, page 311, for tips on avoiding these pitfalls.)

While some information (as discussed in regard to the application form) can be legally obtained, it is important to use the appropriate method. These questions should be avoided:

- Are you a citizen of the United States?
- Are you married?
- Do you have children?
- How much do you weigh?
- How old are you?
- What is your birth date?
- What is your national origin?
- What is your religious affiliation?
- When did you graduate from high school?

It is best to avoid all questions (direct as well as indirect) about an applicant's age, race, religion, sex, or national origin. Otherwise, there is a risk of discrimination.

There are, however, ways to tactfully and legally obtain some of the information that you may want. Consider the following more appropriate questions:

- Did you finish school?
- Have you ever been convicted of a crime?

- Do you speak any foreign languages that might be pertinent to this job?
- Who may we contact in case of emergency?

In addition to the federal legislation prohibiting discrimination, there are state fair employment practices (or FEPs) that must be carefully researched and followed. These state laws may be more stringent than the federal laws. Remember that ignorance of the law is no excuse. It is important to check out your state's Department of Labor Web site for details concerning fair employment practices.

It is best to ask job-related information and avoid any other questions. Straying from job-related information may open the door for legal difficulties later for both the interviewer and the organization.

Reference Checks and Background Investigations

As with most other phases of the selection process, reference checks have various legal sensitivities. Reference checks are a critical component in completing the applicant's overall picture, but they must be conducted carefully to avoid legal issues.

Previous employers can provide good information about job performance. Unfortunately, due to a number of highly publicized court cases, former employers are sometimes hesitant to provide information. Some job candidates who have not been hired because of poor references have successfully sued the former employers. When checking references, then, it is best to obtain a signed release from the applicant giving permission to perform background investigations.

Companies must guard against negligent hiring. For example, if an employee becomes dangerous, the firm can be found guilty of negligent hiring if it did not conduct effective background checks to provide a warning of prior behavior.

It is, therefore, essential to conduct background investigations. They must, however, be carefully performed to protect the rights of job applicants. Be specific when soliciting information from references. Many experts have recommended preparing all questions in advance

> Reference checks are a critical component in completing the applicant's overall picture, but they must be conducted carefully to avoid legal issues.

and using telephone references instead of letters. The letters of recommendation submitted by applicants can be greatly inflated and should be supplemented with telephone checks.

Most organizations that conduct background investigations contact the references that the applicants supply. More organizations today are also verifying the applicant's education and degrees. Some are even requesting valid transcripts to verify the applicant's information.

The Decision to Hire

The final step in the selection process is the hiring decision. Depending on the process and the organization, an individual or a committee can make this decision. This is the time to take into account all information that has been obtained during all the selection process. Compare the qualifications required for the position and those possessed by the applicants. (See Appendix C, page 333, for an employee selection checklist.)

Surveys of selection devices have indicated that some methods are more effective than others. Work samples and references are the most effective methods. These methods, then, should be weighed more heavily in the final decision stage. Personality tests and general cognitive ability tests, found to be some of the least effective methods, should be used with caution.

The decision to hire is not made in a vacuum; it includes several other decisions. Is the person going to be hired at the highest level for which he or she is qualified or where he or she is most needed at the time? This is also the time to make the salary/wage level decision. Will overqualified applicants be hired? Finally, the impact on diversity must be considered with each hiring decision.

The final decision to hire may be made using either a clinical or a statistical approach. The clinical approach takes an overall view of all the information gathered and then the decision-maker makes his or her choice. Since personal biases may influence the decision, different decision-makers are very likely to choose different candidates.

> Compare the qualifications required for the position and those possessed by the applicants.

The statistical approach allows more objectivity in the decision-making process by weighting the selection tools according to their degree of validity. The selection tool with the highest degree of validity is weighted the heaviest. It is then easy to compare the applicants according to their overall ranking based on their scores on each selection method used.

With this statistical approach, an applicant may score very high on one measure and then low on all the others and still achieve the highest rank overall. A minimum level is often identified to ensure that each qualified applicant maintains at least a minimum ranking on each selection device considered. Using the statistical approach creates more agreement among different decision-makers.

The process must be as fair and as equitable as possible. The organization wants to avoid all complaints of discrimination and wants to ensure that the process has been carefully (and legally) carried out. Documentation is key throughout the selection process. Organizations must be able to explain why an applicant was or was not hired.

The decision to hire is a crucial step in the selection process. Candidates are selected to contribute to the firm's competitive advantage. This is the time to ensure that the best candidate for the job is hired.

The job offer may be extended by phone, letter, or, rarely, in a personal meeting. It is important to communicate the decision with honesty and respect to those who are not hired as well. All applicants must be extended every professional dignity. It is good public relations.

Summary

Effective recruitment ensures that the organization will indeed attract the most qualified applicants. Only through attracting talented individuals can the organization create a sustainable competitive advantage. In today's dynamic environment, firms must take advantage of both internal and external recruitment alternatives. Employee referral programs continue to grow in popularity as the competition for talent heats up in the marketplace. Progressive organizations are also taking advantage of technological advances to

> It is important to communicate the decision with honesty and respect to those who are not hired as well.

recruit from a broader labor market. The globalization of business has added to the complexity of recruitment as organizations seek to fill overseas assignments as well. In keeping with the trend across the majority of functional units, human resources must pay particular attention to cost benefit analysis to ensure they are getting the biggest bang for their recruiting buck.

Streetwise Advice

Prepare for interviews
in advance.

- **Ensure that all selection devices are job-related.** Each selection device must be tested to ensure that it is job-related. Otherwise, it may not meet the legal requirements for selection. In addition, each method of selecting applicants will enable you to improve your ability to hire the talented individuals you need to provide your organization with its competitive advantage.

- **Prepare for interviews in advance.** The interview can be the least objective of all the selection devices, especially when the interviewer is not well prepared. Carefully review the job requirements and competencies required of the position prior to the interview. When preparing questions, review the candidate's resume and application.

- **Know the law.** Make sure that you are familiar with the questions that cannot be asked on the application and during the interview. Any inappropriate questions may open the door for discrimination charges against you and your organization.

- **Giving employment references is the flip side of obtaining reference checks. This process of providing and obtaining references is a two-way street.** When you are asked to provide a reference for a former employee, refer the caller to the human resource department. Establish specific guidelines for providing this information. Although your organization wants to ensure that it does not withhold critical information concerning dangerous former employees, care must be taken to protect the rights of these employees as well.

- **Make the decision to hire only after careful consideration of all the information gathered.** The decision to hire is made at the end of the process. It is tempting to allow personal biases and first impressions to influence your decision early in the process. These errors must be overcome to make the decision as objective as possible and to integrate all information gathered in the selection process.

> Make the decision to hire only after careful consideration of all the information gathered.

Orientation: The Acculturation Process

Once employees are hired, they must become acclimated. That is, they must learn how you do things in your organization. Part of being successful on the job is understanding "how things are done around here" and learning about the business. This socialization is accomplished with both formal and informal orientation.

Orientation is the socialization process, the welcome and the initial introduction to the organization offered to new employees. These individuals then have an opportunity to start familiarizing themselves with the firm.

Orientation should be designed to help reduce their anxiety. It is natural that new employees would experience some trepidation, but their comfort level will improve as they are welcomed and as they learn more about the company and about what is expected of them. The orientation is also instrumental in helping reinforce the employees' decision to choose this job—and this company.

This is the reality check. During this stage the firm must work to make new hires more comfortable with the job, the people, and the organization. This is also when the firm begins to communicate what is expected of the new employees.

> Orientation is the socialization process, the welcome and the initial introduction to the organization offered to new employees.

The Importance of Socializing Employees

For all members of an organization to work together effectively and efficiently, they must first understand the culture of their company. This orientation can be accomplished either formally or informally. Most organizations use both methods. Formal orientation is carefully crafted by the firm, while informal orientation occurs during the normal daily activities and interactions that take place.

Every day, dozens of opportunities exist for informal orientation. The key is to establish consistency in the information that is communicated both formally and informally about the company, the job, and the policies. All employees should realize their responsibility in the orientation process—and it should not be taken lightly. This informal contact can be extremely powerful; it can be instrumental in persuading the new hire to leave or stay.

Recognizing the importance of the socialization process, many large organizations like Disney and Procter & Gamble have developed elaborate formal orientation programs. Their orientation programs span several days and reinforce corporate culture, policies, philosophies, and job responsibilities.

TIP

Part of the orientation may be presented in video format. Sometimes a short film on the firm's history begins a formal orientation meeting. Advanced technology such as teleconferencing, for example, enables corporate executives in another location to greet new employees, giving the orientation a personal touch while emphasizing the progressive approach to technology. However, avoid presenting the entire orientation process in a video format. This method eliminates human contact, is too sterile, and is off-putting to the new person.

Most organizations repeat the orientation program for all new hires on a regular basis. Depending on the number and frequency of new hires, this program may be delivered weekly, monthly, or quarterly. Companies that experience hiring peaks (such as retailers) may present concentrated orientation programs that reflect the seasonal hiring crunch. For example, retail firms that hire additional sales associates during back-to-school and holiday seasons may deliver daily orientation programs during these times and then return to a weekly program for the rest of the year.

> Most organizations repeat the orientation program for all new hires on a regular basis.

Corporate Culture

Each organization's culture is different. Although two organizations may operate in the same industry, their cultures are unique. Just as personality is unique to each individual, no two cultures are exactly alike. Organizational cultures may share some specific traits, but the total package that constitutes the culture of the firm will vary from organization to organization.

Culture is defined as the shared way of doing things. It has been compared to glue, as the substance that holds the organization together. Culture is comprised of values, norms, history, artifacts, and myths.

The basic *values* of an organization provide the guidelines for making decisions. For example, a *Fortune* 100 company values creativity. Incorporating this value in its corporate culture gives its employees a decision-making framework within which they can become more innovative.

The values of the founding managers often provide the basis for the organizational values transferred through the years. Sam Walton is a good example. His personal values live on in the organizational values of the employees of Wal-Mart Corporation.

Norms are the appropriate ways of behaving in the organization. These norms may be written or unwritten. Many firms establish norms that address how to communicate and how to address top management. Even though norms are not written in a handbook, they are still powerful for guiding behavior. In one company, the norm is to address all employees by their first name except for the president who is addressed by last name. A right of passage for all new, and uninformed, employees occurs when they call the president by his first name. They quickly learn by violating the norm what is and what is not appropriate behavior in that organization.

History provides an explanation for why things are done the way they are and how the firm got to its current stage. The reason a firm was founded often guides the future direction and actions of its employees, thereby reinforcing the organization's basic values.

For example, some companies may be reluctant to give up long-time markets that are no longer as lucrative as they once were because these markets were their first customers and there is a sense of loyalty and emotional attachment. Or a retail chain may be reluctant to close a store that is no longer profitable because it was the first location. The stories, or *myths,* that are passed from one organizational generation to the next provide insight into the values and norms of the culture. The founding story is often one of the most important myths.

The founding story of the Gap Stores has been used to impress upon new employees the values of the firm, which include the focus on customer service and the need for stock replenishment. The founder tried unsuccessfully to buy a pair of Levi jeans in San

> Many firms establish norms that address how to communicate and how to address top management.

Francisco, the heart of Levi Strauss country. So he built a chain of stores focused on correcting all the negative aspects of retailing stores that he encountered while searching for the jeans. Hearing the story helped new employees understand why high levels of quality customer service were expected of Gap employees and why rapid stock replenishment was so important.

The *artifacts* of the company are the symbols that represent dimensions of the culture. MBNA is well known in the Wilmington, Delaware, area for the green color accents on its buildings and the pins that its employees wear on their jacket lapels. UPS drivers are easily recognized for their brown uniforms. And the Mickey ears are readily associated with Disney.

An awareness of the elements of corporate culture helps employees identify appropriate behaviors and make better decisions. As employees conform to these norms, they bond with their organization, becoming one of the family.

Conformity Versus Creativity

Organizations today walk a very fine line between the need for some level of conformity and the need for creativity and innovation. Unfortunately, high levels of conformity tend to wipe out creativity and innovation in the firm, and vice versa.

The need for creativity and innovation is well publicized today. Organizations have been told repeatedly that they cannot continue to do things in the same old way. Today's changing environment means that companies must rethink their traditional solutions to business problems and approach them in a creative way.

Orientation is designed to create some level of conformity by sharing rules and policies with new hires. A certain degree of consistency, therefore, is achieved with conformity. The organization could not function effectively if there wasn't some level of conformity in the way that things were done.

The question is, how much conformity is appropriate for the company? The need for conformity must be balanced with the need for creativity and innovation.

> An awareness of the elements of corporate culture helps employees identify appropriate behaviors and make better decisions.

The Formal Orientation Process

When possible, the new employee should be met at the door on his or her first day. This greeting makes the employee feel important and more comfortable. It is best if the immediate supervisor can perform this initial greeting or at least send someone from the department to meet the new employee and bring him or her in.

The formal orientation process should be developed with the following in mind:

- Provide an agenda
- Review policies and procedures
- Hold the orientation on the employee's first day whenever possible

TIP

The first day on the job can be very stressful. Part of this is the uncertainty the person is experiencing in a new environment. The formal orientation process can be an effective tool to help reduce some of this stress and uncertainty, if it is used appropriately.

Providing an agenda lets the employees know what to expect in the orientation. An agenda also provides a measure of comfort in informing them of a plan for the program.

Components of the Formal Orientation Process

The important components of the orientation include the following:

- Welcome to the company
- Tour of the facilities
- Introduction to coworkers
- Completion of paperwork
- Review of the employee handbook
- Review of job responsibilities

> When possible, the new employee should be met at the door on his or her first day.

ORIENTATION: THE ACCULTURATION PROCESS

Welcome to the Company

The welcome to the company, which should be given by a corporate executive, kicks off the orientation on a positive note by communicating to the employees that they are important to the firm—and important to the top management. New hires then begin to feel a part of the organization.

Part of the welcome should include an overview of the company. It is important for new employees to understand the business and the industry within which the organization operates. This overview provides the context for the employees' actual job responsibilities as well.

Tour of the Facilities

A tour of the facilities also helps increase the new people's comfort level by helping them feel more "at home" in their surroundings. The tour should not only point out important departments and work facilities but the essentials for everyday working as well. The locations of restrooms, coffee machines, break rooms, the cafeteria, fitness centers, bus stops, and the human resource department should all be part of the tour.

Introduction to Coworkers

To make new employees feel more comfortable, introduce them to the people with whom they will be interacting most closely, usually their direct supervisor and a coworker from their department or unit. The coworker will often serve as an ongoing source of support after the formal orientation process is over.

Mentors can be a great complement to a formal orientation program. They can be either formally or informally assigned and are generally coworkers who provide ongoing support.

> The tour should not only point out important departments and work facilities but the essentials for everyday working as well.

Completion of Paperwork

Essential paperwork should be completed during the formal orientation process. These documents ensure that employees will be paid on time and will receive their benefits (such as enrollment in a medical plan) on a timely basis. Overloading new hires with nonessential paperwork, however, can create an unpleasant experience and overwhelm the employee.

A checklist should be developed to ensure that the necessary paperwork is completed. Overlooked paperwork can lead to employee dissatisfaction early on, especially if it involves late paychecks or missed enrollment dates in key benefits.

TIP

Since more than one individual often processes new employees, a checklist that travels with the employee from one person to the next ensures that nothing falls through the cracks. From a legal standpoint, the checklist is also a technique to ensure that all proper documentation is on hand and the necessary orientation has been addressed. (See Appendix C, page 333, for a sample checklist.)

Review the Employee Handbook

The human resource department staff should go over the employee handbook with the new hires. Staff members should explicitly discuss the rules, policies, and procedures of the firm, paying careful attention to the disciplinary process. This is an opportunity for the human resource staff to emphasize key corporate policies such as the company's commitment to equal opportunity employment, its zero tolerance policies on drugs and violence, its code of ethics, safety programs, and sexual harassment policies.

Review of Job Responsibilities

Now is the time to formally review the employees' job responsibilities to ensure that their expectations are closely aligned with the organization's expectations. A copy of the job description may also be provided at this point.

Critical to understanding expectations is an understanding of the basis for performance evaluation. Human resource staff should review the performance appraisal and discuss standards of performance used to evaluate employees. Taking the time to address this issue now will help to alleviate confusion later.

> The human resource department staff should go over the employee handbook with the new hires.

The Follow-up Session

A follow-up session should be scheduled generally one month to three months after the formal orientation. The follow-up provides an opportunity for employees to ask additional questions and clarify issues that they have encountered in the interim.

The Employee Handbook

The employee handbook provides a great opportunity for the firm to communicate policies and procedures to its employees. Every employee should sign a receipt stating that he or she received a copy of the handbook. This document can protect the company in court if an employee claims to have been ignorant of a policy that he is accused of violating. The standard employee handbook should include, at a minimum, the following components (for a sample table of contents see Appendix A, page 309):

- Welcome letter
- Employment policies
- History of the firm
- Employee benefits

The welcome letter should provide a warm introduction to the organization and give a brief summary of the company and its business. This letter should clearly communicate the firm's commitment to its human resources.

Employment policies should be provided in writing so there is no confusion about whether employees have been advised of these policies. This document also ensures that employees understand critical policies so they do not make mistakes that could embarrass them among their new coworkers. These critical policies include the following:

- Code of ethics
- Disciplinary policy (with grievance procedures)
- Dress code
- Drug-free workplace policy

> Employment policies should be provided in writing so there is no confusion about whether employees have been advised of these policies.

- Equal employment opportunity statement
- E-mail and Internet usage policy
- Employment-at-will
- Performance evaluation system
- Sick policy
- Vacation policy
- Working hours

Employment-at-will policies state that either the employee or the employer may terminate the employment relationship for any reason at any time. This termination, however, is not illegal.

> Employment-at-will policies state that either the employee or the employer may terminate the employment relationship for any reason at any time.

TIP

Contact your state department of labor to determine if your state is an employment-at-will state; not every state is.

It is important to include the disciplinary policy of the firm to avoid future misunderstandings. Part of this policy should include a discussion of due process; that is, how employees can address grievances.

The drug-free workplace policy should also include the company's drug-testing policy and a statement of privacy issues.

If the organization has a written code of ethics (which is definitely recommended), it should be included in the employee handbook. This code explicitly states what is expected of employees—such as appropriate and inappropriate behavior—and usually includes a brief discussion of the consequences of violating the code.

Evaluation: The Final Step

As with any human resource management function, the human resource staff must periodically evaluate the effectiveness of the orientation program. This evaluation ensures that information that is valuable to the acculturation of new hires is being disseminated and that current information is also being shared.

Some organizations solicit the input of recently hired employees in the evaluation. After a period on the job, new hires are asked what was valuable to them and what else they might have found helpful. Their managers can also provide key feedback because they can observe close-up any deficiencies in the information given to their new employees.

Summary

Orientation is a critical component of the new hire process. Effective orientation programs can increase the probability of retaining new employees by helping them bond with the organization and develop a commitment to their new employer. Orientation eases the sometimes painful transition into a new firm. "Learning the ropes" during the socialization process helps new hires become more quickly acclimated to the corporate culture and facilitates assuming their own role in contributing to the overall corporate objectives.

Streetwise Advice

*   **Orientation is more than watching a video.** Although slick videos can present a wonderful introduction to the company and the founding story of the firm, they cannot replace a formal orientation program. Good orientation programs are interactive, providing an opportunity for new employees to ask questions and helping them feel comfortable with the firm—and with their choice of employer. Watching a video falls far short of this objective.

*   **Be aware of information overload.** Try to prioritize information. If large quantities of information are presented to new hires, much of it will be screened out and quickly forgotten. Present what is most important. Be sure to provide critical information in writing so employees can take it away with them and review it at their leisure or refer to it when needed.

*   **Welcome new employees to the firm in a company newsletter.** Seeing their name in print in a company publication makes new employees feel important. Allocate a regular corner of the

> Effective orientation programs can increase the probability of retaining new employees by helping them bond with the organization and develop a commitment to their new employer.

newsletter to welcome new hires. If space permits, include a short biography on each person.

- **Ask an attorney (preferably, one specializing in employment law) to review specific policies before you distribute them in the employee handbook.** Some employees in legal battles have considered the handbook an implied contract. Careful review by an attorney can ensure that you have used appropriate terminology and have met the legal requirements for employment law. For example, use of the term *permanent* employment status following a probationary period could imply lifetime employment, which certainly would not be the employer's intent.

- **The orientation program is just the beginning of the acculturation process.** Acclimation to the organization's culture and the reinforcement of appropriate behavior continues in the training and development efforts and performance appraisal systems of the firm.

- **Think of the orientation program as the company's first impression on new employees.** The quality of the orientation program is a reflection on the organization as a whole. First impressions create lasting impressions. This adage holds true with orientation programs as well. They set the stage for the rest of the employee's employment.

- **Even with employment-at-will, you may not violate an employee's rights or engage in discrimination.** Employees must be treated fairly and with respect.

- **Be sure to conduct orientations for new employees.** If your organization is too small to have enough new employees to hold large-group sessions, use a one-on-one format.

- **Give a welcome gift.** An item with the company's logo is a nice welcome gift that communicates a sense of belonging. A welcome gift doesn't have to be expensive; a coffee cup is a popular gift. You can also present desk calendars, pen and pencil sets, or leather portfolios.

> The quality of the orientation program is a reflection on the organization as a whole.

- Some companies send "welcome aboard" cards that thank employees for accepting employment with their organization.

- **Consider having employees sign an Internet policy as part of the orientation program.** This statement should include specific information on how the Internet can be used and an agreement by the employees not to visit pornographic (or other inappropriate) Web sites.

- **Make sure that new employees' workstations are prepared and well stocked.** A new employee should be greeted with a fully stocked workstation. At a minimum, they should have a desk with stationery/office supplies, a telephone (with procedures for operating the system and activating voice mail), and a computer (with an e-mail address).

> A new employee should be greeted with a fully stocked workstation.

For more information on this topic, visit our Web site at www.businesstown.com

PART III

Maximizing Employee Performance

Every organization is concerned with getting more from its employees. As companies have to produce more with fewer resources, they are showing renewed interest in how to get the most out of each employee in order to benefit overall corporate performance.

Chapter 9: Leverage training and development to maximize employee performance.

Chapter 10: Understand job analysis in the context of collecting data, determining job specifications, and writing descriptions.

Chapter 11: Explore the importance of job design—for individuals and the organization as a whole.

Chapter 12: Use a variety of means to motivate employees to maintain or improve productivity.

Chapter 13: Examine methods of performance appraisal and the reasons behind them.

Chapter 9

Training and Development

L earning organizations are created one employee at a time by training and developing the work force. A collection of life-long learners is the first step toward creating a learning organization. Without an effective training and development program, organizations can quickly fall behind in acquiring the skill sets and knowledge required for a competitive work force.

An organization's ability to compete successfully in today's highly competitive marketplace requires a talented pool of workers. Only by constantly upgrading the skills of its work force can a company achieve and maintain this competitive advantage. Training and development is a never-ending challenge that every organization must address.

> Training improves individual performance, which ultimately improves corporate performance.

The Organizational Role of Training: Meeting Objectives

Training and development has a ripple effect on organizational performance. Training improves individual performance, which ultimately improves corporate performance.

The unprecedented pace of change today forces successful organizations to have a skilled work force that is capable of predicting and reacting to a changeable environment. Only by anticipating the knowledge, skills, and abilities required to compete successfully in the future can organizations meet these challenges.

The pace of technological change in today's workplace is unprecedented. These advances have altered the very way in which work is performed. To keep up with the advanced skills they need to perform their jobs, workers must acquire new skill sets and organizations must retrain them.

TIP

Annual corporate training budgets continue to grow. Although the techniques and topics may change, the one constant is that companies must provide training and development to their people year after year.

Organizations enhance their intellectual capital through training and development. The shift of the American economy from manufacturing to providing services has necessitated a shift in worker skills from skilled labor to knowledge. In this information age, each organization must be committed to acquiring and monitoring knowledge. The majority of this knowledge is housed in the minds of the work force. Thus, companies must be committed to continually offering training and development opportunities to their employees. Training and development is an investment in the work force, which enables the firm to position itself for success in the future. If it stands still, the company will fail.

Although the terms *training* and *development* are usually linked, they address slightly different needs. Training focuses on learning the necessary skills and acquiring the knowledge required to perform a job. Development focuses on the preparation needed for future jobs; it should be considered an investment in the work force since its benefits are long-term

Training and development help fight the obsolescence of human resources. People can become obsolete just like any other resource (i.e., plants and equipment). Training (and retraining) help to combat this problem. Think of training as preventive maintenance.

Most businesspeople today realize that upgrades and additional components are continually needed to keep a computer up-to-date. The same can be said of people. If they do not constantly improve their skills and abilities, workers can fall behind and jeopardize their employability.

As job responsibilities are changed and jobs are redesigned, the skills and abilities required to perform them will change as well. The organization needs to anticipate these changes and provide the necessary training and retraining of its employees. Job training is a continual process that can combat obsolescence and increase corporate productivity.

> As job responsibilities are changed and jobs are redesigned, the skills and abilities required to perform them will change as well.

Assessing Training Needs

Training and development are a multibillion-dollar industry. One survey suggested that over $120 billion was spent on formal training efforts during the year 2000. Each year the training budgets of corporate America continue to increase.

TIP

Most surveys report that training expenditures only capture the cost of formal training programs. American businesses, big and small, spend a more substantial amount on informal training. For example, consider the costs incurred in on-the-job training for a bookkeeper in a four-person office, where an experienced bookkeeper spends a day training the new employee. These kinds of figures are not captured on the annual surveys, which focus only on formal training and usually only on those companies with more than 100 employees.

Needs Analysis

Too often, organizations take a pro-training position, but they spend the dollars foolishly, taking whatever training is available. With such a large financial investment at stake, a systematic approach is more effective. The first step is for the human resource department staff and line managers, who are responsible for determining the training needs of the organization, to conduct a needs analysis.

This stage of the process tries to identify performance deficiencies or gaps between the actual performance and the desired performance of individuals (and the overall organization). Then the analysts need to determine whether training will improve or eliminate this deficiency. (The answer to all performance deficiencies is not always training.) The needs analysis will provide a systematic assessment of the organization, the task, and the employee.

> The overall corporate strategy is the foundation for the assessment of the firm's training needs.

The overall corporate strategy is the foundation for the assessment of the firm's training needs. These needs must be explored within the context of the organization's goals and strategies. In addition, top management must support the training efforts. Training must play a role in helping the organization meet its objectives by identifying and supplying the knowledge, skills, and abilities that will be needed to meet those objectives.

The next aspect of the needs analysis, the task assessment, addresses the specific requirements of the position. It is critical to determine what needs to be done in the job and what qualifications are required to accomplish these tasks. The job analysis provides good insight into this information through the job description and the job specification.

The final piece of the needs assessment is the employee assessment. This phase identifies gaps between the skill requirements of the job and the actual skills possessed by the employee. Training can help close these gaps.

TIP

The bull's-eye technique is an alternative method (or even a complement) for completing a needs assessment for training. The individual jobholder is placed at the center of a bull's-eye target. Through a self-assessment, this individual provides the key information concerning his or her training needs. Each outer layer of the bull's-eye ring represents others with whom the individual works. For example, the individual's supervisor usually occupies the second ring. Other rings can capture information from peers, customers, or anyone else who can provide valuable input into what training needs should be addressed for this individual in this position. The ultimate objective is to paint as complete a picture as possible of the training needs that should be addressed for this individual by soliciting input from a variety of sources.

These three pieces of the needs assessment present a complete picture of the training needed. By combining what the organization needs (such as a commitment to acquiring specific core competencies in technological areas), what the job itself requires (such as advanced technological competence on a new piece of equipment), and what the individual needs (such as the skill to operate this new equipment), the final training needs can be identified.

Once the needs assessment is conducted, it is time to establish the behavioral objectives, which clearly identify the outcomes that are expected of the training program. For example, a behavioral objective for forklift operators may be the ability to safely operate the new forklift model that is being delivered next week. Specific tasks (starting the machine, backing it up, and safety procedures)

> Once the needs assessment is conducted, it is time to establish the behavioral objectives, which clearly identify the outcomes that are expected of the training program.

should be included in the objectives. These objectives are also used in the evaluation stage to determine if the training was effective.

Obtaining Information for the Needs Assessment

The information required for the needs assessment may be obtained from a variety of sources using a wide range of methods. It is important to use as many sources as possible to develop as complete an assessment as possible.

Sources of information include the employee, the employee's supervisor, subordinates, experts in the field, and other people who have performed the job in the past. Any documentation about the job should also be explored. This documentation might include accident reports, performance appraisals, procedure manuals, employment tests, job descriptions, exit interviews, and customer complaints. All of these sources help identify performance deficiencies.

The required information may be gathered using personal interviews (with individuals or groups), observations, group discussions, focus groups, telephone surveys, or questionnaires. These questionnaires may be conducted by fax, e-mail, or paper.

> The required information may be gathered using personal interviews (with individuals or groups), observations, group discussions, focus groups, telephone surveys, or questionnaires.

Learning Principles: One Size Does Not Fit All

Learning is a behavior change that is relatively permanent. Training and development provide learning opportunities. That is, employees change their behavior as a result of the training and development presented.

Before training can be effective, however, employees must want to learn. The basic motivation to learn has been instilled in a larger percentage of the work force as workers recognize that each person must become a lifelong learner in order to succeed.

The Transfer of Training

A critical component of successful training is the effective transfer of knowledge, skills, and abilities from the learning environment to the actual job. If employees only perform the skill in the classroom and do not utilize it on the job, then the training was wasted.

One way to enhance the transfer of training is to make sure that the conditions in the learning environment more closely mirror the actual conditions on the job. To further ensure an effective transfer, the following points should be integrated into the training program:

- Present theory to explain why things are done the way they are
- Provide demonstrations to enable trainees to observe the new behaviors
- Provide opportunities for trainees to practice the behaviors
- Provide feedback (This ensures the behaviors are being used correctly and reinforces the behaviors.)

Meaningful Behaviors

Knowledge and skills are more likely to be transferred back to the job if they are important to the employee. Workers will learn and retain information that is relevant to them more easily and ultimately transfer it to actual performance on the job. Specific knowledge and skills that are related directly to the job or to future job opportunities are also more likely to be transferred back to the job.

Trainers are responsible for making this connection for learners. They must make sure that employees understand the relevance of what they are doing. Trainers must communicate how the trainees' job fits with the rest of the organization and how it contributes directly to the organization's goals.

> Workers will learn and retain information that is relevant to them more easily and ultimately transfer it to actual performance on the job.

Practice

To be more successful in learning, trainees need opportunities to practice the skill. People learn by doing (referred to as *vicarious learning*). Repetition helps employees become more comfortable and more adept at performing the task. Practice also ensures that learners don't easily forget the task.

Few people would be able to learn to ride a bike by just reading about it or hearing a lecture on how to ride. The practice of skills is critical in the learning process for many behaviors.

Reinforcement

Successful training must also be reinforced. The organization must reward employees who transfer training back to the job. If new behaviors are ignored or challenged, they will quickly be extinguished, and the employee will return to the old way of doing things, thus wasting the training.

Reinforcement requires that workers outside the training function support these efforts. As employees return from training, direct supervisors must be aware of the new behaviors and reinforce the behaviors through effective rewards.

> If new behaviors are ignored or challenged, they will quickly be extinguished, and the employee will return to the old way of doing things, thus wasting the training.

On-the-Job Training Options

On-the-job training is conducted while the employee is performing on the job. Usually the supervisor or a fellow employee who has experience with the task provides on-the-job instruction. The vast majority of training performed is on-the-job, which may also involve learning by doing. Some on-the-job techniques include apprenticeships, internships, mentoring, coaching, and job rotation.

Apprenticeships are popular in the skilled trades. An apprentice is placed in a position in an organization in partnership with a school (or, in some instances, with the government or a union) to learn a trade. The apprentice works under a person experienced in the craft. Generally some classroom requirements are specified for the apprentice in combination with the experience gained on the job.

Internships are usually offered in colleges and universities. They are used to assist students in gaining real-world experience. Skills learned on the job supplement the students' classroom learning.

Mentoring has grown in popularity in recent years. Organizations have moved from using informal mentoring programs to formal programs to capture as many of the benefits of on-the-job training as possible. A mentor is an experienced employee who is paired with a younger, less experienced employee to provide guidance. Mentors can be used to coach employees on the job.

Job rotation provides an opportunity for employees to rotate from one job to another, generally for a certain period. For example, an employee may be asked to perform accounts receivable responsibilities for the first four hours of each day and then accounts payable responsibilities for the second four hours of the day. This cross-training benefits the organization by ensuring that more than one employee can perform a specific job.

Lateral moves for managers are the equivalent of job rotation for lower-level employees, but they are of longer duration. The organizational objective is the same for both: cross-training employees. The need for more flexible skill sets and broad-based skills has never been greater. Exposure to as many positions within the organization as possible increases managers' skill sets and helps build important conceptual skills.

Off-the-Job Training Alternatives

Training that is offered away from the job is growing in variety and ranges from videotapes to lectures or formal educational degree programs. Either corporate training professionals or independent trainers can be used to provide off-the-job training. Some of the more common alternatives include college degree programs, professional certification programs, outside meetings, conferences, workshops, and seminars.

> Exposure to as many positions within the organization as possible increases managers' skill sets and helps build important conceptual skills.

Varied Media

Videotapes can be a good learning source for broad topics. Most organizations purchase training videos from companies that specialize in producing these videotapes. Many management topics are also addressed in generic videotapes. The trainer can then customize a presentation after the video to meet specific organizational needs.

Technology-based training is one of the fastest growing training areas. Online courses are one example of this new technology. Computer-based training (referred to as CBT) has responded to the need for just-in-time training. This technology-based training has reduced costs associated with time away from the job. The advantage of computer-based training is its ability to be delivered anywhere and anytime. Another advantage is that the training can be self-paced.

TIP

Much of the research on computer-based training focuses on poor completion rates. Although there are numerous advantages to computer-based training, this problem has yet to be solved. Before implementing a computer-based training program, be sure to address this issue. Some organizations are experimenting with incentives for timely completion.

> Role-playing has been an effective method for teaching management skills and diversity management.

Take It Outside

Many professional associations offer conferences and seminars to update the skills in their industry. For example, the Institute of Management Accountants holds regular training conferences designed to present new knowledge and skills valuable to the accounting profession.

Role-playing has been an effective method for teaching management skills and diversity management. Learners are given an opportunity to role-play what they are learning and then are critiqued afterward. In many cases, these role-plays are videotaped to help trainees evaluate themselves and observe their own behavior.

Like role-playing, simulations, also known as *vestibule training* or *gaming,* create an opportunity to practice job performance. Simulations enable the learner to make mistakes without suffering real-world consequences and repercussions. These methods are especially valuable in training professions such as airline pilots.

Outdoors experiences (also referred to as *wilderness training*) have been used extensively in team building. Groups of employees are taken to facilities especially designed to build team skills. The only way to complete the assigned task, such as climbing a rock wall, is to work with and trust fellow employees. The expectation is that the trust thus built among the team members, and their ability to work together, will be taken back to the job and improve the team's overall performance.

The number of corporate universities increased significantly in the 1990s. Understanding the importance of providing effective training and development to their employees, some larger organizations developed corporate universities that focus on teaching the core competencies they need. Two of the better-known corporate universities are Disney University and McDonald's Hamburger University.

Evaluating the Effectiveness of Training Programs

The training process is not completed once the training is delivered. The effectiveness of the training program must be evaluated. With such significant investments in training programs at stake, evaluation is critical. Companies cannot continue to spend billions of dollars without assessing the effectiveness of these expenditures—that is, the return on their investment.

The following elements should be evaluated:

- Employees' reactions
- Learning that occurred
- Behavior changes
- Impact on corporate objectives

Evaluating the *employees' reactions* involves soliciting feedback on what they thought about the program, the facilities, and the trainers. This is the most common information used in evaluating training effectiveness. Generally, this information is captured in a form handed out at the end of the program. Trainees may be asked if they thought the program was useful. This is a good opportunity to solicit suggestions for improving the program for future learners. Feedback is the most basic information, however; effective evaluation really requires more.

> Companies cannot continue to spend billions of dollars without assessing the effectiveness of these expenditures—that is, the return on their investment.

> The results of the training, including objective measures of the *impact on corporate objectives*, have become more critical to organizations today.

The next level of evaluation addresses what *learning* actually occurred during the program. Then evaluators must determine whether the participants were actually able to master the information presented during the program.

To evaluate what learning occurred, trainees may be asked to take a test. Or in the case of skills, the learners may be asked to take a performance test or complete a simulation test. *Assessing behavior* looks at whether the learners are actually using what they learned. Generally, those employees closest to the trainee, such as the supervisor or peers, observe their behavior. With managers, however, subordinates may be able to observe whether behavior changes have occurred.

The results of the training, including objective measures of the *impact on corporate objectives*, have become more critical to organizations today. For example, cost savings, productivity increases, lower accident rates, or fewer quality defects can be measured to assess the results of the training.

A Special Challenge: Management Development

An organization's success depends in large part on its management talent. There must always be management trainees in the pipeline who are being continually trained and developed in management competencies. As a result, management education and development receives a large part of most organizations' training budgets.

While many organizations provide inside training for lower management levels, the top management ranks are often sent through special university and college programs designed specifically for them. Harvard University provides such well-known programs.

Some of the most popular training topics for managers (across all management levels) include delivering results, managing change, communication, leadership, conducting performance appraisals, motivating the work force, coaching, developing interpersonal skills, negotiation, and managing conflict.

While formal training programs are essential to management development, on-the-job training is also critical. Many critical management skills (such as leadership) can only be learned by doing. Reading a textbook or listening to a lecture will not reinforce these skills.

Recognizing the critical shortage of management talent, many firms have established formal management development programs. New managers rotate from one functional unit to another over a period of months to acquire broad-based skills and to gain exposure to as much of the business as possible. This on-the-job training is usually accompanied by classroom learning.

Career Development: Everyone's Job

Each person is responsible for his or her own career management in today's workplace. A few decades ago, the human resource department and/or the immediate supervisor took on that responsibility. Today's environment makes that almost impossible. Employees can partner with human resource staff members and with supervisors, but the ultimate responsibility for managing his or her career belongs to the individual.

A career path is a road map; it requires a sense of direction and it identifies guideposts along the way. This path provides a focus for the knowledge, skills, and abilities that will be acquired and a plan of action for directing all future actions.

Part of an employee's career development is to recognize what skills he or she has and what skills may be required in the future. A personal SWOT analysis, which identifies individual strengths, weaknesses, opportunities, and threats, is very useful in conducting this kind of an assessment.

Most organizations offer alternative career paths today. Everyone doesn't have to aspire to management positions. Instead, alternative career paths can also be outlined on a professional track.

> Employees can partner with human resource staff members and with supervisors, but the ultimate responsibility for managing his or her career belongs to the individual.

Summary

Training and development has become more critical to organizations as the skill sets required for success change. An ongoing process, training must be constantly monitored and evaluated. Training needs must be systematically identified through a corporate needs analysis, and the programs must be assessed afterward to determine their effectiveness on a routine basis.

Streetwise Advice

- **The goal of every organization should be strategic training.** Your training should be conducted within the context of the overall corporate strategy. Its purpose should be to help employees meet your company's strategic objectives.

- **Most organizations are moving toward the use of core competencies.** Instead of addressing only the specific skills that are required for each position, this method identifies a group of core competencies for groups of jobs—or even for the entire organization. Training efforts can then focus on the development of these core competencies in the work force. This focus builds in a degree of flexibility since broader-based skill sets are acquired that enable employees to perform more jobs with those core competencies.

- **While all organizations must address some type of training and development, the amount of training can be reduced by hiring skilled workers.** Each organization makes the decision either to make or to buy employees. That is, a firm can hire employees with the skills that are needed, thereby buying the skill set (and paying a higher salary for those skills). Or, it can make employees by hiring workers with fewer skills (at lower salaries) and then providing them with the necessary training.

- **The importance of the training function is reflected in the use of the term *human resource development*.** Human resource development (or HRD) coordinates the training and development requirements of the organization.

> Your training should be conducted within the context of the overall corporate strategy. Its purpose should be to help employees meet your company's strategic objectives.

- A wide variety of training is offered across organizations. **Some of the more common training topics include the following:**

  - Conducting performance appraisals
  - Managing diversity
  - Developing interpersonal skills
  - Leadership
  - Listening skills
  - Providing orientation for new employees
  - Problem solving
  - Recruitment skills
  - Selection skills
  - Team building
  - Time management
  - Training the trainer

- Downsizing has placed additional pressure on organizations for training. **As organizations downsize, they need to retrain workers for other positions within the company.**

- Since growing numbers of the population are functionally illiterate, remedial training is on the rise. **In response to the need for more entry-level workers with basic skills, many larger organizations are providing remedial training, focusing primarily on reading, writing, and math. Training in English as a second language is also on the rise in response to the increased number of immigrants.**

- **A good resource for training is found on the American Society of Training and Development's Web site at *www.astd.org.*** Providing training opportunities communicates that your work force is valued and that your organization is willing to invest in them.

- **The trend is for more organizations to provide company-specific training with corporate universities.** Corporate universities enable firms to customize management development to address the unique challenges of their business and industry.

> As organizations downsize, they need to retrain workers for other positions within the company.

The acquisition of skills and knowledge is presented in the context of the company and its business processes.

- **A large part of management development is reading.** Reading should not be confined to just trade publications. Managers should be encouraged to read very broadly. Innovative ideas come from unlikely sources. It is important for managers to be generally well read.

It is important for managers to be generally well read.

For more information on this topic, visit our Web site at www.businesstown.com

Job Analysis

Chapter 10

J ob analysis has become a critical function of human resource management that drives many other HR functions. An effective job analysis process provides an understanding of all the jobs in the organization, including the responsibilities each involves and the qualifications necessary for a person to successfully discharge those responsibilities. This process enables the organization to better determine its human resource needs—both current and future.

The EEOC is clear about the critical role of job analysis in providing information to make better recruiting and selection decisions. Job analysis is the beginning of the process to determine job-related information used in all the human resource functions.

> Human resource professionals work in partnership with the line managers to successfully provide critical information in order to conduct the analysis.

The Process of Job Analysis

The human resource department has traditionally had the ultimate responsibility for the job analysis process. In most cases today, however, human resource professionals work in partnership with the line managers to successfully provide critical information in order to conduct the analysis.

The Purpose

A job analyst is a human resource specialist who performs the job analysis. This person may be a company employee or a consultant. In some cases, the person acting in the role of analyst may be the supervisor or line manager of the job being analyzed.

The degree of detail gathered will depend on budget and time constraints. However, the types of information to be obtained from the job analysis include:

- Interactions with other jobs
- Knowledge, skills, and abilities required (i.e., education, experience, and aptitudes)
- Machines and equipment required
- Physical work conditions encountered (where appropriate—such as exposure to hazardous materials)

- Specific procedures used
- Specific tasks performed on the job

This information paints a picture of the job responsibilities, how they are performed, and the knowledge, skills, and abilities needed to perform these responsibilities successfully.

Sources

The data of the job analysis process is critical. Care, then, must be taken to select the methods and sources for this data.

A variety of sources are generally used to gather information during the job analysis process. Sources must be experienced and familiar with the job being analyzed. In addition, the more sources used, the greater the likelihood that the information will be complete and accurate.

In the vast majority of cases, the employees currently performing the job will be the number one source of information. The employee's manager or supervisor is another likely source for accurate information. Employees who performed the job in the past may also provide additional insights.

TIP

When using the current employee as a source of information for job analysis, exercise caution. Employees are likely to inflate their responsibilities and somewhat exaggerate the importance of their tasks.

In many cases with specialized jobs, an expert in the field may provide valuable information. In some larger organizations, industrial engineers may also be tapped as good sources of information. They are familiar with a wide range of jobs in the organization or at least with a specialized field of job categories.

In some rare instances, the job analyst may actually perform the job for a specified period to learn more about the responsibilities and how they are performed. This method could only be used in manual jobs requiring fewer or no specialized skills. And then afterward, the analyst may conduct his or her own job analysis.

> In the vast majority of cases, the employees currently performing the job will be the number one source of information.

Data Collection Methods

There are a variety of ways in which this data may be gathered. These methods may include observing the work being performed, work samplings, conducting interviews, completing questionnaires, and using standardized instruments.

Observations

Observing workers on the job can provide good insight into the essential functions of the job. Observers may keep a diary of the functions performed. Workers may also be videotaped on the job. Job analysts can then compile a list of essential functions from watching this video.

Observation tends to be more effective with some jobs than with others. It is easier to observe manual jobs. When analytical thinking skills are required, however, it is not always possible to observe all of the essential functions being performed. A certain amount of contamination also occurs as people become aware that they are being observed. Data may become less accurate as workers change the way they would normally perform the job.

> A certain amount of contamination also occurs as people become aware that they are being observed.

TIP

Care must be taken when using the observation method to gather job analysis data. As a society, Americans are more geared toward activity (that is, doing things). Time spent thinking is often viewed inaccurately as idle time—or worse, as doing nothing. Observers, then, must carefully monitor all work behaviors—thinking and doing.

Work Sampling

A variation of the observation method is work sampling. Instead of observing all the actions of a worker over an extended period (perhaps each workday for a week), random samples of the work are taken for specified shorter periods. However, work samples must be representative of the entire job. With cyclical work, for example, gathering samples from times that are not representative of the entire job may result in skewed data. Enough preliminary information must be gathered about the job to be able to determine appropriate timings for the work samplings.

Interviews

Interviews can be conducted one-on-one or in a group setting. The face-to-face nature of interviews provides an opportunity for clarification. Employees tend to overstate their skills. They may exaggerate the importance of the tasks they are performing and the complexity of the job, especially when they believe that the job analysis is being conducted to determine compensation.

The use of multiple sources in interviewing can help improve the accuracy of the information being gathered. A structured interview form is recommended. The interview technique is time-consuming and can be costly, especially considering the cost of training the interviewers. However, if the job analysis is not conducted at all—or is conducted inappropriately—it can cost the organization even more in the long run.

> The use of multiple sources in interviewing can help improve the accuracy of the information being gathered.

Questionnaires

The most popular method for gathering job analysis data, a questionnaire is a relatively quick, low-cost technique for gathering more standardized information. The company can use a standardized questionnaire or develop one of its own. Checklists can also be used to solicit data, but they must have a complete list of all job tasks.

Some organizations use questionnaires in tandem with other techniques. The questionnaire can be used and then followed up with interviews for further clarification.

Standardized Instruments

There are also a number of standardized job analysis instruments, such as the position analysis questionnaire and the functional job analysis. With these quantitative techniques, analysts can compare rankings across jobs, which can be especially important when job analysis is used for compensation purposes.

The position analysis questionnaire (or PAQ) requires that each job be analyzed in terms of 194 specific tasks commonly found in a variety of jobs. The PAQ uses six scales to determine the degree to which these standardized tasks are performed in the job being analyzed. The PAQ services software then generates a job score based on the responses.

For example, one section gathers data on information sources. The questionnaire solicits feedback on the role of written materials, quantitative materials, and mechanical devices as sources of job information. The job analyst then determines the extent to which the employee actually uses these sources of information to perform the job.

Functional job analysis, another popular quantitative technique used to gather information, examines the degree to which data, people, and things are involved in the functions of a job. Once again, the analyst completes this instrument.

The critical incident method is a qualitative technique that focuses on behaviors that are critical for job success. Some incidents may focus on ineffective behaviors as well as effective ones. The key is to be able to differentiate between the two types. This method is also important in developing performance appraisal systems.

Quantitative techniques enable analysts to rank jobs in terms of the tasks performed and then use those rankings to compare jobs. For example, a firm could use this information to help determine pay rates for different jobs. Qualitative techniques, however, may provide greater insight into the complexity of some tasks. To generate a more complete picture of the job requires the use of both kinds of methods.

Generating Documentation

The job analysis process generates two key documents: the job description and the job specification. Together, they provide a complete picture of the job and the qualifications of the person who will be able to successfully perform the job.

> Functional job analysis, another popular quantitative technique used to gather information, examines the degree to which data, people, and things are involved in the functions of a job.

The Job Description

The job description is a critical document in the organization. It identifies the job title and lists the responsibilities and essential functions of the job.

While the specific format varies from organization to organization, most job descriptions contain the following common elements:

- Job title
- Job summary
- Job duties

The *job title* is significant for a number of reasons. The title must reflect the work that is actually performed and where the job is located in the corporate hierarchy. For instance, the job title differentiates a junior accountant from a senior accountant. These designations reflect the organizational level of each job. The analysis must also take into account the psychological impact of the title. People respond to the status of their job titles.

The *job summary* is just what the name implies. It should include a thumbnail sketch of the job. The job summary differentiates this job from all others in the organization.

The essential functions are listed in the *job duties* section. All of the functions listed must be job-related. If nonessential functions are listed, the firm may be open to legal challenge.

Essential functions are often listed in the order of importance. The most important functions are listed first and the other functions listed in descending order of importance. Functions may also be weighted according to their importance; that is, the more important the function is to the successful performance of the job, the higher the weight assigned.

Some firms prefer to list essential functions in order of the time required to perform them. For example, the job description for an accounts payable clerk may list the essential functions with the percentage of time that management expects the worker to devote to each of the functions:

> The most important functions are listed first and the other functions listed in descending order of importance.

- Voucher, code, approve, and mail bills (40 percent)
- Maintain customer AP files (25 percent)
- Key data (10 percent)
- Generate AP checks (10 percent)
- Submit routine AP reports (5 percent)
- Prepare purchase orders (5 percent)
- Implement process improvements (5 percent)

The Job Specification

The job specification is the second critical document generated by the job analysis. This document, however, focuses on the person performing the job rather than on the tasks being performed (which are addressed in the job description). It specifies the knowledge, skills, abilities, and characteristics required to effectively perform the job. These specifications may include the following:

- Education (such as college degrees or professional certification)
- Experience
- General characteristics (such as good communication or team player skills)
- Specific knowledge (such as foreign language proficiency or software program proficiency)

> This document, however, focuses on the person performing the job rather than on the tasks being performed.

TIP

The law and court rulings have been clear in the use of criteria listed in job specifications. Only those specifications that are truly job-related may be identified. Any specifications that are not job-related may be challenged in a court of law.

Overcoming the Challenges to Job Analysis

The process of conducting a job analysis must be explained to employees, and they must understand their role in the process. Anxiety levels tend to be higher if employees don't know the reasons for the job analysis.

The changing nature of the business environment means that the results of the job analysis may quickly become obsolete. The process should be one of continuous review to respond to the changing nature of jobs. An analysis should be performed every three years—if few changes are occurring in the job.

Since job descriptions often require updating and revising, the process can be time-consuming and expensive. However, software programs are available to streamline the process.

To help standardize job analysis information, each organization should create its own form to record results. This form will help verify that complete information has been obtained and enable comparisons to be performed across jobs. The form can also make it easier to update and revise the information as necessary.

Companies may choose to customize existing questionnaires. But if jobs are changing rapidly and frequent job analyses are being performed, it may be too expensive to develop all the necessary questionnaires.

> To help standardize job analysis information, each organization should create its own form to record results.

How Job Analysis Fits with Other Human Resource Functions

A clear understanding of the responsibilities of every job and the qualifications necessary to successfully perform in that job drives a variety of other human resource functions. The job responsibilities and the job specifications serve as valuable input to the planning, recruitment, selection, training and development, compensation, and performance appraisal functions.

The job analysis is the foundation for the human resource planning process. By identifying the knowledge, skills, and abilities required for current jobs and future jobs, the job analysis has gathered the basic information for the planning function. In addition, the job analysis benefits the hiring process. Without full knowledge of the responsibilities of a job, there cannot be a good match between the person and the job. This information also helps the company decide where to recruit candidates.

Selection of the best-qualified applicants depends on an evaluation of their abilities. This evaluation must be conducted in light of the job-related duties. The data gathered in the job specification helps determine the best tools to use in the selection process also.

This job analysis process has been especially important in complying with the Americans with Disabilities Act. Some recruiters may assume that an applicant with a disability is unable to perform a specific job, especially if the responsibilities are not clear. As a result, the applicant may have a legal claim against the company. An effective job analysis process allows the manager to review detailed job-related information, and he or she may conclude that the applicant can indeed perform all of the responsibilities listed for the job, thus avoiding a lawsuit.

> Information generated from the job analysis also provides guidelines for training new employees.

Information generated from the job analysis also provides guidelines for training new employees. Once the gap is identified between the knowledge, skills, and abilities required of the new employee and those that are actually possessed, training needs can be determined.

If similarities in knowledge, skills, and abilities are found across several jobs in a job family, the firm's training program can target these skills. This cross-training may also be important in mapping individual career paths if the same general knowledge, skills, and abilities are identified for a family of jobs. The flexibility of the work force is also enhanced as employees are trained for job families instead of individual jobs.

The job analysis also provides the data necessary to determine compensation. Wages are formulated by considering the knowledge, skills, and abilities required in the job. Those jobs requiring higher levels of knowledge and skills are generally paid higher wages. The responsibilities of the job also impact pay. Salaries are often higher for jobs involving hazardous circumstances or dangerous responsibilities.

Summary

An effective job analysis process provides input to many of the other human resource management functions. While data collection methods and sources may vary, the end result is the development of the job description and the job specification. These documents are especially critical to a firm's recruitment, selection, compensation, and performance appraisal systems. The job analysis process has also been extremely important in helping organizations comply with EEO guidelines by generating job-related information for use in all human resource management functions.

Streetwise Advice

- **An effective job analysis can reduce the risk of legal difficulties.** Job analysis provides objective measures for making human resource decisions. This output has been especially helpful in responding to the Americans with Disabilities Act.

- **In response to the rapid changes in many jobs today, the job analysis process has shifted its focus in some organizations.** Rather than focus on specific job tasks and responsibilities, some companies are identifying several core competencies. These general skill sets provide the basis of the job analysis.

- **A good source of information for smaller organizations is the *Dictionary of Occupational Titles*.** If a firm is unable to perform a job analysis, the *Dictionary of Occupational Titles (DOT)* may be used as a reference. The *DOT* provides standardized job descriptions that can even be retrieved online. The company can then customize the description for its own use. Six-digit codes are used to categorize 20,000 jobs. These codes serve as points of external reference for job analysts when gathering data. The first choice, however, is to perform your own analysis if possible.

- **Job analysis can be an important component of the career planning process**. A job family can provide natural transitions for employees' career paths. With similar skills (though on different levels), individuals can plot their career path. For example, within accounting a possible career path may be as follows:

  - Accounts payable clerk
  - Junior accountant

> Job analysis provides objective measures for making human resource decisions.

- Senior accountant
- Assistant controller
- Controller
- Vice president of finance

- Each organizational level within the job family provides a natural career path.

- **Most organizations perform job analysis on a rotating basis.** Since the job analysis process can be very time-consuming, all jobs within the organization are not analyzed at one time. Certain job families may be analyzed every two years while others may be analyzed on a less frequent or more frequent basis, depending on the changes being experienced in the jobs.

- **When analyzing management positions, use the management position description questionnaire (referred to as the MPDQ).** This instrument uses thirteen factors generalized across the majority of management positions.

- **Use computerized surveys as well.** Computerized surveys can reach many people at a low cost. In some cases, the survey is placed on the company's intranet. Surveys may be administered at specified times (controlled through the posting of the survey) and are more easily returned to the survey administrators (with the click of a button).

- **In some cases, job analysis may take a future-oriented position (rather than a present position).** With a rapidly changing business environment and regular technological advancements, the job analysis provides an opportunity to look to the future. That is, job analysts may include information concerning new equipment or technology to shape the way the job will be performed in the near term. This orientation ensures that the organization will be prepared by planning the staffing needs, recruitment, selections, compensation, and training. Knowing that changes are likely to occur and then ignoring them is a

> Certain job families may be analyzed every two years while others may be analyzed on a less frequent or more frequent basis, depending on the changes being experienced in the jobs.

waste of effort. If change is coming, it should be incorporated into the process as soon as possible.

* **Use as many sources as possible to solicit information for the job analysis.** If only the incumbent is asked about the job, he or she is likely to give an inflated picture of job responsibilities. Asking more elicits a more complete and accurate picture of the actual job.

* In some organizations, workers may be asked to maintain a diary of their job activities. **Job analysts then use this diary as the starting point to perform their analysis of the job.**

> In some organizations, workers may be asked to maintain a diary of their job activities.

For more information on this topic, visit our Web site at www.businesstown.com

Job Design

The design of jobs today has become even more critical as segments of the work force demand more challenging work. Changing technology, advanced communication, and changing organizational structures have all impacted job design. To be more responsive to the rapid pace of change, jobs must have some degree of built-in flexibility. This flexibility is achieved through careful attention to job design.

Job design is the process that determines the responsibilities of a job. This process considers how tasks and responsibilities will be allocated throughout the organization, what employees need in order to perform these tasks, and how all the jobs in the organization are interrelated and aligned with one another.

> Careful attention to job design can create a win/win situation in which both high satisfaction levels and high performance levels are achieved.

The Impact of Job Design on People and the Organization

Job design impacts employee satisfaction levels and performance (and ultimately the performance of the organization). Careful attention to job design can create a win/win situation in which both high satisfaction levels and high performance levels are achieved.

Effective job design takes into account the requirements of the organization, the person performing the job (especially in terms of knowledge, skills, and abilities), and opportunities for job satisfaction. Dull, boring, routine jobs can create low levels of satisfaction and motivation in the work force for most employees. Jobs can be designed to build in satisfaction and motivation.

TIP

Competitive pressures for organizations to perform better and improve productivity levels drive some changes in job design. Organizations constantly have to do more with less. Sometimes this can be achieved with job redesign efforts. Jobs can be redesigned to build in higher productivity levels.

Job design is a concern for every organization. Traditionally, job design applied only to manufacturing jobs. Today, however, every job in every industry is a candidate for job design—or job redesign. Even office design is given careful consideration today.

Increasing work productivity and job satisfaction are two primary reasons for engaging in job design. Effective job design, including alternative work arrangements, enables organizations to attract workers and to retain employees. Older workers are retained in those organizations that rethink the way that work is being performed to better accommodate their employees' needs for more flexibility.

Scientific Management and Job Simplification

At the turn of the century, the Industrial Revolution changed forever the way work would be performed. With the demise of the craft system, the focus switched to how to simplify work. Adam Smith's work with pin makers emphasized the importance of designing work that focused on the performance of one piece of the entire task.

Smith, an economist who sang the praises of the division of labor, suggested that this job specialization would enable the worker to become adept at one job instead of having to perform the entire task and never becoming skilled in any one facet. As the work was divided into many specialized tasks, overall productivity increased.

> With the demise of the craft system, the focus switched to how to simplify work.

The modern assembly line is an outgrowth of this concept. The system of mass production breaks down a major job (such as the manufacture of an automobile) into hundreds or thousands of smaller tasks. When they concentrate on repeatedly performing only one small task within a larger job, workers become very skilled and are able to make improvements in their task. The worker who specializes in adding the right tires to every automobile manufactured on the assembly line becomes very good at it as he performs it day in and day out. This automobile plant is able to achieve higher productivity as each worker becomes skilled at the one specialized task that he or she performs on a routine basis.

Job specialization provides many advantages. These benefits include:

- Increased proficiency from repetitive performance
- Less time transferring from one task to the next (since only one task is being performed)
- Increased probability of creating equipment specifically designed to help in the performance of the job
- Lower worker replacement costs since the firm needs to hire someone with only the one skill

Unfortunately, there are disadvantages to job specialization as well. While the organization is concerned with improving productivity, job simplification/specialization often leads to higher levels of boredom and dissatisfaction as workers perform routine work. This dissatisfaction often leads to increased absenteeism, which will ultimately impact the productivity of the firm.

The scientific management era was launched during the last decades of the nineteenth century. Frederick Taylor, known as the father of scientific management, conducted research on job design at the Midvale Steel Works. He suggested that it was management's responsibility to design jobs in the one best way and then, it was the workers' responsibility to perform the work in that one best way.

> While the organization is concerned with improving productivity, job simplification/specialization often leads to higher levels of boredom and dissatisfaction as workers perform routine work.

TIP

Frederick Taylor also proposed the systematic hiring of employees. That is, he recognized the need to consider what tasks would be performed and then carefully match the applicant with the job. Taylor suggested that performance levels could be improved through this systematic hiring. This concept is still used today with the job specification criteria.

Time and motion studies were used to determine the best way to perform a job. Using a stopwatch, industrial engineers observed workers in their jobs. The engineers then determined how the job should be performed, including when to take breaks, how long the breaks should be, what tools to use, and how to perform the work.

Unfortunately, the human element was not considered in this approach to job design. The individual's role in job design was captured in the job characteristics approach.

Using the Job Characteristics Model

Hackman and Oldham's Job Characteristics Model provides insight into the way that jobs might be designed and redesigned. The model provides a conceptual framework that guides line managers and human resource managers in designing more motivating work.

According to the model, three critical psychological states are instrumental in improving motivation:

- Experienced meaningfulness of the work
- Experienced responsibility of the outcomes of the work
- Knowledge of the results of the work

Hackman and Oldham identified five core job dimensions that would influence these psychological states and thus improve worker motivation. The core job characteristics are skill variety, task identity, task significance, autonomy, and feedback.

Skill variety refers to the number of different tasks that are performed by the person on the job. Greater skill variety enables employees to use a broader range of talents, which makes the job more interesting. *Task identity* is the portion of the total job that the person performs. The importance of the task, or the degree to which the job impacts others, is the dimension referred to as *task significance.* The amount of control that the worker has over the way in which the work will be performed is known as *autonomy,* and it also includes the employee's discretion in scheduling his work. The degree to which the employee knows how effectively she is performing is the *feedback* dimension.

Job designers, then, should keep these five core job dimensions in mind. Building in more tasks to be performed, assigning a greater portion of the total job, and ensuring that the tasks being performed are important (and that the employees understand the importance of their tasks) addresses the experienced meaningfulness of the work.

> The core job characteristics are skill variety, task identity, task significance, autonomy, and feedback.

Increasing the amount of control that employees have over the way their work is performed will improve their responsibility for the outcome. For example, if an employee is empowered to decide what equipment will be utilized and when the maintenance for that equipment will be performed, the increased responsibility will make her more concerned about the outcome of her work. A system that enables employees to see how they are doing and that provides regular information about their work (rather than having to wait for management to tell them how they are doing) increases the critical psychological state of feedback.

Using the Job Characteristics Model as a guide, organizations should consider the following suggestions when designing jobs:

- Whenever possible, combine fragmented job tasks into one more meaningful, larger job that generates more ownership of the job.

- Encourage managers to give up some control. Allow employees to make more decisions regarding their work (including planning and prioritizing), thereby increasing their autonomy. Delegate contact with customers to them.

- Make sure there is direct feedback concerning their performance. Recognizing effectiveness instills a sense of pride in workers. For example, one company decided to send weekly error reports directly to employees instead of to their supervisors.

Using the core job dimensions to design or redesign a job will ultimately result in improved motivation, higher quality performance, higher levels of satisfaction, decreased absenteeism, and decreased turnover.

Options to Designing Jobs

In the past, job design techniques focused on job specialization to make the job smaller. Workers were trained to perform one small piece of a larger task. Today's organizations are trying to overcome the problems of narrowly focused jobs by designing more motivating jobs. Three

> Whenever possible, combine fragmented job tasks into one more meaningful, larger job that generates more ownership of the job.

of the more popular options being considered are job enlargement, job rotation, and job enrichment.

Job Enlargement

Variety can sometimes improve motivation levels. Job simplification brought such specialization that boredom set in with the routine nature of the job. With job enlargement, however, adding responsibilities can combat some of this boredom and reduce some levels of employee dissatisfaction.

This design option adds tasks that are on the same responsibility level to the job. Although some of the boredom is alleviated by increasing the variety of tasks, no real control or responsibility is added. For example, job enlargement on the assembly line mentioned earlier might mean that the worker who was adding the right tires to automobiles might be given the responsibility of assembling the left tires as well.

Small work teams can also use enlargement. For example, an organization may train three individual employees who perform three sequential tasks to perform all three tasks. There are, however, some disadvantages with job enlargement. Training costs increase because employees are trained for more than one job. Pay issues also crop up as employees expect to be paid more for performing more tasks. And while boredom is initially reduced, it returns over the long term since employees are still only performing tasks on the same responsibility level.

> With job enlargement, adding responsibilities can combat some of this boredom and reduce some levels of employee dissatisfaction.

Job Rotation

Job rotation also adds tasks to a job. Employees are rotated on a systematic basis from one job to another. The tasks are still on an equal responsibility level, as with job enlargement, and still routine.

With job rotation, the employee performs one task for a portion of a day (or a portion of a week) and another task for the balance of the day (or the week). The premise of this option is that more than one task is being performed by the worker, which increases skill variety.

Although boredom is temporarily reduced with an increased variety of skills, it usually returns since employees are still performing tasks on basically the same responsibility level. Once again, this option raises a compensation concern as employees are asked to do more without a salary adjustment. Job rotation is, however, a good option for training since it creates a flexible, multiskilled work force.

TIP

Job rotation provides an excellent opportunity for employees to acquire new skills and to increase their employability. As employees acquire more skills and learn to perform more jobs, they become more valuable to the organization (and to other organizations as well). Single-skill workers are more vulnerable to downsizing and lay-offs. Multiskilled workers have the best chance of retaining their jobs or finding new jobs when the time comes to make a change.

Job Enrichment

An outgrowth of Frederick Herzberg's work on motivation (Chapter 12), job enrichment is another approach to job design. This option gives employees tasks with additional authority. Job enrichment has become a popular approach because it helps improve employee motivation by responding to the need for intrinsic rewards. This option increases both the variety of tasks being performed and the level of control a worker has.

TIP

Any job design technique should be carefully matched with the unique needs and values of the employees being impacted. The organization must use discretion in selecting the most appropriate techniques. This caution is especially important with job enrichment, which is not a one-size-fits-all solution for every employee in today's work force. Not every employee wants an enriched job. Before investing the time and expense necessary to enrich jobs, human resource staff should talk to the employees to determine what they would like to see in their job.

While job enlargement adds responsibilities on a comparable level, job enrichment, also known as *vertical loading*, adds higher-level responsibilities to the job. Regularly adding new responsibilities

> While job enlargement adds responsibilities on a comparable level, job enrichment, also known as *vertical loading*, adds higher-level responsibilities to the job.

also helps employees experience opportunities for growth, achievement, and challenge.

Increasing the difficulty of tasks and accountability can enrich jobs. Other options may include adding the responsibilities for planning, controlling, or evaluating the work, duties historically performed by supervisory personnel. Job enrichment, then, requires managers to give up some control, as they delegate responsibilities to enrich their workers' jobs.

Ergonomics Today

More equipment and machinery is being used to streamline operations and redesign work across all industries. As this move to integrate advanced technology increases, organizations must ensure that people receive the proper attention in this new design effort. Organizations no longer try to fit machinery to their employees. The task today is just the opposite: to fit the people with the machinery.

This task must also take into account the diverse work force. Not every person is the same size or even reads at the same grade level. Machinery must be adjustable to accommodate differences among people. In addition, as much as possible, machinery and equipment must be standardized to ensure safe operating procedures. For instance, most on/off switches flip the same way and, increasingly, universal symbols are being used to avoid confusion.

Computers and advanced technology are increasingly being used to handle routine tasks. As a result, employees are able to take on more challenging work.

> More equipment and machinery is being used to streamline operations and redesign work across all industries.

TIP

Ergonomic concerns are no longer just being addressed in manufacturing plants. The office is now the target of many ergonomic efforts to reduce workplace injuries and improve employee productivity.

Flexible Designs

Flexible job designs today include alternative work arrangements. These designs involve not just the way that work is performed, but also how and when and where it is performed. Some flexible work arrangements include:

- Compressed work week
- Flextime
- Job sharing
- Telecommuting

Flexible work alternatives can provide valuable opportunities for employees to match their work schedules and their lifestyles. Personal lifestyles may dictate that some people seek part-time employment or telecommuting positions. Organizations that don't have flexible work arrangements may miss out on talented employees.

Compressed Work Week

The compressed work week has become especially popular. Instead of working a forty-hour work week in the traditional five days, employees work fewer days. However, they do work longer hours each day. The most common variation is the 4/40. Forty-hour weeks are worked in four days, or four 10-hour days.

One variation of the 4/40 enables employees to have every other Friday afternoon off. The four hours are added across nine working days to total a two-week period of eighty hours. With the 4/40 week, employees have an extra day off during the week for their personal use. In the case of working parents, this can mean one less day of day care. Although the compressed work week can involve some scheduling issues and added worker exhaustion, in general, both organizations and individuals benefit from the arrangement.

Flextime

More organizations have recognized that not every job has to be performed during the same working hours. They have used flextime

> Instead of working a forty-hour work week in the traditional five days, employees work fewer days.

to improve customer service levels and to provide employees with more flexibility in their own lives.

With flextime, workers are given some discretion in selecting their work hours. In many cases, employees are asked to work specific core hours, generally the critical peak hours when more employees are needed. Workers can then decide what combination of hours that overlap these core hours they would like to work.

In a flextime arrangement with core hours from 11:00 to 2:00, employees have many options. Although employees are required to work eight hours a day, they may choose to work any combination of hours that includes the period from 11:00 to 2:00. Some of these options include working from 8:00 to 5:00, 6:00 to 3:00, or perhaps 11:00 to 8:00. Flextime allows employees to select the hours that best fit their own needs.

Job Sharing

Job sharing is an option that provides part-time opportunities to employees who might otherwise be lost to the organization. In cases where talented workers do not want a full-time position, two part-time individuals may choose to share a full-time position and divide the work. The employees may split the day or split the week to reach forty hours between them.

Job sharing benefits both the individuals and the organization. Organizations that are flexible in presenting job-sharing options may be able to attract or retain excellent employees who are not interested in full-time positions. These companies gain the talents of two individuals and pay less for benefits.

The employees benefit by experiencing less stress. They are working the hours that best suit their lifestyles and are not trying to overextend themselves with a full-time position. Many often report that they feel more job satisfaction and enthusiasm for their work because the work and nonwork aspects of their lives are in balance.

> Job sharing is an option that provides part-time opportunities to employees who might otherwise be lost to the organization.

Telecommuting

There are growing numbers of telecommuters today in the American work force. Millions of employees work from remote locations via electronic links to their employers. These locations may be their homes or electronic cottages.

The virtual office terminology reflects the fact that with advanced technology, employees don't necessarily have to work only from their homes or electronic cottages. Some may work from their cars, from airplanes, from hotel rooms, or from anywhere they might be. Traveling sales associates often work from virtual offices.

Telecommuters enjoy the flexibility of matching their work style to their lifestyle. Some people prefer to avoid the time, aggravation, and expense of commuting to work each day. They prefer to stay at home in their bedroom slippers, avoiding the interruptions of their coworkers. Organizations enjoy cost savings on office space. Some organizations have also reported that telecommuting employees have higher job satisfaction levels and increased productivity.

> It takes a certain amount of self-discipline to be a telecommuter.

TIP

Telecommuting is not for everyone. It takes a certain amount of self-discipline to be a telecommuter. Organizations must carefully assess the work habits, job involved, and employee characteristics to determine if telecommuting is an option. Some extremely social employees select out of telecommuting, knowing that it would not be a good fit for them. A company cannot trust employees to self-select out in every case. Therefore, there should be some general guidelines that govern telecommuting.

Teams

Teams are used extensively in organizations today. This approach has had a significant impact on the design of work as individual workers have given way to teams to accomplish tasks. Some of the more popular team concepts used today include the following:

- Cross-functional teams
- Quality circles
- Self-directed teams
- Virtual teams

Cross-functional Teams

Cross-functional teams have grown in popularity to combat the functional silo mentality. In many cases, the employees of a specific functional unit only see the organization through the lens of their unit. That is, marketing people see the organization from the marketing perspective—often to the exclusion of all other considerations. The same is true of accounting, human resource, and operations employees.

Cross-functional teams enable accountants to work with marketers, engineers, and human resource professionals. This approach provides a richer work experience. As teammates share their own perspectives, everyone learns more about the interconnected nature of their work.

For example, cross-functional teams are able to get products to market faster. As the linear nature of work is abolished, representatives from each functional area can share information and work together to cut development time.

Quality Circles

In quality circles, or work improvement teams, eight to ten volunteer employees from one department meet once a week in a participative environment to discuss quality issues and make suggestions on quality improvement to management. Although quality circles have been the most popular in manufacturing environments, they can be valuable in service industries also.

The return on investment has been reported as high as 800 percent in some organizations. For success to be achieved at these levels, the organizational culture must be consistent with the employee involvement team concept. The culture must embrace empowerment and participation. In addition, management must be committed to this approach and any skepticism must be overcome. Short-term successes can help demonstrate the results that can be achieved.

In quality circles, or work improvement teams, eight to ten volunteer employees from one department meet once a week in a participative environment to discuss quality issues and make suggestions on quality improvement to management.

Self-Directed Teams

Self-directed teams, or self-managed or autonomous work teams, have replaced many of the traditional work groups. These teams have no traditional supervisors; instead, they use team leaders. This approach cuts down on bureaucracy as the team is given control of its work.

Autonomous work teams generally result in improved productivity and quality. In many cases, organizations also experience reduced turnover, reduced absenteeism, and improved quality of work life. There are, however, disadvantages as structural changes impact management. Many first-line supervisory positions are eliminated and those that remain are changed drastically in the move to empower team members.

Virtual Teams

Virtual teams are some of the newest innovations in the team approach. With the advanced technology and communications systems available, employees who are geographically dispersed can still work together on teams. E-mail, teleconferencing, and videoconferencing bring these team members closer together without actual face-to-face interaction.

There are numerous advantages to this concept. Regardless of location, the "right" team for the job can be assembled and decision-making tends to focus more on the facts than on emotional issues. The major disadvantage of the virtual team, however, arises from this issue as well. The richness of face-to-face communication is impossible with virtual teams. Different group dynamics must be used.

Summary

Job design continues to be an ongoing challenge as work force values, skill sets, and technology change and as organizational structures shift. Although many options are available today, there is no one-size-fits-all solution. Organizations must customize these alternatives to best meet the unique challenges presented in their own culture and to best meet the needs of their unique work force.

> With the advanced technology and communications systems available, employees who are geographically dispersed can still work together on teams.

Streetwise Advice

- **There is no one-size-fits-all approach to job design.** Before undertaking any design or redesign project, consider the people who will be involved. Different people will respond differently to design approaches.

- **The trend toward empowering the work force has substantially impacted the design of jobs today.** As the work force is empowered, employees are given more control over the decisions that impact their work and the way that work is performed. With an increasing number of knowledge workers, it makes sense to have the workers who are most knowledgeable make the decisions about how the work will be performed.

- **Job design does not just apply to individuals performing jobs.** Progressive terminology today refers to the design of work systems, which opens the door for groups and teams as well.

- **Re-engineering is the radical redesign of work.** Re-engineering requires rethinking the way all work is being performed—and if the work is even necessary.

- **Members of quality circles are usually from the same department.** More cross-functional quality circles are being used. Broader quality issues are considered in these cross-functional units.

- **As jobs are redesigned, changes must be made in other human resource documents.** Job descriptions, job specifications, and standards for performance appraisal must reflect redesigned jobs. There is a definite ripple effect.

- **Not every employee is a good candidate for telecommuting.** Although many employees sing the praises of telecommuting—especially its flexibility and freedom—it is not an alternative for everyone. Some employees need the social interaction of their coworkers and are unhappy in a solitary telecommuting arrangement.

> As the work force is empowered, employees are given more control over the decisions that impact their work and the way that work is performed.

- ***Technostress* is the new term coined to reflect stress created by redesigned work.** As computer technology is designed into more jobs, it creates technostress. The nature of computer work may exclude human contact, diminishing interpersonal relationships and increasing this new stress.

- **More employees are downshifting.** More aging baby boomers are opting to choose careers that better match their lifestyles, often working fewer hours and taking less demanding positions. Some studies have estimated that over 4 percent of baby boomers are downshifting. Organizations, then, must respond with more flexible work arrangements.

> To effectively design motivating jobs, recognize that job redesign is not performed in a vacuum.

- **Work teams can be viewed as job enlargement on a group level.** A large task is presented to a team of workers who decide how the work will be performed. For example, you can redesign a traditional department with three workers performing distinct functions by letting them decide how the larger job of the group will be accomplished.

- **Job design doesn't always improve productivity.** To effectively design motivating jobs, recognize that job redesign is not performed in a vacuum. It must take into account changing environments, technology, knowledge, skills, and abilities. Most important, however, the personal preferences of the employees must be considered.

- **Groupware is used for virtual teams.** Software for virtual teams—referred to as *groupware*—is utilized for holding meetings and group decision-making. Several large software companies (such as Microsoft) market this software.

- **Telecommuting is also being called *flexiplace*.** The term *flexiplace* reflects the flexible workplace; that is, technological advances now make it possible for workers to work wherever they want.

Motivation:
The Old
and the New

M otivation is an integral component of every human resource function. Every organization wants to provide the appropriate motivation to ensure that each employee works to his or her full potential, providing a win/win opportunity for both the organization and the employee.

Motivation remains a key managerial function today. A lack of motivation can cost an organization millions of dollars, whereas an effective motivational program can help create a competitive advantage in the marketplace that is hard for competitors to overcome. Effective motivation also helps build a loyal work force.

> Motivation remains a key function of both line managers and the human resource department.

Why Motivate? The Productivity Challenge

Motivation remains a key function of both line managers and the human resource department. Even a century of research has not solved all the mysteries. There is no single solution. Given the diversity of the work force and the globalization of business today, the need to treat each employee as a unique individual has never been greater.

Motivation helps explain why people do the things they do. Understanding motivation can help shape the behavior of people in the workplace. The overall performance of an organization depends on its ability to motivate individual employees. In general, motivated employees will work harder to accomplish organizational objectives.

TIP

Motivation continues to be ranked as a top concern for managers. The complexity of the issue has increased with more generations in the work force than ever before—and each with different sets of values and loyalties. The best advice continues to be customization. The best motivational tools are customized to meet the unique needs and values of each individual in the workplace.

Productivity gains in American businesses are not what they once were. The United States now ranks twelfth in the world in increased individual worker output.

Reducing labor costs isn't the only answer, and sometimes it isn't even the most appropriate solution to productivity issues. Organizations can improve productivity levels by cutting the cost of inputs and/or improving the transformation of inputs into outputs. Motivation is one way to improve transformation processes.

Motivation provides a number of issues for human resources. To motivate individuals, human resource staff must have the necessary abilities as well as the resources for effective training and development programs.

Traditional Motivation Theories

A review of the traditional motivation theories will provide a basic understanding of how to motivate today's work force. Motivation theories help provide insight into why people behave the way they do and what energizes them. Each of these theories adds to an improved implementation of motivational tools that can be used.

Maslow's Hierarchy of Needs

The hierarchy of needs theory, developed by psychologist Abraham Maslow, has helped explain human behavior. Maslow's theory, which postulated that humans have an explicit priority list of needs, has provided insight into the differences among employees as well as the changes in motivational drives across time for one individual.

A clinical psychologist, Maslow proposed that five basic needs drive human behavior. That is, these five needs create a tension that results in action. The five needs (starting with the lowest level, or *most* basic, need) are as follows:

- Physiological needs
- Safety needs
- Affiliation needs
- Esteem needs
- Self-actualization

> Motivation theories help provide insight into why people behave the way they do and what energizes them.

The Theory

People are first and foremost motivated by basic *physiological needs,* which include the need for water, air, and food. The behaviors people engage in are driven first by the need to fulfill these needs. For example, when the organization provides employees with an appropriate salary and meal breaks, it is addressing physiological needs.

Once these basic survival needs are met or satisfied, the second-level needs, for *safety,* kick in. The need for safety includes having order and a safe environment. The organization can meet these needs with safe working conditions and job security.

The third level is *affiliation* and acceptance. Maslow originally preferred the term *belongingness.* People need others and need to fulfill social contact with other people. Opportunities that organizations provide for cultivating friendships and working with others address these social needs. The company can also address these needs by helping employees balance work and nonwork issues (such as spending time with family outside the organizational setting).

Once the need for affiliation is satisfied, the need for *esteem* motivates behavior. Esteem can be both internal and external. People are driven by the need for self-respect (internal) and by the need for recognition from others (external). When the organization provides opportunities for career advancement, shows appreciation for employees, gives raises based on merit, and provides status symbols (such as titles), it is helping its employees fulfill the need for esteem.

The highest level need is for *self-actualization.* Only after the four lower-level needs are met can people be motivated by self-actualization. This need is for people to reach their full potential and develop themselves. The armed forces refer to self-actualization in their advertisement to "be all you can be." The organization can also provide opportunities for individuals to develop their skills and increase their autonomy on the job.

Self-actualization is different from the other four needs in that it cannot be satiated. Although people can fulfill the other four needs, the need for self-actualization might be thought of as a moving target. Once the personal goals are met, they are immediately replaced with higher goals to meet greater potential. Maslow also

> People need others and need to fulfill social contact with other people.

suggested that a small percentage of the population meets the need for self-actualization.

Intuitively, Maslow's theory makes sense, and it has been quite popular. This theory helps explain why all people are not motivated by the same tools. Employees can be found at all different levels in this hierarchy, depending on what need is motivating their behavior. As a result, different tools are necessary to motivate workers to higher performance levels. What works for one employee will not necessarily work for another.

The Application

A young employee who is a recent college graduate with school loans and who is saving for an apartment may be motivated by financial incentives. Concentrating on safety and security needs, she would see the additional money as a means to fulfill her need to get an apartment.

An older employee with a family, however, might be at a higher level need of affiliation. He might be better motivated by additional time off from work to fulfill family obligations or responsibilities. The financial incentives offered to the younger employee might not motivate the older employee, depending on either individual's priorities.

Maslow also suggested that people's needs change over time. As workers age and experience life changes, they are motivated by different needs. The movement along the hierarchy is usually upward (toward self-actualization), but it may also be downward in certain situations. That is, Maslow believed that people could regress if something happened to remove the fulfillment of any of the higher-order needs.

For example, if a married woman is working on self-actualization and then her husband dies, she may regress. If she was financially comfortable and then finds herself in considerable debt, she might very well be motivated by basic physiological needs like putting food on the table (versus working to reach her full potential as before).

Maslow's work helps underscore the importance of individualizing motivational tools. Everyone has different needs. The organization must determine how best to meet those needs to motivate the work force to higher performance levels—with higher satisfaction levels as

> As workers age and experience life changes, they are motivated by different needs.

well. According to Maslow, the key is to know which level of needs is motivating each employee. He also suggests that continued monitoring is necessary to identify any changes that could make former motivational tools ineffective.

Herzberg's Motivator-Hygiene Theory

Frederick Herzberg's theory of motivation, called the Two Factor Theory or the Motivator-Hygiene Theory (Herzberg, Mausner & Snyderman, 1959), was based on interviews with 200 engineers and accountants. Herzberg's major premise was that satisfaction and dissatisfaction are not really opposite ends of one continuum. Rather, he proposed that the opposite of satisfaction is no satisfaction and the opposite of dissatisfaction is no dissatisfaction. This distinction is crucial to understanding this theory because each continuum uses a different set of factors to move employees from one end to the other.

> To move an employee from dissatisfaction to no dissatisfaction, a set of factors, referred to as *hygienes*, is used.

To move an employee from dissatisfaction to no dissatisfaction, a set of factors, referred to as *hygienes*, is used. These factors are extrinsic to the work itself. These context factors are then dissatisfiers and include working conditions or the work environment. Herzberg considers pay a hygiene. Providing employees with new carpeting or a newly paved parking lot are also examples of hygienes. The absence of these factors can create dissatisfaction in the workplace.

TIP

Although Herzberg considered pay a hygiene, researchers trying to replicate this employee motivation study have not found similar results. Several surveys indicate that job satisfaction is now the number one motivator. The practical role of pay in the motivation of the work force is still being debated. Other researchers have concluded that pay is a motivator, not a hygiene. Unfortunately, the jury is still out on this one.

According to Herzberg's theory, using hygienes to motivate workers (moving them to satisfaction) will not be successful. Hygienes can only move an employee from dissatisfaction to no dissatisfaction. To really motivate an employee, a different set of factors, called *motivators*, must be manipulated. Motivators are satisfiers or factors that are intrinsic to the work itself. Increased job autonomy, challenge, increased responsibility, and recognition for a job well done are all good examples. These are the factors, according to Herzberg, that will move an individual from dissatisfaction to satisfaction.

The problem is that management has traditionally focused on hygienes to motivate the work force. This quick fix has been ineffective, removing dissatisfaction but not creating satisfaction. Management must focus on the factors that are intrinsic to the work itself (such as opportunities for achievement) to create high satisfaction levels and motivate the work force.

The hygienes must be met before employees can be motivated, but an inordinate amount of attention should not be given to these factors if satisfaction is the goal. Based on this recommendation, Herzberg's work has led to the growth of job enrichment (see Chapter 11).

McClelland's Learned Needs Theory

David McClelland developed a theory of motivation referred to as the learned needs theory, manifest needs theory, or acquired needs theory. McClelland suggested that three needs drive behavior. These needs are a function of personality and of each individual's interaction with his or her environment. McClelland identified the need for:

- Achievement
- Affiliation
- Power

While everyone possesses all three needs (though in varying degrees), one becomes dominant in each person and drives the individual's behavior. Different needs account for the differences in people's behavior, according to McClelland.

The need for *achievement* is reflected in being goal oriented, engaging in competitive behavior, seeking challenge, taking risks, and taking personal responsibility to resolve problems. The need for

David McClelland developed a theory of motivation referred to as the learned needs theory, manifest needs theory, or acquired needs theory.

achievement is important to the success of entrepreneurs. The employee who has a high need for achievement should be given challenging assignments with increased responsibility and concrete, regular feedback.

The need for *affiliation* is seen in those people who want to be liked and to enjoy close relationships. These individuals need approval and join many groups for the social interaction. They would rather be part of the group than the leader. Employees with a high need for affiliation make excellent mentors and team members. They should be given opportunities to work closely with others and to help train coworkers.

Most managers are motivated by a need for *power*. These individuals tend to seek out authority. They like to have control and they enjoy competitive situations, especially when they have a competitive edge. Employees who are driven by a need for power should be given as much control over their job responsibilities and as much autonomy as possible. They generally perform better when working alone.

Equity Theory

Equity theory, a social comparison theory, was developed by social psychologist J. Stacey Adams. Most individuals use equity theory on a regular basis. They may not recognize it by name, but they use it just the same.

An individual compares the ratio of his or her inputs and outputs to the ratio of someone else's inputs and outputs. For example, you come to work early each day, rarely take a lunch, work late twice a week, have a graduate degree, and have been on the job for three years. These are your inputs; they are what you bring to the organization. If you make $30,000, this is your output or your reward; that is, what you get in exchange for your inputs.

Joe in the next cubicle works the regularly scheduled hours, has just finished his undergraduate degree, and has been working in the company for one year. You believe that his salary is $32,000. You perceive this as inequitable. That is, the ratio of your inputs and outputs to Joe's inputs and outputs is not equal. Your inputs are greater than Joe's and your outputs is less than Joe's.

> Most managers are motivated by a need for *power*.

According to equity theory, then, you must bring this relationship back into equity. To do so, you can decrease your inputs, increase your outputs, or leave the job. Since few people have the power to increase their output (their salary), most will decrease their inputs, which results in a loss for the organization. A hard-working employee now is reducing her work efforts because she perceives an inequitable relationship. On the other hand, an employee may see an inequitable relationship in reverse. That is, he will perceive a ratio that is not in balance unless he increases his inputs or reduces his output. Since it is rare for an individual to ask for less pay, he will, in all probability, increase his inputs to the job.

Human resource departments and line managers can help create perceptions of equity by ensuring that rewards are fair and that employees are treated equitably. Interestingly enough, when employees do not really know how much a coworker earns, they usually overestimate the salary, perceiving an inequitable relationship. This perception, then, may result in the employee reducing her inputs and ultimately hurting the organization. (Compensation issues are discussed in Chapter 14.)

Expectancy Theory

This theory was developed by Victor Vroom, a psychologist and professor of organization and management at Yale University. Expectancy theory suggests three primary components of motivation. These components are valence, expectancy, and instrumentality. Valence refers to the value that an individual places on the reward to be earned. Expectancy is the degree to which the individual believes that she has the necessary skills and abilities to work at this level. Instrumentality is the belief that the employee holds that his hard work will lead to the reward.

Attention to all three components can improve an organization's ability to motivate its work force. First, organizations must create rewards that employees will value. If workers do not value the rewards offered, they will not be effective. Companies must also ensure that their work force possesses the skills needed to succeed. And finally, organizations must create a climate of trust.

> Human resource departments and line managers can help create perceptions of equity by ensuring that rewards are fair and that employees are treated equitably.

TIP

The key role of managers in motivating with expectancy theory is to clarify expectations and the paths by which employees can achieve their rewards. Managers and the human resource department must know what rewards employees value. If the reward is not valued, it will not be an effective motivational tool.

> Reinforcement is the control of behavior through the utilization of rewards.

To effectively motivate workers using expectancy theory, managers should also remember to clearly identify objectives for their employees and then specify the steps required to meet these objectives. In addition, employee performance must be linked to rewards. Only high levels of performance should be rewarded.

Reinforcement Theory

Reinforcement is the control of behavior through the utilization of rewards. This theory has also been referred to as *behavior modification* since behavior can be modified (or manipulated) through the use of rewards.

The basic premise of reinforcement theory is that behavior is shaped through the administration of positive and negative consequences. The law of effect states that behavior that is met with a positive consequence has a greater likelihood of being repeated. Behavior that is met with a negative consequence has a greater likelihood of extinction. For example, if you stay late to complete a report for your superior and then you are given a valued reward for doing so, you are more likely to stay late again if asked. If, however, you stay late and it is never acknowledged, you are much less likely to repeat that behavior. That is, it is not likely that you will work late again.

New Approaches to the Motivation of Employees

Motivation is a product of the interaction between individuals' needs and their working environment. Motivation theories help provide an understanding of needs. The human resource department and line managers can build an appropriate environment to foster motivation.

A key to effective motivation is to create a positive work environment that enables employees to be self-motivated. Creating a climate in which each individual can meet his or her own goals ultimately benefits the organization.

An organization that fosters a positive environment supports its individual workers. This organization provides training and development opportunities and shows appreciation. The corporate culture emphasizes participation, empowerment, and tolerance for risk.

Empowered employees tend to be more motivated. Empowering the work force creates a feeling of ownership; it is a demonstration of trust. The managers must let go of power and of decision-making. Given more autonomy, workers make more decisions and often take initiative. A participative work force also presents more creative solutions.

Employees who are participating in the decision-making process (especially as it pertains to controlling their own jobs) tend to be more satisfied and more committed to the organization, which translates into higher levels of motivation. To achieve this commitment, however, the organization must share information and knowledge, provide skills that employees need, and listen to its employees.

The organization must also tolerate risk. Creativity comes with mistakes. Employees who are afraid of being punished for mistakes will not be creative and innovative.

The management's style of philosophy management also impacts worker motivation. Douglas McGregor, an industrial management professor, proposed a theory that focused on the assumptions managers make about their employees.

According to McGregor, the assumptions held by managers influence the environment within which workers operate. Theory X managers assume that workers must be closely supervised and monitored. They assume that work is not natural for employees and that, given a chance, employees will play instead of work. Theory Y managers, on the other hand, assume that work comes as naturally to people as play. They believe that giving workers flexibility and latitude will reward the organization with creative output.

McGregor believed that these assumptions influence the work of employees. Overall, the Theory Y manager is more effective in

> Employees who are afraid of being punished for mistakes will not be creative and innovative.

motivating a work force. The heavy-handed approach of the Theory X managers removes any self-motivation.

TIP

Do not assume, however, that there is no place for the Theory X manager. Although the Theory Y manager is more effective in many situations, the Theory X approach is appropriate in some situations with individual employees. Managers must use their discretion and judgment to pick which approach is most effective as they move from one unique circumstance to another.

Are We Having Fun Yet? Humor in the Workplace

The world is so serious. And today's society is said to be the most humorless in history. Societal problems burden everyone. Business seems so serious, but part of creating an environment supportive of high levels of performance is to develop a culture that embraces humor. Everyone appreciates a good laugh and a funny incident. Humor and levity can help combat some of the effects of stress in the workplace.

Humor plays a crucial role in the life of every organization. Although some organizations still resist its use as an interpersonal tool, the importance of humor as an important part of any healthy organization is growing. Humor in the workplace brings both personal and organizational benefits.

Humor can refresh the spirit and open the mind. In a tense situation, humor can reduce stress and defuse anger. If a conflict is rising to dangerous levels, a humorous comment can clear the atmosphere. People can use humor as an intervention strategy. Humor provides an opportunity to view the situation from a new perspective. After people laugh, it becomes almost impossible to hang on to anger. Humor can also alleviate monotony.

During team building, humor can be used as a powerful bonding tool. When coworkers share humbling, funny experiences, everyone seems more human. People see each other as more

> Humor and levity can help combat some of the effects of stress in the workplace.

approachable. This humility helps the team bond and creates a sense of belonging.

Humor is also valuable in training. Numerous psychological studies have shown that a humorous example will increase the learner's retention of a concept by more than 50 percent. Listeners also tend to tune in more when humor is used in training.

A person's sense of humor is also related to creativity. People with a well-developed sense of humor are usually more creative. In some cases, humor can provide the opportunity to think more creatively and to arrive at more innovative solutions to old problems.

Furthermore, there is a direct correlation between humor and advancement. As a general rule, those employees with a good sense of humor are given more opportunities for advancement than those who are humorless. Workers with a good sense of humor generally have creative problem-solving skills and are often perceived as more positive in nature.

However, humor can be overdone. There is a fine line between positive humor and dysfunctional, negative humor, and it can be crossed very easily. Coworkers should never be the subject of a joke; this can be discriminatory. People must know when the use of humor is appropriate and also when it is not.

Incentive Plans

To be effective, rewards must be linked to employee performance. Any incentive plans must also be customized to meet the unique needs of each individual. Management must know what is important to its employees and then provide incentives that are meaningful to them.

The work force today is not homogeneous. Each worker has unique needs. A fair and equitable incentive system will customize rewards to meet the variety of needs of a diverse work force.

Effective incentive plans must also be creative. Since different needs motivate different people, the incentives must fulfill a variety of needs. The trend is toward incentives that are not financial in nature. For example, gift certificates, additional time off, dinners, and sports equipment are being used more widely today. Plaques,

> There is a fine line between positive humor and dysfunctional, negative humor, and it can be crossed very easily.

certificates of appreciation, and public recognition have also been used effectively to improve motivation. A handwritten note from a superior in the organization doesn't cost the firm a thing, but it is extremely effective in reinforcing good work behaviors.

Summary

Managers and human resource department staff must create an environment in which each employee is motivated to contribute to his or her full potential. Managers must transform the way they think about motivation. The human resource department is responsible for developing policies that create a motivated environment in which employees are empowered, trusted, and encouraged to take risks.

> Praise can be a great motivator. It must, however, be administered appropriately to be most effective.

Streetwise Advice

- **Praise can be a great motivator. It must, however, be administered appropriately to be most effective.** Praise must be specific. To ensure that the appropriate behavior is repeated, clearly articulate the behavior being praised. The individual must also understand why this behavior is important and how it helps the organization meet its objectives.

- **Contrary to popular belief, money is not the prime motivator.** Job satisfaction is the number one motivator. In fact, money does not truly motivate individuals who score high in the need for achievement, according to David McClelland's acquired needs theory. These individuals are already highly motivated intrinsically.

- **No one theory explains all human behavior.** The most appropriate theory depends on the person and the situation. A complete understanding of a wide range of motivation theories increases the probability of being able to understand more of what motivates people.

- **Effective motivating today requires creative approaches**. There is no single way to motivate all employees across the board.

- **Creative incentives can motivate employees to high performance levels, often without large financial investments.** Some organizations have successfully implemented the following incentives to better motivate their work force:

  - Concert tickets
  - Impromptu recognition parties or lunches
  - Keys to the building
  - Stock options
  - Tickets to sporting events
  - Tickets to the theater
  - Weekend travel vouchers

- **Equity theory can use standards or surveys as methods of comparison.** The salary surveys conducted by most industries can be used to compare inputs to outputs.

- **Respond, respond, respond.** When employees provide feedback or suggestions, be sure to listen and respond to their comments. Your failure to respond may make your employees wonder if they are being heard.

- **Employees are motivated by consideration and respect.** Managers who extend common courtesies to employees in their attempt to balance all facets of their lives are appreciated and often "rewarded" with higher performance.

- **One of the biggest problems with motivating today is that managers are using the same techniques that they used nearly twenty years ago.** As workers have changed, the techniques that will effectively motivate them have also changed.

- **The approach to motivation is a key component of an organization's culture and often reveals important information.** Organizations that believe workers can easily be replaced don't invest in their employees. Employees receive this message and

> When employees provide feedback or suggestions, be sure to listen and respond to their comments.

respond with less loyalty and a tendency to leave the organization in greater numbers.

- **Poor performance cannot always be assumed to be a problem of motivation.** If an employees is slipping in performance, review his past performance appraisals. Performance is a function of ability, motivation, and environment. If employees don't have the right skills, they can't perform well. They may, indeed, be motivated, but they may not have the necessary skills to be successful.

> Performance is a function of ability, motivation, and environment. If employees don't have the right skills, they can't perform well.

For more information on this topic, visit our Web site at www.businesstown.com

Chapter 13

Appraising Performance

T he performance appraisal process is a key human resource function that is closely integrated with compensation, training, and career planning. Only by effectively evaluating the performance of each individual employee can the overall organization's performance be improved.

The performance appraisal is the systematic evaluation of employees' performance. Once the appraisal is conducted, feedback can be given on any adjustments that are needed to improve each employee's performance and, ultimately, the organization's performance.

Appraisals are conducted for two major reasons: evaluation and feedback. When used for evaluation, the appraisal provides input for decisions on promotions, transfers, demotions, terminations, and compensation (salary increases).

When used for feedback purposes, the appraisal focuses on the development of the individual, including the identification of coaching and training needs. The job analysis process determines standards of performance, which are clearly communicated to the employees and used as the basis of evaluation in the performance appraisal process.

> The job analysis process determines standards of performance, which are clearly communicated to the employees and used as the basis of evaluation in the performance appraisal process.

Why Conduct Performance Appraisals?

Performance appraisals are a critical component of reinforcing appropriate behaviors within the organization and of helping employees understand how to avoid inappropriate behaviors. The evaluation of performance also enables the organization to provide feedback to employees concerning their work and to identify areas that are in need of improvement.

Performance appraisals may be formal or informal. Although most firms implement the formal appraisal system, the informal evaluation is equally important. Both systems should be used. The formal evaluation process is generally conducted at least once a year. Some organizations may conduct evaluations on a more frequent basis (such as twice a year). A company form is generally used and the direct supervisor sits down with the employee being appraised to discuss his or her performance. The informal appraisal should be conducted on a regular basis throughout the appraisal period.

The informal phase of performance appraisal becomes critical in annual evaluations. Employees cannot wait a year to find out what they are doing well and what they are doing poorly. Informal, periodic updates keep the employee on-track and help shape work performance more effectively. Informal appraisals also ensure that the formal appraisal does not come as a surprise to the employee. Constant updates prepare the employee for what to expect in the formal evaluation.

Understanding Reinforcement Strategies

According to the law of effect, behaviors that are followed by positive consequences are more likely to be repeated. On the flip side, behaviors that are followed by negative consequences are less likely to be repeated. Organizations, then, must focus on the systematic positive reinforcement of appropriate behaviors to increase the probability that they will be repeated. And they must not provide positive reinforcement for inappropriate behaviors. There are four reinforcement strategies:

- Positive reinforcement
- Negative reinforcement
- Punishment
- Extinction

Positive reinforcement is the administration of positive consequences to increase the probability that an appropriate behavior will be repeated. To be the most effective, however, the positive reinforcement must be given as soon as possible after the behavior and must be contingent on the desired behavior.

Behaviors that are positively rewarded after a long period are often not repeated. Therefore, informal appraisals must be conducted so employees know which behaviors are appropriate and which are inappropriate, without having to wait until the end of the appraisal period. Positive reinforcement must also be used only when the appropriate behaviors are exhibited. Otherwise, the positive reinforcement will result in inappropriate behaviors being repeated.

> According to the law of effect, behaviors that are followed by positive consequences are more likely to be repeated.

TIP

A classic *Harvard Business Review* article addressed this concept in the 1970s. Unfortunately, organizations are still not heeding this advice. Employees must be rewarded only for those behaviors that are acceptable to the organization.

Managers must guard against the tendency to reward inappropriate behavior. Rewarding other behaviors and hoping this will propel employees toward appropriate behaviors is not going to happen. Only the appropriate behaviors should be rewarded. Employees will not make the connection with what behavior is wanted if another behavior is rewarded.

Negative reinforcement, or *avoidance,* involves avoiding a negative consequence by engaging in the appropriate behavior. If an employee knows that she will be locked out of a meeting if she is late, she will more likely come to the meetings on time (the appropriate behavior) to avoid being locked out (the negative consequence).

The least effective, and most overused, of the reinforcement strategies is *punishment.* Used to discourage inappropriate behavior, punishment has several disadvantages. Rather than changing the offending behavior, the employee who is being punished focuses his or her resentment on the person doling out the punishment. In some cases, this strategy has resulted in employee sabotage. In addition, punishment does not permanently abolish the inappropriate behaviors. These behaviors are simply not exhibited temporarily.

Extinction involves the removal of any reinforcers. Extinction is most effective when combined with other strategies. The inappropriate behavior will reappear if it is reinforced since it is not really unlearned, but rather just not exhibited.

For example, extinction can be used to change the behavior of the proverbial class clown (or organizational clown). The clown entertains the class with inappropriate behaviors and is rewarded by laughter. Even though the teacher admonishes the clown, the laughter reinforces the behavior; that is, the behavior is positively rewarded with peer approval. If, however, the teacher asks the class (without the clown present) to stop laughing—and they do—the reinforcement is removed and the behavior is not exhibited.

> Rewarding other behaviors and hoping this will propel employees toward appropriate behaviors is not going to happen.

The Performance Appraisal

A variety of performance appraisal methods are available. They can be divided into comparative and absolute methods.

Comparative Methods

The comparative methods develop the employee's relative standing as compared to other employees. These methods include ranking, forced distribution, and paired comparisons.

With *ranking*, employees are ranked numerically from best to worst. If six employees make up the unit, the best performing employee would be ranked one, and so on through number six. However, this ranking provides no real feedback about the employees' performance.

The number one-ranked employee may be outstanding while numbers two through six are marginal at best. There is no way to determine this with the ranking. The differences between employees are not known; there is no indication of the degree of performance gaps between individuals. The advantage of this method is that the rater cannot give everyone a high rank.

The *forced distribution* method requires the rater to distribute a certain percentage of employees in each ranking category. For example, the following distributions may be used:

Outstanding	5%
Above average	10%
Average	60%
Below average	15%
Unsatisfactory	10%

If the department has forty employees, the forced distributions would be as follows:

Outstanding	2
Above average	4
Average	24
Below average	6
Unsatisfactory	4

> The comparative methods develop the employee's relative standing as compared to other employees.

TIP
Forced distribution helps the organization control salary budgets. Knowing what percentage of employees managers are required to slot into each category makes budget projections more successful. Since specific salary increases correspond to specific performance appraisal categories (e.g., an average performer will receive a 3 percent increase), the organization is in a better position to forecast the required funds for salary increases.

Absolute Methods

The absolute methods include the checklist, the graphic rating scale, the critical incident diary, and the behaviorally anchored rating scale. *Checklists* include a list of statements describing positive and negative behaviors that may be exhibited on the job. If the employee exhibits the behavior, the item is checked off. If he does not exhibit the behavior, the item is left blank. (See Appendix C, page 332, for a sample performance checklist.) For example, a checklist may include some of these items:

❑ Exhibits creativity when faced with new problems
❑ Regularly fails to meet deadlines
❑ Gets along well with others and displays good team player skills

A variation of this method is the weighted checklist. Rather than considering each statement to be of equal importance, behaviors may be weighted differently. Points are assigned based on the organizational value placed on that behavior.

The *graphic rating scale* provides a ranking scale (usually one to five) for behaviors. One end of the scale represents unsatisfactory performance and the other end represents outstanding performance. The rater checks the ranking that reflects the degree to which the employee exhibits that behavior. An overall rating can be calculated by averaging the individual rankings.

For example, a scale may be constructed as follows:

1	2	3	4	5
UNSATISFACTORY	BELOW AVERAGE	AVERAGE	ABOVE AVERAGE	OUTSTANDING

> The absolute methods include the checklist, the graphic rating scale, the critical incident diary, and the behaviorally anchored rating scale.

The graphic rating scale is one of the most popular methods of performance appraisal. It is easy to use and easy to understand. The forms are easy to revise, and the method is not usually very time-consuming for managers.

A *critical incident diary* requires raters to keep a diary for each employee that describes very successful or unsuccessful performance. The diary must record incidents as they occur. To be effective, very specific details of the behaviors, the context within which the behaviors were performed, and the consequences must be recorded. Although the technique takes time, it provides a good recap of the entire performance appraisal period—if kept up-to-date.

Behaviorally anchored rating scales (BARS) focus solely on employee behaviors. The method avoids any evaluation of attitudes. It uses a numerical rating scale with a description of behaviors that correspond to each of the ratings.

The development of BARS is expensive and time-consuming. It is difficult to develop since it must identify all the work behaviors of the job and then specifically describe that behavior in the range from unsatisfactory to outstanding.

> A *critical incident diary* requires raters to keep a diary for each employee that describes very successful or unsuccessful performance.

Who Should Conduct the Appraisal?

Traditionally, the direct supervisor conducts the performance appraisal because he or she has the most direct information concerning the individual's performance. Today, however, the appraisal process includes many others who have knowledge of the employee's performance, including the supervisor, the subordinates, peers, customers, and even the employees themselves.

TIP

More organizations are developing customer service measures (or CSMs) to use in the 360-degree appraisal system. Customers are asked to appraise the performance of employees based on these measures. The CSMs are also used as goals for the employees. Ultimately, pay should be tied to the attainment of these customer service measures.

With 360-degree evaluation, the firm tries to paint a more complete picture of the employee's performance by using a full circle of people familiar with the employee's work. Direct supervisors today often know less about the actual work being performed by their employees.

The Interview: Ten Tips to More Effective Performance Interviews

The performance interview is the face-to-face discussion that occurs between the employee being evaluated and the evaluator. (See Appendix A, page 311, for tips on conducting more effective performance appraisal interviews.)

> Plan the best time to conduct the appraisal interview, have all the required documents ready, be familiar with the appraisal form, and plan for quiet time that is free of interruptions and phones.

1. Plan, plan, plan. Plan the best time to conduct the appraisal interview, have all the required documents ready, be familiar with the appraisal form, and plan for quiet time that is free of interruptions and phones. Be sure to advise the employee in advance of the scheduled time for the interview.
2. Let the employee talk. Solicit feedback and comments. This is not a time for one-way communication. Focus on discussing the areas in which there were discrepancies between the employee's evaluation and your evaluation.
3. Start on a positive note. Express your appreciation to the employee for her contributions to the firm. Discuss some of the positive aspects of the performance appraisal at the beginning, and be sure to end on a positive note as well.
4. Make sure the appraisal is not a surprise. Use this time in the appraisal interview to formalize what has already been discussed informally with the employee concerning his performance.
5. Tell the employee up-front about your agenda. Include the format of the interview and review the reason for conducting the appraisal. (This discussion should only reinforce what the employee already knows.)
6. Remind the employee of the performance standards. Since these are the standards against which the employee's behavior

is being evaluated, they should be reiterated. Also solicit her feedback on the appropriateness of these standards.

7. Open a discussion about the areas that need improvement. Solicit input from the employee about how he thinks he can improve. Also let him make suggestions about how he thinks you can help him to make the necessary improvements. Then be ready to provide that support.

8. Ensure that the employee has a clear understanding of the appraisal given. Don't just hand a copy of the appraisal form to the employee; explain your ratings. Allow her sufficient time to ask questions and clarify any points of concern.

9. Develop a plan of action including input from the employee before ending the appraisal interview. Base this plan on the employee's strengths and weaknesses discussed during the appraisal interview. Set objectives that provide the basis for evaluating performance for the next appraisal. This plan of action may also include career planning information.

10. Focus on behaviors when evaluating performance and cite specific examples of these behaviors. Avoid any discussions of personality; this can lead to legal difficulties.

> Ensure that the employee has a clear understanding of the appraisal given.

The Use of Discipline: The Road to Corrective Action

Progressive discipline is an effective method that organizations use to shape the behavior of employees. In progressive discipline, the seriousness of the violation of company policies and procedures matches the discipline administered. The following is the progressive disciplinary process traditionally used:

- Verbal warning
- Written warning
- Termination

The degree of the disciplinary action taken increases with the seriousness of the offense or the increasing frequency of the violations. For less serious infractions, a *verbal warning* is generally given to the employee. If the behavior continues, a *written warning* is placed in the employee's personnel file and discussed with the employee. Steps to correct the behavior are outlined. This written warning should contain a time table for improvements and the consequences for not making the required improvements. The consequence is usually *termination*. (See Appendix C, page 335, for a sample disciplinary form.)

> The key to the disciplinary process is fair and impartial administration.

TIP

Effective discipline should not focus on punishment. Instead, it should focus on changing job behaviors. Too often the organization emphasizes punishing employees rather than trying to change their behavior.

The key to the disciplinary process is fair and impartial administration. That is, the policy must be perceived as fair, and it must be consistently administered among all employees. For example, if two employees come to work one hour late, they must both be treated in the same way. One cannot be terminated while the other is given a verbal warning.

A grievance procedure must also be available. Employees must be able to appeal any disciplinary actions taken against them. This appeals process may be to an individual or to a committee within the organization. To improve the perception of the fairness of the disciplinary process, this right of appeal must be clearly communicated to all employees.

When All Else Fails

The last step in the disciplinary process is termination. When all other steps have failed to improve the employee's performance and/or behavior, termination may be necessary. (See Appendix C, page 331, for a termination checklist.)

Every terminated employee should have an opportunity for an exit interview. During this interview, the employee can discuss his or her employment experience and perhaps provide some insight into human resource issues.

The line manager is responsible for the actual notification of termination. To prepare, managers should keep the following guidelines in mind when conducting a termination interview:

- **Don't let the discussion drag on.** State your position and end the discussion; hold it to under fifteen minutes. Be clear about the termination; it is not up for discussion.

- **Be sensitive about when the discussion takes place.** Try to avoid holidays, birthdays, Friday afternoons, or the day before or after a vacation.

- **Be prepared with all of the severance information.** If an outplacement agency is used, be sure to include the contact information.

- **Treat the employee with dignity and respect.** End on a positive note by expressing good wishes.

Summary

Performance appraisals are instrumental in changing employee behavior by improving performance, reducing inappropriate behaviors, and increasing productivity. Only through the use of an effective performance appraisal system can employees' behavior be shaped and modified. Remember, improving employee performance will improve corporate performance.

Streetwise Advice

- **Document, document, document**. Keep detailed records of the specific behaviors of all your employees.

- **Recognize that both the interviewer and the employee are nervous during the appraisal interview.** Decrease your anxiety level by being well prepared. Take advantage of any training that is offered by the organization to better understand the use

> Be sensitive about when the discussion takes place. Try to avoid holidays, birthdays, Friday afternoons, or the day before or after a vacation.

> Have employees sign their evaluation forms and provide them with a copy.

of the appraisal form and how to better conduct appraisal interviews.

- **To communicate that you value the employee's feedback, approach the evaluation as a tentative document.** Once the employee has had an opportunity to discuss her perspective in the interview, finalize the appraisal. This recognizes that the employee does have input into the process; some things may change as a result.

- **Have employees sign their evaluation forms and provide them with a copy.**

- **Managing the appraisal of marginal employees may be more difficult.** When evaluating marginal performers, keep control of the interview and don't allow it to become confrontational. Pulling rank will escalate an already difficult situation. Remember that this can be a very emotional time, and the employee will most likely exhibit defensive reactions. If you feel threatened, call for security.

- **A key to avoiding legal difficulties is being consistent with all employees and documenting performance.** Use the same evaluation procedures and standards for all employees. Using one set of standards for one employee and another set for another employee can lead to lawsuits. Documentation helps you cite specifics—both for the employee's benefit during the evaluation stage and perhaps in court if you are challenged.

- **Communicate openly and honestly with employees concerning their performance on a regular (and informal) basis.**

- **No one specific performance appraisal system is successful in avoiding all legal difficulties.** The key is the administration of the system—not the system itself. Managers should be trained in the use of the method selected, in the use of the appraisal form, and on how to conduct the interview. Role-playing with videotapes is quite effective. Training helps ensure that standards are uniformly applied to all employees being appraised.

- **Begin and end the performance appraisal interview on a positive note.** This is called the sandwich technique. You must be sure, however, that the employee hears and understands the discussion of improvements and weaknesses held "in the middle." The danger is that he focuses only on the positive information.

- **To increase the probability of a positive outcome when legally defending a poor performance appraisal, provide organizational guidance to help the employee improve.**

- **Courts tend to rule more favorably when organizations have attempted to assist poor performers in increasing their performance.**

- **A single global measure of performance is not recommended. One measure is more easily distorted and tends to be less objective.**

- **Conduct sixty-minute performance interviews. An hour provides time for two-way communication. The average interview in reality, however, lasts fifteen minutes, which does not provide sufficient time for a discussion.**

- **The performance appraisal interview may even be divided into two separate sessions.** The first session may address the past performance and the actual evaluation. The second session may address the action plan for the future.

> Courts tend to rule more favorably when organizations have attempted to assist poor performers in increasing their performance.

For more information on this topic, visit our Web site at www.businesstown.com

PART IV

Maintaining Human Resources

Organizations have placed increasing importance on retaining their employees. Recognizing the high cost of turnover and the high cost of recruiting new employees, more companies are seeking effective techniques to retain their employees.

Chapter 14: Explore the role of compensation and benefits in employee retention programs.

Chapter 15: Learn to recognize the importance of effective hiring and signs of trouble among the staff.

Compensation and Benefits

Chapter 14

C ompensation and benefits are provided in exchange for the employees' contributions to the organization. An effective compensation program can help shape performance and improve job satisfaction as well.

Compensation is the reward package that employees are given in exchange for their job performance. An organization must provide a fair exchange for the knowledge, skills, and abilities its workers provide. Offering fair and equitable compensation makes employees feel valued.

A compensation package is comprised of two components: direct compensation and indirect compensation. Direct compensation is the money paid for work; that is, wages or salary. Indirect compensation is the benefits portion.

The Role of Compensation Programs

Compensation is one way for an organization to "put its money where its mouth is." If it values something (such as teamwork, diversity, or customer service), then the company must openly reward these things in order to reinforce its objectives and values.

Compensation can be critical in motivating employees. They are more likely to be motivated when they feel their contributions are being fairly and equitably rewarded. Compensation is a reward system. It reflects the employee's value to the firm and in turn impacts his or her sense of self.

An effective compensation plan helps the organization attract, and retain, skilled employees. Compensation can also be used to encourage workers to learn new skills and to exhibit appropriate behavior. Employees who are rewarded for performing well will, in turn, provide good role models for others.

If, in an ideal organization, individual goals are aligned with organizational goals, then the organization will meet its goals when all the employees meet their goals. Rewarding employees (by providing equitable compensation) for meeting their own goals, therefore, brings the organization closer to achieving its overall goals.

> An effective compensation plan helps the organization attract, and retain, skilled employees.

Terminology: Wages Versus Salaries

The difference between working wages and executive salaries is clearest in context, but it can be boiled down to this: Wages are determined by the work; salaries are determined by the job.

Wages

Wages are hourly rates. Employees are paid based on the amount of time they work. Employers must know the minimum wage required by law when determining wages. People in operating jobs are usually paid hourly rates. They must work the time to receive their wages.

For example, if an employee is paid $6 an hour and works the following hours, the wages paid will reflect only the hours worked.

Hourly Wages	
Hours Worked	**Amount Paid**
8 hours on Monday	$48
3 hours on Tuesday	$18
6 hours on Wednesday	$36
2 hours on Thursday	$12
8 hours on Friday	$48

> Employees are paid based on the amount of time they work.

In some companies, the compensation system, also called a *piece-rate system,* may be based on the work completed. Each employee is paid for each unit produced. Garment workers may be paid a predetermined sum for each shirt they produce. For example, if it took ten hours for one garment worker to produce three shirts at a piece rate of $4, he would be paid $12. If another employee took three hours to produce three shirts, she would also be paid $12.

Salaries

Salaries are compensations based on an annual or monthly basis. The actual time worked on the job is not a pay determinant. (In some less common cases, the salaries might be expressed in a weekly rate.) Professionals and managers are traditionally paid salaries.

For example, a salaried employee who makes $2,500 a month would be paid the same amount regardless of the actual number of hours he worked during each month. If a manager worked 40 hours the first week, 44 the second week, 48 the third week, and 50 hours the fourth week, her compensation is $2,500 for the month. If the same salaried employee worked 30 hours, 40 hours, 38 hours, and 35 hours for the four weeks in the next month, she would still be paid $2,500.

Alternative Pay Systems

The general formula for compensation has traditionally been that the more complex or dangerous the job, the more compensation is paid. Seniority and the position of the job in the organization determined the compensation. Now there are more creative compensation systems. Employers are no longer concerned solely with the tasks performed.

A growing trend is to pay people for the knowledge, skills, and abilities they acquire. The underlying premise is that the organization is paying now to acquire the skills that it will need later. As a result, when the skills are needed, the firm will not have to search for them. This ability to anticipate future needs improves the company's long-term competitive position and increases their flexibility in responding to future challenges.

Skill-based, or *knowledge-based,* pay is an example of this trend. Employees are paid for having acquired knowledge and skills, regardless of whether they are actually used in the current job. The more skills or knowledge the employee has acquired, the bigger the compensation package.

Pay-for-performance systems tie compensation to performance. Employees who perform at higher levels (regardless of time on the job) receive greater compensation than their poorer performing counterparts. Workers who contribute more to the organization's performance are rewarded with higher salaries.

More organizations have moved to a compensation system known as broadbanding, in which several pay grades are combined

> The general formula for compensation has traditionally been that the more complex or dangerous the job, the more compensation is paid.

into one band (hence the name). Instead of having three pay grades with the following ranges, one band is created:

Pay grade 1	$17,500–30,000
Pay grade 2	$22,000–40,000
Pay grade 3	$30,000–60,000

The new band combines pay grades 1 through 3 and ranges from $17,500 to $60,000.

This system provides a more flexible approach to compensation. The focus becomes the job responsibilities and the development of new skills instead of the pay grade for the job. Employee growth is no longer reflected in the move from one pay grade to another, but rather by increasing responsibilities, performing more of the activities found in the band, and moving up the band.

Special Issues in Compensation

Several compensation issues require careful analysis by the human resource department and top management. These issues include the firm's general compensation policy, the importance of external equity, internal equity, pay secrecy, and pay for performance. Many organizations are still debating these issues.

Compensation Policy

Organizations must decide on a compensation policy. This policy should include how people will be paid, a seniority policy, and external equity. Organizations must decide if they will pay employees for the value of the job being performed (and the contributions made to the organization) or if pay will be based on the skills acquired by the employees.

In addition, companies must decide how differences in pay rates will be determined. Many organizations use seniority (time in service), regardless of performance, to determine pay differentials. An average performer who has been in the job for ten years may make significantly more than an outstanding performer who has only been

> Several compensation issues require careful analysis by the human resource department and top management.

on the job for two years. Seniority as a basis for determining pay differential is common in union environments.

TIP

Compensation policy is often a reflection of an organization's overall view of the value of their human resources. Those organizations that place a high value on their human resources often structure compensation policies to provide fair and equitable compensation.

Equity is the assumption that the longer an employee is with an organization, the more experience they have and, therefore, the greater their contribution. This system can be used as a retention tool to encourage longevity with the organization.

Pay for performance does not consider seniority. The pay differentials reflect performance differences. The better the performer is, the greater the rewards (pay). This system, however, depends on a reliable performance evaluation system.

External Equity

Since no organization operates in a vacuum, the external environment must be taken into account, especially when examining compensation. Each organization must decide if its policy will lead, meet, or lag its competition. That is, each company develops a policy to pay their employees above the market, at the market rates, or below the market.

Some organizations have a reputation for paying more than the going rate for the industry because they want to hire the best and the brightest in the field.

Although the firm incurs additional expense by paying above the market, this policy does improve retention. Employees who think of leaving the organization won't usually be able to find many better paying jobs. Instead, they would more likely be faced with a pay cut if they leave. There is also a positive perception of a company when its compensation is above the market. These employees are perceived as having a higher status within the industry.

If the company is in a high-growth phase, it is more likely to pay above-market compensation. The company must be able to quickly attract the talent in order to keep up its pace of growth.

Other organizations would rather pay a competitive wage that simply meets what the competition is offering. They may be able to compete on the basis of other issues, such as a prime location with free company parking. Providing compensation at comparable market rates usually means that the basis of competition is with other benefits. Pleasant working conditions or exceptional medical insurance may balance out pay. Companies engaging in a stability strategy (where the company is holding steady and is not engaged in growth or retrenchment) are more likely to pay at the market rate.

Other organizations may pay wages below the competition—either out of economic necessity, or in exchange for other favorable working conditions such as a flexible work arrangement. The firm may attract lower-quality employees, but it will save money.

In a loose labor market (experiencing high unemployment), companies paying below the market may still get some talented, qualified workers since job applicants have fewer employment opportunities. A big disadvantage of paying below the market, however, is that employees usually know they are being underpaid (relative to the competition) and this knowledge can be demoralizing. The organization may experience lower retention rates as employees leave for higher paying jobs with competitors. Finally, the performance of the company may be further negatively impacted as the more talented employees leave and less talented employees remain.

Companies engaged in a retrenchment strategy are more likely to provide compensation below the market, because the focus of retrenchment is on cutting costs. Labor is a big cost to the firm so paying below the market can help trim costs.

The condition of the local labor market may also impact this decision. When the demand for workers in a specific field exceeds the supply of these workers, many firms may be forced to raise their compensation to attract applicants. Management philosophy is yet another factor in the compensation decision. Those management teams that place a high value on their people generally pay higher wages.

> A big disadvantage of paying below the market, however, is that employees usually know they are being underpaid (relative to the competition) and this knowledge can be demoralizing.

TIP

Although most employees think of their paycheck as their compensation, it is only part of their compensation. The total package is comprised of all the financial rewards and benefits provided by the organization in exchange for the employee's contribution.

Of course, the company's ability to pay will also impact the compensation policy decision. A firm will pay below the market if it can't afford higher salaries. Its ability to attract employees with other benefits will impact the compensation policy. If many of the other benefits it offers make a firm an employer of choice, it may be able to offer compensation below the market. However, the reverse may also be true. If there are unfavorable working conditions, a firm may be forced to offer above-market compensations in order to attract talented employees.

> Internal equity is the establishment of compensation levels that reflect the worth of the job to the organization.

Internal Equity

Companies also make decisions on the subject of internal pay equity. Internal equity is the establishment of compensation levels that reflect the worth of the job to the organization. Employees basically ask if they are being paid fairly in exchange for what they are giving to the organization as compared to the pay of their fellow employees. Organizations, then, must address any perceptions of internal inequity before employees lose their motivation, confront other employees, or bring legal action.

Job evaluations help establish a perception of internal equity within a firm by determining what pay level is appropriate for each job, given its contributions to the organization. This evaluation compares the knowledge, skills, abilities, and responsibilities required to perform a job successfully with the requirements for other jobs within the organization.

TIP

Equity theory helps explain how employees perform this comparison. They evaluate the ratio of their inputs to outputs as compared to the ratio of someone else's ratio of inputs to outputs. They then determine if this relationship is equitable or inequitable. A perceived inequity (such as not being paid enough) can cause an individual to leave the organization.

Pay Secrecy

Organizations must decide the level of pay secrecy that they desire. Although a few decades ago, the majority of organizations demanded that employees keep their pay secret from coworkers, this is not the norm today.

The trend today is toward the use of open-pay systems. The reasoning is that it may motivate the rest of the work force to see that high-performing individuals are rewarded more. A company's level of pay secrecy (or openness) doesn't have to be at one extreme or the other. A firm may simply choose to open up information on pay grades and share information about where jobs fall in these grades.

Pay Compression

Big differences in experience or performance are not always reflected in big differences in pay. Instead, two pay levels may be compressed.

When the external labor market drives up starting salaries, organizations are likely to see more pay compression. The starting salaries of new employees begin to rapidly approach the salary levels of those employees in the same positions with more time on the job and more experience. That is, there is little difference between the starting salaries and seasoned employees' salaries. Consider the pay rates for these accountants:

> When the external labor market drives up starting salaries, organizations are likely to see more pay compression.

Pay Rates		Salary Today
Starting salary two years ago	$21,000	$23,000
Starting salary last year	$22,000	$23,800
Starting salary this year	$23,500	$23,500

The accountant hired last year now has one year's experience with the firm and is making only $300 more than this year's new hire. If the trend continues, it could prove disastrous to the perception of internal pay equity.

The firm must decide if it must raise the current employee's salary. Starting pay may even surpass the experienced individuals' salary, creating issues with internal equity. In this example, the accountant hired two years ago (now with two years' experience in the job) is making $500 less than the new accountant just hired. The firm must decide if it wants to raise the salary of the accountant with two years' experience. The firm may have to explore some creative rewards and examine the effects of starting salaries on internal equity.

TIP

Pay compression may also be of concern between management and nonmanagement ranks. This compression may make it harder to recruit management. As the compression occurs, managers may question whether the small differential in pay is adequate compensation for their additional responsibilities.

Determining the Worth of Jobs

> Fair and equitable compensation systems depend on effectively determining the worth of each job in the organization.

Fair and equitable compensation systems depend on effectively determining the worth of each job in the organization. Job evaluation, the method used to determine this worth, ensures that internal equity is more likely to be achieved.

There are several different methods of determining the worth of jobs in an organization. The most popular methods include:

- Job ranking
- Job classification/pay grades
- Point system
- Factor comparison

Regardless of the system used, the job description and job specification (generated during the job analysis) are the key documents on which the decisions are based.

The most simplistic system of job evaluation is *job ranking*. It is best suited to organizations with few jobs. The jobs are ranked according to their contribution to the business. The most important jobs are ranked higher (and paid more) than jobs that are less important. It is difficult, however, to determine differentials between jobs.

In the *job classification* method, descriptions are written of each grade to differentiate it from other classifications and to determine competencies. As new jobs are designed, they are placed into one of these categories according to the descriptions. These descriptions may include broad categories of responsibilities (e.g., routine work or independent judgment), knowledge, skills, abilities, specialized training, and education (such as specialized subject matter).

Then the jobs are grouped into classifications or pay grades and the classifications are ranked by their contribution to the business (as in the job-ranking method). The firm must decide how many grades it wants; the average is around nine.

The use of job classes helps differentiate between workers. There are different job grades established within a class. For example, accounting positions may be differentiated as follows:

Accounting clerk	Entry level (little or no experience)
Junior accountant	Middle level with more experience and accounting education
Senior accountant	Extensive experience, higher education, and/or professional certification

In the *point system* the various elements of a job are assigned point values. This method uses compensable factors; that is, the elements of a job that are compensated, such as skill level requirement, proficiencies, or working conditions. The total of all compensable factors is then calculated to arrive at a single point value for each job. A point manual must also be developed to ensure the objectiveness of the system as well as consistency in evaluating jobs.

For example, the following point system may be used to examine the educational component of every job in a company:

10 points	High school diploma
25 points	Associate's degree
50 points	Bachelor's degree
70 points	Master's degree
100 points	Doctorate

> In the *point system* the various elements of a job are assigned point values.

In the *factor comparison* system, a scale is developed as the standard measurement against which all jobs are compared. Compensable factors are agreed on and then those factors are used to measure all jobs. The most common compensable factors used in this system are job responsibility, skills and abilities, physical requirements, mental requirements, and working conditions/environment.

Common jobs in the organization are then selected as benchmarks and ranked according to the agreed-on compensable factors. Then the factors' relative importance in the total compensation (i.e., the percentage of compensation generated from this factor) is determined. The resulting chart with factors and compensation is used as the basis (or benchmark) for ranking other jobs.

Using this method, it is easier to compare jobs and to tie differences in the jobs to pay. However, the process of developing the system is difficult, expensive, and time-consuming. In addition, this method is more subjective.

> Pay structure involves the determination of pay levels for each job class and the differentials within these classes.

Pay Structure

Pay structure involves the determination of pay levels for each job class and the differentials within these classes. For example, if there are six pay grades/classes, a minimum, midpoint, and maximum amount is determined along with the range for each class. Overlap is often designed into the system so the high range of one grade overlaps the low range of the next grade.

A sample pay structure may be presented as follows:

Grade Level	Minimum	Midpoint	Maximum
Grade 1	$15,000	$17,500	$20,000
Grade 2	$17,500	$24,125	$30,000
Grade 3	$20,000	$35,000	$50,000
Grade 4	$30,000	$50,000	$70,000
Grade 5	$45,000	$72,500	$100,000
Grade 6	$65,000	$120,000	$175,000

Executive Compensation

In recent years, popular business publications have printed annual surveys that report executive compensation packages along with company performance. Executive compensation has been found to be excessive. While most hourly employees receive annual increases averaging 3 or 4 percent, executive increases for the same period have averaged 45 percent. In 1980, the average chief executive officer (CEO) was paid 42 times more than the average manufacturing employee. In twenty years, this rate increased to more than 325 times.

The most astounding fact is exposed when examining company performance in relation to CEO compensation. Executive compensation has increased at rates far greater than profits. In fact, these surveys continuously report firms with huge financial losses whose CEO compensation packages show substantial increases during the same periods.

Perceptions of equity are violated when executives are paid so much more than the average worker, especially in hard economic times. Executive perks (such as company jets and limos) sometimes continue as workers are laid off, which perpetuates feelings of internal inequity.

As these excesses come under closer scrutiny, increased involvement by both shareholders and the boards of directors will ensure that reforms are instituted. More firms are starting to use short- and long-term measures to help tie company performance to executive pay. Organizations are also using multiples to control CEO pay. For example, Ben & Jerry's had publicized in their early years the low multiple of their executive pay as compared to their lowest paid employee.

Executives are also given golden parachutes; that is, if their employment does not work out, they may receive a large severance package often paid over several years. These kinds of arrangements offend the average employee's sense of fairness when it is possible for them to be laid off with only two weeks' severance.

> Perceptions of equity are violated when executives are paid so much more than the average worker, especially in hard economic times.

Types of Benefits

Benefits are often referred to as indirect compensation (since they are not expressed in financial terms). Once called fringe benefits, this terminology sent the wrong message when it became such a large percentage of the total compensation package. Benefits on average approach 50 percent of an employee's total compensation. Now they are just referred to as benefits.

Benefits are used to attract employees and improve the satisfaction level of the work force. As a result, firms want to remain competitive in their offerings. Benefits should be carefully selected to meet the needs of the individual firm's work force.

The Standard Package

> There are both required benefits and voluntary benefits that employers may offer.

There are both required benefits and voluntary benefits that employers may offer. Some voluntary benefits have become so popular that many employees feel they are entitled to them. However, benefits that are not required by law are only provided at the discretion of the employer.

The required benefits an employer must offer are as follows:

- Social security
- Unemployment compensation
- Workers' compensation

While most organizations offer a host of additional benefits, these three benefits are the only ones required by law.

Social security provides income (though rather limited) for retirement. It also provides for survival benefits and disability. If a covered individual dies before retirement age leaving children under the age of eighteen, the children may collect survivor benefits based on the earnings of the decedent. If a covered worker becomes totally disabled (prior to sixty-five years of age), he or she is eligible for benefits and Medicare kicks in.

Unemployment compensation is a subsistence payment that is administered by each state. The employer pays a premium into a fund for unemployment. Only three states—Alabama, Alaska, and New Jersey—require payments to these funds from employees as well.

Unemployment compensation continues for a fixed period under specific conditions mandated by law. This time period usually is twenty-six weeks. For example, voluntary terminations are usually excluded from the benefits. Familiarity with state legislation is essential to ensure compliance. *Workers' compensation* is paid entirely by the employer and is offered to protect the employee from hardship as a result of any injuries sustained while on the job. Every state has a compensation law governing the requirements of each firm.

Both physical and emotional injuries are covered under workers' compensation. Emotional injuries are the fastest growing sector of workers' compensation claims. Stress-related injuries are a large part of this growth today.

Voluntary Benefits

As with their moral and ethical positions, preferred employers make an effort to go beyond the letter of the law when providing benefits. Some of the more popular voluntary benefits include:

- Child/elder care
- Insurance
- Pension plans
- Severance pay
- Supplemental unemployment
- Time off with pay
- Wellness programs

Child/Elder Care

Childcare has become very popular as a voluntary benefit. With an increasing number of working mothers, childcare has become a real concern for many employees. Companies offer a wide range of benefits such as company-paid on-site day care facilities, referrals to recommended child care facilities, reimbursements, and subsidies. All of these offerings help establish a "family friendly" image for the firm.

Closely related to childcare is the issue of elder care. With people living longer, many require additional care. Today's working generation has been referred to as the sandwich generation since they are responsible for childcare and elder care (as they assume the responsibility for the care of their aging parents). As employers try to assist

> As with their moral and ethical positions, preferred employers make an effort to go beyond the letter of the law when providing benefits.

employees in balancing work and family issues, attention to elder care is helping to ease this burden. A limited number of firms are providing on-site facilities and more are providing referral services.

Insurance

Although many employees think that insurance, especially medical insurance, is a standard benefit, it is not a required benefit and is provided at the discretion of the employer. As medical insurance has become more expensive, employees have had to shoulder much more of the cost by paying a higher percentage of the premiums. Health insurance is the most common type of insurance offered. Many companies also choose to offer prescription plans, vision, and dental plans. Life insurance and long-term disability are becoming more popular offerings as well. Some larger companies have even chosen to fund their own health insurance to better control rising costs.

> Although many employees think that insurance, especially medical insurance, is a standard benefit, it is not a required benefit and is provided at the discretion of the employer.

Pension Plans

Pension plans are retirement income provided to employees. These plans generally require contributions from both the employer and the employee. The 401 (k) is a tax-deferred savings for retirement to an investment account. The 403 (b) is the comparable plan for a nonprofit organization. As more employees move from job to job, they are more likely to take their funds with them when they leave an organization and roll them into a new retirement investment.

Severance Pay

When employees are terminated, they are given severance pay, which is financial assistance until they land their next job. There is a wide variety of pay from organization to organization. Some companies pay two weeks to every employee leaving their employ; others use formulas to determine the number of weeks to be paid, often reflecting time in service to the company. For example, an employee of ten years would receive ten weeks' severance while an employee of two years would receive two weeks' severance pay.

Supplemental Unemployment

Supplemental unemployment benefits are paid to employees who are temporarily laid off. This benefit, which is intended to supplement unemployment payments, is common in the automobile industry where there are more regular layoffs. These layoffs often occur when a plant is closed for a specified period for retooling. Supplemental unemployment benefits help bring the employee's pay during these layoffs closer to their full pay so the employee can wait out the layoff and return to the employer when needed. These pay levels in the auto industry often approach 95 percent of the regular pay.

Time Off with Pay

Most employees today feel that they are entitled to time off with pay, but this benefit is offered only at the discretion of the employer. Most organizations offer an average of ten paid holidays. The most common include the following:

- New Year's Day
- Martin Luther King Day
- President's Day
- Memorial Day
- Fourth of July
- Labor Day
- Columbus Day
- Thanksgiving
- Christmas

> The trend is to require employees to take their vacation each year and not carry it over from one year to the next.

Vacation time is also a popular time-off-with-pay benefit. Although vacation pay varies from organization to organization, seniority generally determines the number of weeks an employee is allowed to take per year. The trend is to require employees to take their vacation each year and not carry it over from one year to the next. The belief behind this stipulation is that employees need time away from the job to rest and relax and that they will return refreshed and more productive.

Most organizations also offer sick days, another paid-time benefit. Employees generally accrue sick time through time in service.

Then when an employee is unable to work due to illness, he or she is still paid.

Companies are increasingly using personal days to accommodate their diverse work force. Offering fewer paid holidays and more personal days enables employees to better meet their individual needs (such as religious holidays or personal occasions).

Wellness Programs

Organizations can help contain costs by keeping their work force healthy. Wellness programs are growing in popularity and variety. Aimed at keeping workers well, these benefits can include organized exercise programs, paid health club dues, on-site gyms, programs to quit smoking, stress management programs, and weight loss programs. These programs have been found to decrease health care costs and the number of sick days used, thus positively impacting the organization's bottom line.

Employee assistance programs have also grown in number. These programs may assist employees with substance abuse problems, violence, marital difficulties, stress, or emotional problems. A large number of firms provide referrals for employees to find counseling outside the firm. Larger organizations may actually provide the counseling in-house.

Creative Options

Other perks offered by the company can include company cars, company stock, uniforms, discount rates for automobile insurance, legal advice, time off to do community service, financial planning, discount rates for home owner's insurance, or the use of frequent flier miles earned on the job.

While every organization must pay attention to the market to be aware of what benefits the competition is offering, the critical issue is to meet the needs of the work force. Flexibility is the key in most cases. This flexibility is reflected in the widespread use of cafeteria-style benefit plans. Employees are allowed to choose their benefits from a list. They are allotted a specified amount of money to allocate across the benefits offered by the firm. These plans have proved valuable to many organizations. Employees have become

Aimed at keeping workers well, these benefits can include organized exercise programs, paid health club dues, on-site gyms, programs to quit smoking, stress management programs, and weight loss programs.

more informed about the cost of their benefits and might not take them as much for granted.

Summary

With the high cost of compensation—both direct and indirect—organizations are paying particular attention to crafting their compensation policy. The key is to ensure that their compensation rewards past performance and encourages high levels of current performance to help the organization better meet its organizational objectives. The compensation package today must be flexible enough to meet the needs of a changing workplace.

Streetwise Advice

- **Texas, New Jersey, and South Carolina have different workers' compensation laws than the rest of the states.** Employers have the option of paying into the state fund. Each manager should be familiar with the laws of each state in which the firm operates since the states vary quite a bit in their legislation.

- **Employees have become savvy about compensation negotiation.** With more information readily available, employees have a better understanding of what fair compensation is. There are salary sites available on the Internet and professional associations publish annual surveys on compensation. More organizations are sharing their salary information in these surveys.

- **You must be aware of the state laws governing minimum wage.** Some states have higher minimum wages mandated than the federal laws. In some cases, city legislation addresses wages in specific industries.

- **Managing compensation is a continuous process.** As jobs are routinely evaluated, the firm must assess the impact of these changes on the compensation system in order to ensure that the system remains equitable and meets strategic objectives.

> The compensation package today must be flexible enough to meet the needs of a changing workplace.

- **Assess the effectiveness of benefit programs regularly.**
  A benefits audit should be conducted regularly. With the high cost of benefits, programs should be reviewed periodically to ensure that the firm is offering the benefits that the employees want—and at a good price.

- **Benefits must vary with international operations to reflect local and regional cultures.** To be effective operating in the global arena, benefits must be adapted to local cultures. For example, in England, time off to move and longer bereavement leaves are generally provided as voluntary benefits.

- **Everyone who performs the same job is not necessarily paid the same amount.** With individual pay differentials, the factors determining pay differences must be job-related to avoid discrimination charges. These factors may be based on seniority or performance.

To be effective operating in the global arena, benefits must be adapted to local cultures.

For more information on this topic, visit our Web site at www.businesstown.com

Retention Strategies

Chapter 15

15: RETENTION STRATEGIES

O rganizations are finding it more difficult to retain employees today. This lack of commitment leaves in its wake soaring expenses that companies must incur to find replacements and a negative impact on the morale, efficiency, and productivity of the remaining work force. To avoid these costly situations, employers of choice are creating more effective retention strategies in an effort to encourage higher levels of commitment to the firm and a more loyal work force.

Employees are one of the most important resources of an organization. If they are nurtured, cared for, and supported, they will provide valuable contributions.

All about Commitment

Job satisfaction is how positive an employee feels about his or her job. When an individual's expectations of the job (or the organization) are not met, he will probably experience job dissatisfaction. Research studies have identified certain factors that influence job satisfaction, such as compensation, recognition, relationships with other organizational members (especially peers and direct supervisors), opportunities for training, and challenge.

An employee's level of job satisfaction, therefore, impacts her level of commitment to the organization and determines how likely she will be to remain with the organization. Withdrawal from the company can be seen in absenteeism rates (reflecting a temporary withdrawal) or in turnover rates (reflecting a permanent withdrawal).

Absenteeism can be both voluntary and involuntary. Voluntary absenteeism is perceived as avoidable whereas involuntary absenteeism is unavoidable. An organization can control voluntary absenteeism by using both positive and negative reinforcement strategies. When a company creates rewards for perfect attendance (such as a monthly cash bonus), it is using positive reinforcement. When a company issues warnings to workers with high absenteeism rates, it is using negative reinforcement.

As any good marketer knows, it costs less to retain a customer than to recruit a new one. The same principle applies to employees.

> When an individual's expectations of the job (or the organization) are not met, he will probably experience job dissatisfaction.

In light of the increasing costs of recruitment and selection, each organization must make a commitment to hire effectively and then to retain those talented individuals. Most firms cannot afford the cost of high turnover since it is controllable to some extent.

The Cost of Turnover

Defined as the number of workers who leave the firm during a specified period (usually one year), turnover is an expensive proposition for any organization. A firm's turnover rate is also a measure of the effectiveness of the human resource department's policies and programs to retain employees.

Examining the Problem

There are many reasons for turnover. Some turnover results simply through attrition. There is a natural movement of workers into and out of organizations. Employees retire or die. They are laid off during the valleys of the business cycle (such as retail sales clerks after the Christmas season) or during unexpected economic downturns.

Turnover can also be voluntary or involuntary. For example, if an employee is terminated, the turnover is involuntary because the employee did not leave of his own accord. But if an employee decides to leave because she gets a better offer from a competitor, the turnover is voluntary.

Organizations are particularly concerned about the number of employees who leave to accept another job. Had the organization been employing better retention strategies, these workers might have stayed. Knowing that some turnover is natural, a company must take proactive measures to hold this number down as much as possible.

The rate of turnover can provide a good insight into the climate of an organization. Higher turnover rates may be associated with lower work force morale and poor management skills. If this is indeed what is happening and word spreads throughout the industry, the organization will find it increasingly difficult to attract skilled workers.

To avoid this situation, corporate management must determine what an acceptable rate of turnover is for their company and what

> Organizations are particularly concerned about the number of employees who leave to accept another job.

they can do to stop employees from leaving. The first step is to understand why the work force is dissatisfied. Some of the more common reasons employees cite for deciding to leave their employer include a lack of growth opportunities, poor management, high stress levels, better pay in another organization, better growth opportunities in another organization, and a desire to relocate to a new area.

> Turnover starts an avalanche of costs, both direct and indirect.

The Direct Costs of Turnover

Turnover starts an avalanche of costs, both direct and indirect. Some of the direct costs, associated with replacing the employee and training the new hire, may include:

- Communicating the vacant position
- Administering the recruitment function
- Screening the applicants
- Interviewing (line manager) the candidates
- Administering selection tools/tests
- Meeting the candidate
- Conducting background investigations
- Giving drug tests
- Preparing new employee training materials
- Conducting training sessions (including orientation)
- Giving on-the-job training

There are also costs associated with separating the former employee from the firm, such as:

- Administering paperwork/meetings
- Conducting exit interviews
- Paying severance pay/package, vacation time, sick time

The Indirect Costs of Turnover

Turnover also brings with it indirect costs. For example, if the employees who are leaving are well liked by the firm's clients, customer loyalty may be affected. As new employees learn their jobs, the quality of the products and services they provide may also suffer.

Impact on Morale

High turnover levels can also negatively influence the remaining work force. Morale may plummet and stress levels may rise as workers take up the slack for the departing employees. Morale also suffers when employees who are integral to the work force leave a firm. Coworkers then worry about completing their own work. The loss of a popular employee also makes remaining employees wonder if they've missed important signs. A stampede of employees can result, known as the "domino effect."

TIP

Human resource staff and line managers should be aware of turnover as an indicator of more serious problems. Turnover rates that exceed the norm or exceed what is normal in an organization should always be investigated.

Impact on Productivity

Turnover can also impact productivity. When skilled workers leave, the less skilled employees have to fill in temporarily, often performing at significantly lower levels. Even when the new employees are hired, productivity suffers as a result of the learning curve.

As human resource department personnel and line managers spend time replacing departing employees, their productivity suffers. They are not engaging in activities that contribute to organizational objectives. Considering that the average interview takes about sixty minutes (with about fifteen minutes of preparation time), the overall impact for high turnover rates can be staggering.

Hidden Costs

In addition, there are the hidden costs of turnover. If, for example, an employee leaves the firm after a short time, there is no chance for the firm to recover its full investment. This investment includes all the expenses incurred in recruiting, selecting, training,

> Turnover rates that exceed the norm or exceed what is normal in an organization should always be investigated.

and orienting the person to the firm. Then the company must incur all those expenses again in finding a replacement.

Most industries are relatively small in terms of how quickly news travels. High turnover rates can send the message to competing firms that you are weak. Competitors may choose to make a strategic move by targeting market share or attempting to hire away what is left of your talent. Other companies may see you as a takeover target (and at a bargain basement price). Yet others may see you as a less desirable strategic partner and thereby provide fewer business opportunities. With the tremendously high cost of turnover, it pays to address retention strategies. In the long run, retention strategies save the company money.

> Effective hiring to improve retention requires that attention be paid to the organization-job-person fit.

Effective Retention Begins with Good Hiring Practices

Effective hiring to improve retention requires that attention be paid to the organization-job-person fit. To improve retention, it is no longer enough to fit the person with the job. The person must also fit the organization. This fit increases the probability of staying with the firm for a longer time.

The choice of recruitment sources actually impacts the retention of employees. Some sources have proved to be more effective in recruiting employees who stay with the organization for longer periods. Informal internal recruitment methods and word-of-mouth have traditionally yielded the best retention rates. Talented individuals are recognized by their informal networks and are often referred to jobs by these networks.

The use of realistic job previews (referred to as RJPs) has also improved retention. Telling an applicant about the negative aspects of the job also helps improve retention. The applicant will become disillusioned with the firm and lose trust in the employer if he is only told about the positive aspects of the job. Once he comes onboard and discovers the negative aspects of the position—and he surely will!—he is likely to leave.

While these general conclusions are drawn across a broad category of firms, each organization will find methods that are effective in increasing retention. Recruitment methods should be analyzed to determine their retention rates, and any methods that are not effective should be eliminated.

Other Retention Strategies

Retention is a management philosophy that trickles down from the top of the organization. Management must see retention expenses as a sound investment that improves long-term performance. The top management team must view employees as valuable assets that must be nurtured and supported.

Happy employees are more likely to remain with the firm for a long time. Compensation packages and working conditions go a long way toward helping employees achieve happiness on the job, although they are certainly not the only means of retaining employees.

Directed Efforts

Fair Compensation

Pay for performance can improve employee retention by linking compensation to performance and by providing a motivational tool to encourage employees to continue working at a high level and to stay with the organization. This system may also have a secondary benefit. Those employees who are not performing at high levels will feel discouraged and may very well leave the organization. Or they may see the value of improving their performance to gain additional pay. Both of these outcomes can result in a stronger work force with better performing individuals. In effect, the pay for performance system may help the firm "clean house."

> If top-performing workers do not think that they are being fairly compensated, they are likely to leave.

Less effective compensation systems may create higher levels of turnover. If top-performing workers do not think that they are being fairly compensated, they are likely to leave. The consequence is not just higher turnover, but the loss of talented workers who are needed to meet the organization's objectives. Thus, the firm may be left with only the poorer performing workers, which will also negatively impact performance.

Fair compensation is a reflection of the employee's perceived value to the organization. That is, people believe the pay they receive is a message from the organization about how valued they are. If they are recognized (demonstrated through fair compensation), they are more likely to remain with the firm.

The benefits offered by the firm as part of the total compensation package also influence the retention of employees. Providing benefits that are of value to the employee will also make them more likely to remain.

Lifestyle Benefits

HR Focus magazine reported the findings of a survey concerning benefits. Twenty percent or more of the survey respondents cited the following benefits as the most effective in retaining employees:

- Casual dress days
- Entertainment and service discounts
- Larger raises
- More input on policies/procedures
- More flextime options
- More office social events
- More vacation/leave time
- Performance bonuses
- Telecommuting options

> The quality of work life and the balance of work/nonwork issues have become even more important to employees.

Some of these benefits, such as employee input or casual dress days, don't cost the company anything to implement. The message being sent to employers in these surveys is that lifestyle benefits can improve retention rates. The quality of work life and the balance of work/nonwork issues have become even more important to employees today. Carefully crafting benefits can help employees better achieve this balance.

Recognition

Recognition of employee contributions is critical in retaining employees. An organization must be vocal in recognizing the good efforts of its employees. This recognition can be as small as a handwritten thank-you note expressing appreciation for the employee's contribution to the organization. More employees would like to receive additional freedom, control, and autonomy in recognition for a job well done.

TIP

Recognition for employee contributions provides tremendous opportunities for organizations. To reap the maximum benefits, organizations must be creative. Many times, it is a simple matter of asking employees what they want and what they value.

Good Management

Good management is important in keeping people with the firm; that is why the effectiveness of management should be assessed on a regular basis. Bad management is often cited as a top reason that employees leave a firm. Every organization has good and bad managers. The key is to address on a timely basis management problems that result in high turnover rates.

Training and Development Opportunities

Training and development opportunities have become a crucial retention tool. Employees who are receiving training tend to be more loyal to the firm, more knowledgeable, and more skilled. This continued development of employees, then, increases the employee's value to the organization.

TIP

The popular business press conducts annual surveys to determine those companies considered "employers of choice" or "the best companies to work for." These surveys, which are published in the business journals, enable other companies to see what is being done in those organizations to improve employee satisfaction.

Advancement Opportunities

As additional training is received, employees also want opportunities for advancement. These opportunities for advancement top the list for "employer of choice." It is better to transfer a talented employee to

> Bad management is often cited as a top reason that employees leave a firm.

another department than to have her leave the firm to work for a competitor. Promotions from within also have a positive effect on other employees who realize that good performance is rewarded. Lateral moves also become important as opportunities for growth.

Consider Indirect Solutions

Individual differences must be recognized. Companies should avoid trying to fit every employee into their corporate mold. This strategy leaves no room for individuality. Instead, let employees put their personal touch on their cubicles and offices. Too many rules and too little flexibility snuff out creativity and negatively impact morale.

A Caring Environment

Creating a caring environment helps improve retention. When the company helps an employee who is going through tough times, that employee will remember and bond more with the firm. Helping employees balance work and family issues can create a high level of commitment.

Two-Way Communication

Open, sincere communication ensures that employees stay plugged in and helps them better identify with the firm. Open communication also helps employees perform better because they have more information to act on and better understand the context within which they are working.

Two-way communication provides an opportunity for management to hear what the employees are saying. The firm must value their input and even solicit it. This effort will pay off for the organization as it taps into what its employees think; after all, the employees are closest to the "real" work of the organization.

Consistent Policies and Practices

Consistency in human resource policies and practices will help retain employees by increasing their perception of fairness within the organization. Knowing they are treated fairly and equitably is important to workers.

> When the company helps an employee who is going through tough times, that employee will remember and bond more with the firm.

Listening to Employees: Signs of Trouble

Absenteeism Rates

Absenteeism rates may provide an indicator of trouble. Since voluntary absenteeism is temporary withdrawal from the organization, it may precede permanent withdrawal. Therefore, the firm should closely monitor absenteeism rates.

Of special concern should be changes from what is normal. A firm can determine what "normal" is by benchmarking its absenteeism rate against industry information and employee surveys. These surveys are conducted by professional associations (especially in the human resource field) and private consulting companies (such as Hay Associates) and the results are published in many trade journals. If a firm's absenteeism rate is significantly higher than the industry's, it should determine the cause.

TIP

Having an open-door policy is a good early warning system. This policy gives employees the opportunity to talk openly with management about their concerns. In turn, the organization often has time to respond before the employee actually decides to leave. But an open-door policy must be more than lip service. Management must be ready, willing, and able to listen to the concerns being voiced—and then do something about them.

The second signal of a problem is a change from the firm's historical absenteeism rate. A jump in the number may be a forecast of turnover. The figures should be examined to see if there is a concentration of this increased absenteeism. For example, if the increase occurs in one department, a close examination of that department should be conducted to determine the causes. The key is to correct the problem before it causes people to leave.

> Management must be ready, willing, and able to listen to the concerns being voiced—and then do something about them.

Changes in Performance

Performance appraisals also provide an opportunity to assess an employee's performance. Significant changes in an employee's performance may signal a problem. The manager must identify the underlying causes because the change in performance is hurting the overall productivity level of the organization and may lead to the loss of a formerly good employee.

The performance appraisal interview is also a great opportunity to solicit information about how the organization is doing. The manager has a chance to ask employees if they are happy, if they feel supported, if they have problems, if they are challenged, and if they would like to see their work environment/conditions changed.

Signs of Burnout

> If several employees are experiencing burnout, the company needs to review the benefits it is providing.

Early signs of burnout can be an indicator of possible trouble and may eventually lead the employee to leave. Burnout is especially common when employees are trying to unsuccessfully balance work and family issues. These employees need to get help before they decide to leave the firm. Help can be in the form of assigning coworkers to ease the workload temporarily or perhaps referring the employee to an assistance program for counseling.

If several employees are experiencing burnout, the company needs to review the benefits it is providing. The organization may not be offering effective benefits to help employees balance their work and nonwork issues or perhaps the job design needs to be re-evaluated. Companies have to fight the tendency to take advantage of people by consistently working them long hours. In the long run, this behavior is likely to prompt the employee to leave.

Other Means of Listening

Attitude surveys are a valuable tool to test the climate of the company, which has a direct impact on the level of employee commitment. These surveys solicit the employees' opinions on the jobs they perform, their direct supervisors, their peers, and organizational policies. Attitude surveys should always be anonymous to ensure that employees can be more honest in their feedback. The results of the survey will point out what is being done well and what areas need to be improved. These areas of improvement should be the critical focus. Management may even ask workers for suggestions to address these shortcomings.

Employee satisfaction surveys can be conducted in-house or by outside consultants. If surveys are not possible (due to cost constraints), focus groups can be used, in which small groups of employees are gathered to discuss specific organizational issues.

The Exit Interview: A Heads-Up

Each employee who leaves the organization should be given an exit interview. This interview is considered one of the best retention strategies that a company has at its disposal. It provides the human resource department an opportunity to tell the employee about his benefits and any information concerning his separation. Perhaps more important, this is an opportunity to obtain information from the employee concerning his perception of the organization—and his reasons for leaving the firm. Both face-to-face interviews and questionnaires may be used to solicit information such as the following:

> Each employee who leaves the organization should be given an exit interview.

- ❏ Advancement opportunities
- ❏ Changes that could decrease turnover
- ❏ Compensation (pay and benefits)
- ❏ Condition of morale
- ❏ Differences between the firm and the new organization
- ❏ Openness of communication
- ❏ Organizational policies and practices
- ❏ Perception of fairness in human resource policies
- ❏ Perception of fairness in supervision
- ❏ Perception of growth opportunities within the firm
- ❏ Perception of management/supervision
- ❏ Positive and negative aspects of the job
- ❏ Reason for leaving the firm
- ❏ Training opportunities
- ❏ Workload

A skilled human resource interviewer may be able to solicit extremely valuable information that can impact the turnover rate of other employees. Understanding the reasons for turnover is the first step in correcting the problems. Those who are leaving the organization have little to lose when being honest about their reasons for departing. This information, then, should be acted upon to improve the overall turnover rate.

TIP

Use an exit interview checklist to ensure that all the bases are covered. The checklist includes all the benefits discussion and final paycheck (with vacation or sick pay as appropriate). A checklist is provided in Appendix C (page 330).

To gather the information and then fail to act on it is useless. This often means that the interviewer must provide sensitive feedback to managerial personnel. However, this valuable information can be used to make changes necessary to improve the retention of other talented employees.

> Organizations must carefully nurture and support their work force in order to improve retention rates.

Summary

Hiring talented individuals for the organization is critical. But that is only the first part of the challenge. Once these employees are hired, they must be retained. Organizations must carefully nurture and support their work force in order to improve retention rates—and ultimately, improve organizational performance.

Streetwise Advice

- **More than half of your employees will leave the organization within five years. In some job fields, this rate is even higher as demand for these positions increases.**

- **Benchmark turnover rates.** Rather than accepting your turnover rate, compare it to those of your competitors. You might also benchmark against some of the company practices of organizations with lower rates.

- **Treat employees as the valuable assets they are.** Treating employees as though they are replaceable will only encourage the more talented employees to leave the organization often in search of appreciation and recognition.

- **Don't assume all turnover is bad.** Turnover can be beneficial; it is called *functional turnover.* If marginal or poorer performing employees leave the organization and are replaced with better performing workers, overall productivity may improve.

- **E-mail makes it easier to conduct attitude surveys and to administer them on a more regular basis.**

- **As loyalty to a company decreases, turnover rates will remain a concern.**

- **Today's employees are expected to change jobs on an average of every two and a half years.** This generation of workers does not spend a career with one company, but rather builds a resume and a skills portfolio while moving from company to company. The use of effective retention strategies, however, can improve these turnover rates.

- **Exit interviews should be used as an opportunity to probe for useful information to make improvements and as a public relations tool.** The exit interviewer should be positive and ensure that the employee leaves on a good note. Be sure to extend best wishes for his or her new job and express appreciation for contributions to your organization. Allowing the employee to leave on a positive note leaves the door open. Some employees may decide to return to the organization if things don't work out in the new company. If you use an off-the-shelf employee satisfaction survey, try to customize it to your organization's needs. It will be considerably more effective.

- **Build in fun.** Be sure to include fun in your organization. For example, one college schedules back-to-school barbeques for faculty each September and gives Butterball turkey gift certificates to all its employees at Thanksgiving.

> This generation of workers does not spend a career with one company, but rather builds a resume and a skills portfolio while moving from company to company.

- **Keep in mind that the benefits you offer that attract new employees to the firm may not be effective in retaining employees.**

- **Don't just offer training opportunities to top performers**. These opportunities can be beneficial to marginal performers as well. Training can improve their skills and productivity and improve their commitment to the organization and its goals.

- **Remember that little things count**. If you ask your employees to work additional hours, provide a lunch or dinner to show them you appreciate their hard work and extra contribution.

- **Hold informal meetings.** Don't wait until there is a crisis. Meet informally on a regular basis to solicit feedback about how the organization is doing, what they like, what they don't like, what is working, and what is not working. Ask them to recommend changes.

- **Don't solicit information on an employee satisfaction survey that you are not willing to take action on. This practice only leads to increased employee dissatisfaction.**

- **Retention bonuses are being used just as signing bonuses have been used.** Some organizations even provide team retention bonuses. If the entire team is still with the company after a specified period, the bonus is paid to every team member.

- **Companies make a concerted effort to survey their customers to learn what they want and then they provide it**. The same holds true for employees. To retain employees (just like customers), survey them regularly to determine what they want to remain with the firm—and then provide it!

> Some organizations even provide team retention bonuses.

For more information on this topic, visit our Web site at www.businesstown.com

PART V

Human Resource Trends

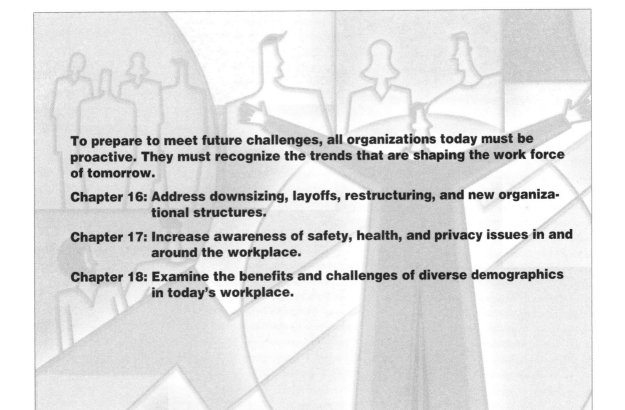

To prepare to meet future challenges, all organizations today must be proactive. They must recognize the trends that are shaping the work force of tomorrow.

Chapter 16: Address downsizing, layoffs, restructuring, and new organizational structures.

Chapter 17: Increase awareness of safety, health, and privacy issues in and around the workplace.

Chapter 18: Examine the benefits and challenges of diverse demographics in today's workplace.

Downsizing, Layoffs, Restructuring, and New Organizational Structures

Chapter 16

As organizational operations become less effective and as organizations position themselves for improved competitive advantage, they need to explore new organizational structures to respond to the challenges of the business world. Many external changes have had a substantial impact on organizational structures. As a result, organizations have begun to pay attention to the message that they must be responsive, agile, and flexible in order to meet the challenges of a dynamic world.

To be responsive—that is, to be able to respond quickly to changes in the external environment—an organization must rethink the way it is structured and the way in which jobs are performed. This restructuring will cause a ripple effect throughout the organization that impacts the personnel who will be performing those jobs and the skills they need to possess.

> Downsizing has been the organizational response to changes in the economy (especially slower growth rates), the increase in international competition, and changes in work force composition.

The Impact of Downsizing

Over the past two decades, downsizing has become one of the most popular strategies. As firms have downsized successfully and have experienced positive reactions from their shareholders and Wall Street, other companies have adopted the strategy. Some estimates suggest that more than 100,000 employees are laid off nationwide each month.

The popularity of this strategy, however, has caused a major problem. Some organizations have downsized unnecessarily. Since to be effective, corporate strategies must be aligned with the unique strengths and weaknesses of the individual organization, copycat methods rarely work.

Downsizing has been the organizational response to changes in the economy (especially slower growth rates), the increase in international competition, and changes in work force composition. And not just blue-collar workers are affected. Entire management layers have been eliminated. These flatter organizations are supposedly more responsive to changes in consumer preferences/tastes.

Downsizing is the organizational effort to create a lean company that can become more efficient and achieve increased levels of productivity. This strategy reduces labor costs by reducing the number of positions within the organization. Theoretically, then, the company should be able to reallocate resources to improve organizational performance.

TIP

The business press has reported that current downsizing wears pinstripes. That is, today's downsizing is impacting more managers than ever before.

Usually adopted to cut costs, downsizing is no longer used just during periods of economic downturn. The term *rightsizing* has been adopted by organizations that believe they are on the "right track." However, years ago the *Wall Street Journal* coined the term *dumbsizing* to reflect the fact that this strategy really does not reduce costs. In most organizations, reducing payroll expenses has not produced improved profit positions.

An organization usually implements a downsizing strategy to achieve better results in the following areas:

- Cash flow
- Competitive position (including increased market share)
- Customer satisfaction
- Streamlined decision-making
- Employee motivation
- Productivity
- Profits

> Downsizing is no longer used just during periods of economic downturn.

Unfortunately, in the overwhelming majority of cases, downsizing does not achieve these results. Not even half of the organizations that downsize have been able to reduce costs.

The number of management layers does decrease, ultimately flattening the organizational pyramid and leaving fewer people to perform the same amount of work. During this process, the employees' psychological contract with the employer no longer implies long-term employment. Downsizing eliminates feelings of job security.

TIP
The flattening of the organizational pyramid has created other structural challenges as well. The most notable is a broader span of control. With fewer management layers in most organizations, managers are being asked to supervise larger numbers of employees.

Downsizing creates a number of problems that must be addressed, such as:

- Decreased productivity
- Increased job insecurity
- Lack of trust
- Low morale
- Reduced employee satisfaction
- Survivor issues

> Layoffs generally demoralize the work force.

Layoffs generally demoralize the work force. The remaining employees tend to experience higher levels of job dissatisfaction and lose trust in management. As round after round of layoffs occur, employees begin to experience increasing feelings of job insecurity. This insecurity usually results in decreased productivity as workers worry about the future of their jobs and whether they will be the next ones to go. The downward spiral in productivity will increase as better performers seek employment elsewhere, before they, too, lose their jobs. Downsized firms should expect an increased number of resignations within the first year.

Handling Layoffs Tactfully and Addressing the Survivors

Layoffs are unpaid leaves of absence. In some cases, employees may be called back at a future date. Layoffs can be an effective strategy, but they must be handled appropriately. Knowing how and when to implement the strategy is half the battle.

To be effective, organizations must plan the downsizing effort. This plan must emphasize improvements in productivity instead of across-the-board cuts and must actually involve employees. The plan and the reasons for it should be clearly communicated. And finally, the people involved must be supported—both those who are laid off and those who remain with the organization.

The need for planning cannot be overemphasized. The downsizing strategy must be well organized and well thought out. Management should carefully assess the firm's human resources and consider alternatives to the strategy. It is essential to set clear objectives and dates for implementation.

Rather than planning cuts across-the-board, specific areas should be targeted for productivity improvements. If units are already lean, cuts may actually decrease productivity. The key is to evaluate each area of the firm and focus on ways to improve productivity. It may be that redesigning the work process will enhance production.

Making the Decision

Part of the planning effort should include whom to lay off and how to make that decision. Generally, the two most common methods are seniority and employee ability.

When seniority is used as the deciding factor, the length of service with the company determines who stays and who doesn't. The most recently hired employees are the first to be laid off. This method, commonly seen in union environments, appears to be more objective and holds no surprises for the work force. There is little opportunity for bias. The disadvantage is that seniority ignores the talent and skills of employees who may be valuable to the firm.

When employee ability is used to determine layoffs, decisions are based on the employee's skill level and performance on the job. Better performers will remain with the firm. Companies may use proficiency tests to make this determination. With this method, the firm is better able to maintain productivity with their good performers. However, it is hard to standardize abilities, so the method may appear to be subjective.

Involving the employees who are being impacted in the decision process can make the changes easier to implement. Communicating openly and honestly with employees can also increase the probability

> When seniority is used as the deciding factor, the length of service with the company determines who stays and who doesn't.

of successfully implementing the strategy. Workers should be told the reasons for the downsizing. This kind of communication will help build trust in management and reduce some feelings of job insecurity.

Handling the Layoffs

Two issues in downsizing are often overlooked. As organizations cut costs across-the-board, they don't always handle the layoffs with tact or provide support to those individuals who remain with the firm.

Support and care must be used in dealing with those who are being laid off and those who remain with the company. It is important to communicate as far in advance as possible with those employees who are being laid off. The treatment of these workers has significant ramifications on the employees themselves, their families, the community, and the employees who remain with the company.

> Support and care must be used in dealing with those who are being laid off and those who remain with the company.

TIP

Severance pay is not a required benefit. Although many employees feel they are entitled to a severance package, by law they are not. Organizations provide severance at their own discretion.

Severance pay should be as generous as the firm can afford. This pay helps employees financially as they seek new jobs and sends a clear message that the company cares about them. Whenever possible, the firm should also consider some outplacement assistance to help employees obtain new employment.

Outplacement is a valuable support tool. Through these services, employees who are laid off can receive help in their job search, career counseling, assistance in preparing resumes, administrative support (such as the use of telephones or computers), training in interviewing skills, and referral services. Although usually performed by an outside firm specializing in these services, outplacement may also be provided by an in-house department (generally an extension of the human resource department). Providing outplacement services also sends a good message to the remaining employees that they work for a caring organization.

All employees must be treated with dignity and respect. It doesn't cost the organization anything to be kind, respectful, and supportive of these workers, and it can have a powerful public relations effect. This good press will extend to the local community as news travels about how well employees are being treated. The organization is seen as having a heart.

When laid-off employees are treated poorly, those who remain with the firm begin to re-evaluate their "luck" in retaining their jobs. For example, a petroleum firm in Texas handled layoffs so poorly that one remaining employee was quoted as saying that he felt that he "worked for a bunch of sadistic idiots."

Moving On

Survivors' guilt manifests itself on the job in many ways. As the remaining employees see their friends laid off, they experience mixed emotions. They don't feel so lucky to have a job when they find themselves working harder to make up for their peers.

Survivors suffer significant problems that are often overlooked. Although survivors are often called "lucky," they don't always feel lucky. They usually experience decreased motivation, increased worry over their jobs, and increased turnover rates.

The organization must make a concerted effort to build trust with the remaining staff. The first step is open, honest communication. Survivors must be told when the layoffs are over. The system of determining who is laid off must also be communicated and it must appear to be fair. Management should be open about the survivor's anxiety and stress. The firm may also offer counseling.

As the survivors take on the additional responsibilities of their coworkers, they often need training in performing these tasks effectively. Providing these training opportunities demonstrates that the company is investing in them.

Since the future of the organization's performance depends on these survivors, career planning should be considered. Planning will help rebuild trust and reduce some of the anxiety concerning job security.

> As the remaining employees see their friends laid off, they experience mixed emotions.

Everybody's Restructuring

Recognizing that the old structures and ways of doing things are no longer appropriate and do not really work in today's world, most organizations are trying new structures and processes. Organizations are restructuring to do more work with fewer employees. Putting a restructuring strategy into effect, however, requires that the organization rethink how the work will be accomplished.

Since 1980, over three-quarters of the Fortune 1000 companies have restructured. And this restructuring effort has resulted in more than 3 million employees losing their jobs.

Instead of running the risk of downsizing, some organizations have opted to use *temporary workers*. This option avoids the cycle of layoffs, hires, and more layoffs. The use of temporary workers is a hedge against the highs and lows of the business cycle. This strategy has been especially popular in the banking industry.

> The use of temporary workers is a hedge against the highs and lows of the business cycle.

TIP

Restructuring simply for the sake of restructuring is a waste of time and money. Organizations must carefully craft a restructuring plan that capitalizes on their unique set of strengths and weaknesses, regardless of what their competitors are doing. Simply imitating another organization's strategy is seldom successful.

Increasing the number of part-time workers also increases a firm's flexibility. The hours worked by part-time employees can be increased or decreased to meet the needs of the firm—and layoffs are avoided.

Some organizations are using *early retirement buyouts* to encourage older workers to leave the company before their normally scheduled retirement.

Instead of layoffs, some firms may *reduce work weeks*. The firm can still reduce labor costs without laying off people. These cuts are achieved by having workers shorten their work week, perhaps from forty to thirty-five hours.

Reduced shifts are yet another alternative. This method reduces the hours of the company's operation. The firm may reduce the number of employees per shift or even reduce the number of hours per shift (perhaps from 8-hour shifts to 6.5-hour shifts).

New Organizational Structures

Any restructuring effort will impact human resources in a variety of ways. All of these changes have human consequences that must be dealt with. Most restructuring results in a loss of jobs, and the organization has to decide how the job losses will be handled.

An organization must make several decisions about their human resource policies when restructuring. These alternatives include the following:

- No-layoff policy
- Method of termination
- Temporary layoffs versus permanent layoffs
- Wage cuts

No-Layoff Policy

Some organizations have adopted a no-layoff strategy. Although this strategy is employee-friendly, it is not always possible. Economic conditions may force a company to revise a no-layoff policy. Then, more harm will be done if the company has to reverse its decision. A no-layoff policy lets employees know they are valued. Often if their skills are unique, a no-layoff policy is a good long-term approach. If employees with rare skills are laid off during economic downturns, they may not return to the organization when the business cycle improves, which will leave the company in a weakened condition to compete.

This strategy does not mean that the size of the work force remains the same. The work force is reduced through attrition, reassignment, or leasing to other firms.

When a company reduces the work force through attrition, it decreases the total number of employees without actually laying off employees, usually by implementing hiring freezes and not replacing departing employees. A hiring freeze temporarily halts the recruitment for any newly created positions or openings. One of the biggest

> If employees with rare skills are laid off during economic downturns, they may not return to the organization when the business cycle improves, which will leave the company in a weakened condition to compete.

disadvantages of attrition is the increased workload for the remaining employees.

Reduction of the work force can also be achieved simply by not replacing any employees who leave, either voluntarily or involuntarily. Since hiring involves costs other than salaries, the company can save substantial expenses by not filling positions.

Reassigning workers can also help an organization redeploy, rather than lay off, their human resources. As one unit needs additional workers and another needs fewer, employees can be retrained and reassigned. Too often, balances are not achieved in organizations. There are layoffs in one area while hiring is fast and furious in another.

The reassignment of workers must be handled with care, however. The tendency is for better performing workers to take advantage of the opportunity to be reassigned and retrained. Poorer performing workers are not as confident and may not seek out these opportunities. This tendency may leave the unit in a weakened position with poorer performing individuals remaining if reassignments are not carefully monitored.

> Reassigning workers can also help an organization redeploy, rather than lay off, their human resources.

Temporary Solutions

Workers may be temporarily loaned to other firms instead of being laid off. Although not a widespread strategy, loaning out workers has provided an alternative to layoffs. In some cases, workers may be loaned to a charitable organization or another firm. The aerospace industry has a history of loaning employees to competitors. Not all organizations are comfortable with this. Some firms prefer to loan employees only to noncompeting companies.

Worker loan-outs generate goodwill while keeping employees' skills up-to-date until they can return to the company. They often learn from the other job and then bring this knowledge and new skills back to the company when they return.

Changing organizational structures have also impacted the career paths of employees. The linear career path (traditionally referred to as the upward mobility "fast track") is extremely rare today. With fewer management layers and employees working until older ages, the spiral career path with lateral moves and a zigzag pattern up the organization is more common today.

As baby boomers occupy positions for longer periods, the organization has to consider alternative means of career growth for younger workers. Transitory careers are more the norm as younger workers seek opportunities for professional growth, often across several organizations.

Does the Box Have to Be Square?

When economic hardships occur, sometimes a longer-term solution is needed. To better meet the challenges of the changing marketplace, tinkering with old structures doesn't always work. Sometimes the entire company needs to be restructured.

Some of the new organizational structures that have become more common include the electronic corporation, the shamrock organization, the upside-down pyramid, and strategic alliances.

E-Corps

More firms are now considered e-corps; that is, electronic corporations that are conducting business over the Internet.

Shamrock Organizations

The shamrock organization depicts the firm as a three-leaf clover with each leaf representing a different type of worker. One leaf represents the traditional permanent employees holding full-time positions. The second leaf is the contract employee group. These employees assist the permanent employees with daily functions. And the third leaf is comprised of those employees who are workers who help out temporarily when needed. Not surprisingly, more growth will be experienced in the last two leaves of the shamrock.

Upside-Down Pyramids

Some organizations have literally turned their pyramid structures upside down to reflect the importance of their customers. Rather than depicting top management at the apex of the pyramid, the new view places top management at the bottom and customers at the top.

> Some of the new organizational structures that have become more common include the electronic corporation, the shamrock organization, the upside-down pyramid, and strategic alliances.

The responsibility of each organizational level is even viewed differently. Top management's responsibility is to develop and communicate the mission and strategic direction of the firm to the middle managers. These middle managers then provide support to the operations people who are servicing the customers.

Strategic Alliances

Strategic alliances have grown in popularity as organizations have heeded the advice to "stick to the knitting." That is, more firms are identifying their core competence and then focusing on it. All other nonessential functions–those that do not directly contribute to the core competence–are outsourced. The organization then develops strategic alliances with other firms to deliver these nonessential services.

These relationships are fluid. As the needs of the organization change over time, the strategic partners will also change.

The Impact of Teams on Organizations

In restructuring, the most popular trend has been the move to teamwork. All organizations have begun to use teams. The value of teamwork has been well documented. There are, however, human resource consequences that must be addressed when a team approach is implemented.

Teams are groups of employees who come together to meet a common goal. Everyone on the team is accountable for the achievement of this goal. Effective teams are diverse and the skills of the members complement one another. The team approach has been adopted to improve customer service, improve the quality of products, increase employee participation (especially in decision-making), and positively impact employee satisfaction levels.

Yet to effectively implement a team approach, the firm must change. Employees must receive training in team skills, such as group decision-making, communication, group dynamics, intergroup dynamics, and conflict resolution. On cross-functional teams, members learn to work with members from different functional areas. As a result, accountants work with marketers, engineers, and so on–not just with other accountants.

Team members must also become multiskilled. That is, they must learn how to perform more than one job on the team. More funds,

> Teams are groups of employees who come together to meet a common goal.

therefore, must be available for training. Regular performance appraisals must be conducted to ensure that team performance–rather than individual performance– is the focus. Finally, rewards and compensation must emphasize team results.

Virtual teams are increasing in popularity. These team members meet electronically, even though they may very likely be geographically dispersed. Here, team members must be trained in using the appropriate technology. They must also realize that without face-to-face interactions, the communication process becomes more difficult.

The Role of Human Resources in High-Performance Organizations

More companies are recognizing the importance of striving to become high-performance organizations (referred to as HPOs). An HPO is designed to enable people to contribute to their full potential and to achieve high-performance levels for the organization. People are considered the organization's most important resource–the very means by which the high-performance levels will be achieved. Human resources are at the center of the organization; they impact everything else.

The HPO's human resource policies are designed to enhance the productivity and knowledge of the work force. The emphasis is on managers as coaches and on teamwork instead of individual effort. Training is critical to ensure that knowledge, skills, and abilities are continually enhanced. The HPO has a few core components–and key to the list is the focus on people. The core components of an HPO are as follows:

> Human resources are at the center of the organization; they impact everything else.

- Commitment to employee involvement
- Commitment to the team approach
- Commitment to continuous improvement
- Commitment to organizational learning
- Integration of technology

Employee involvement is integral to the HPO. A commitment to participative management and empowerment provides opportunities for employees to contribute to the organization to the fullest extent possible.

High-performance organizations utilize the *team approach* to work. Most of these are self-directed work teams, emphasizing employee involvement at this team level.

True HPOs never rest on their laurels. Integrated across all they do is an organization-wide commitment to continuously improve. The ongoing development of the firm, all the processes within the firm, and the people supporting that organization is critical. This *continuous improvement* ensures that the firm is fast and can respond quickly to the changes occurring in the marketplace.

A commitment to *organizational learning* goes hand-in-hand with the focus on continuous improvement. The HPO must ensure that new information is constantly gathered and used to make changes to improve performance. The firm must constantly monitor the external environment for new information that impacts its business.

Technology has become critical to all businesses today. In the HPO, technology is integrated throughout the firm. The high-performance organization requires changes—in structure, processes, and people. Perhaps one of the most significant changes is in middle management. By empowering more employees and using more self-directed work teams, the HPO either must eliminate or must radically redesign many middle management positions. Part of the responsibility of the human resource department is to help middle managers in this transition.

> By empowering more employees and using more self-directed work teams, the HPO either must eliminate or must radically redesign many middle management positions.

Summary

The bell has been sounded and organizations have been warned. Only the fast and responsive will survive. Organizations must rethink the timeworn structures of the past century. New organizational structures must be adopted that enable faster responses to environmental changes. These transformations mean greater responsibilities for the human resource departments in helping organizations re-create themselves, their work, and their people.

Streetwise Advice

- **Change downsizing terminology in some circles.** The term *rightsizing* is said to better reflect what organizations are attempting to achieve–the right size work force.

- **Change the organizational mindset.** A lack of upward mobility is not a sign of failure. Rather, alternatives such as lateral moves are signals of success today. But this new mindset must be clearly communicated and reinforced throughout the organization.

- **Use the contingent work force to increase your organization's flexibility.** Contingent workers are both temporary and part-time workers whose schedules can be adjusted up and down to better meet the changing demands of the marketplace.

- **Familiarize yourself with the WARN Act.** The Worker Adjustment and Retraining Notification (WARN) Act mandates that companies provide sixty days' notice of a plant closing or layoff of fifty or more employees.

- **Make sure outplacement programs are in place before layoffs begin. Employees should be able to avail themselves of the services immediately.**

- **Carefully analyze the downsizing option before implementing it. Downsizing has had more negative impacts on the financial performance of organizations overall.** Hamel and Prahald, business writers and coauthors of *Competing for the Future* (Harvard Business School Press), refer to downsizing as "corporate anorexia." Although the organization is leaner, it has not necessarily improved its financial health.

- **Be sure to manage the rumor mill during layoffs.** Honest communication should provide employees the opportunity to ask about the rumors they hear.

- **Fight the urge to centralize during downsizing.** Increasing the participation and involvement of employees will be much more beneficial.

> Be sure to manage the rumor mill during layoffs. Honest communication should provide employees the opportunity to ask about the rumors they hear.

- **Help your organization guard against being caught in a deficit cycle.** A deficit cycle is a downward spiral of deteriorating performance. As the organization fails to learn, the same mistakes are repeated. Each time the problem arises, there are fewer resources to deal with it—and less probability of success in responding to it—until the firm perishes.

A deficit cycle is a downward spiral of deteriorating performance

For more information on this topic, visit our Web site at www.businesstown.com

Chapter 17

Safety, Health, and Privacy Issues

E very organization is responsible for creating a safe, healthy workplace for its employees. Society is placing greater pressure on businesses to address new challenges that impact workers' health and organizational productivity, including stressors from work, home, and the external environment. New health threats and new equipment are continually evaluated for their impact on workers' safety and health.

> Establish an environment that is safe and free from known hazards and harms to employees.

Safety and the Legal Environment: OSHA

The Occupational Safety and Health Act of 1970 requires companies to establish a safe and healthy workplace. This act consists of three main stipulations that employers must address:

1. Establish an environment that is safe and free from known hazards and harms to employees
2. Obey the regulations and standards established by the Occupational Safety and Health Administration
3. Maintain safety records of injuries and illnesses on the job

The Occupational Safety and Health Act created three agencies: the Occupational Safety and Health Review Commission (OSHRC), the National Institute for Occupational Safety and Health (NIOSH), and the Occupational Safety and Health Administration (OSHA). The OSHRC is the judicial agency established to hear appeals for citations. The NIOSH was created to conducted safety research, which is critical input for establishing workplace regulations. For example, NIOSH researches what safe levels of various chemicals or noise levels in the environment should be.

The most visible of the three agencies is the Occupational Safety and Health Administration. This agency creates and enforces the regulations for safety in the work force. OSHA is responsible for establishing interim, permanent, and temporary standards as appropriate. OSHA often requires inspections to ensure enforcement of the regulations. These inspections are more likely to occur in a company that has had a serious illness, injury, or death.

Trained representatives of the Department of Labor conduct these inspections, which may be triggered by employee complaints, the specific hazards involved (such as an emphasis on those employers handling a certain substance), a serious injury, death on the job, or a random selection. Most inspections are unannounced. On arrival, the inspector explains what will occur, reviews the organization's safety records, conducts an inspection of the facility, talks to employees concerning safety issues, and then reviews the findings of the inspection.

Should a violation of OSHA standards be found, the inspector issues a citation that must be posted in the location where the violation was found. The company is given fifteen days to contest a citation.

TIP

Some organizations use their safety record as a marketing tool. Many manufacturing facilities with impressive safety records post signs at their entrance to notify the public of the number of accident-free workdays that have passed. This kind of a safety record is also a selling point for customers, suppliers, and potential job applicants.

> Some organizations use their safety record as a marketing tool.

Employers are in violation of OSHA standards if they meet the following conditions:

1. They fail to create a workplace free of hazards.
2. The company knows about the existence of a hazard.
3. This hazard resulted in death, illness, or injury.
4. The death, illness, or injury was preventable.

Employers may take a number of steps to develop an effective safety program. These steps can include the following:

- **Ensure the involvement and support of top management.** Top executives must also be safety role models. Other organizational members will take their cue from top management.

Have first-aid equipment available in every area of the organization and make sure employees know how to use it in case of an emergency.

- **Make one department accountable for the safety program.** In most cases, the human resource department will take responsibility for this program.
- **Solicit employee suggestions and use them.** Employee participation will improve commitment to the implementation of the safety measures. Conversely, ignoring employee suggestions will negatively affect motivation.
- **Investigate every accident and determine the cause.** Corrective action is essential to prevent recurrences. Pay particular attention to patterns or trends in accidents.
- **Make safety training a priority.** Emphasize each employee's responsibility for safety.
- **Have first-aid equipment available in every area of the organization and make sure employees know how to use it in case of an emergency.**
- **Provide incentives for safety compliance.** Giving rewards for implementing safety measures institutionalizes and reinforces new behaviors.

TIP
To reinforce a commitment to safety, include a safety policy in the employee handbook.

Safety and Health Concerns

Some of the safety and health workplace concerns include the handling of hazardous substances, occupational diseases, smoking in the workplace, cumulative trauma disorder, and sick building syndrome.

OSHA's Hazard Communications Standard specifically addresses *hazardous materials*. This arm of OSHA requires that an employer train employees in the handling of any dangerous materials. Employers must also complete Materials Safety Data Sheets (MSDSs), which inform workers about each dangerous chemical.

All employees must take the following steps to comply with OSHA's requirements in regards to hazardous substances.

- Prepare a list of all the hazardous chemicals present in the workplace
- Complete an MSDS for each chemical and distribute the sheets to employees
- Develop a system to effectively communicate information about these hazardous substances
- Provide hazardous substance training for all appropriate employees

Occupational diseases are long-term health issues created by exposure to hazardous materials on the job. These materials can be absorbed, inhaled, or ingested. For example, coal miners can contract black lung disease from coal dust and shipyard workers can contract lung cancer from asbestos.

Smoking in the workplace became a safety issue when second-hand tobacco smoke was identified as a life-threatening carcinogen by the Environmental Protection Agency. As a result, smoking has been restricted or prohibited in the vast majority of organizations.

TIP

Some companies do not permit any smoking on their grounds. One particular company has a facility located on several acres. Since it does not permit any smoking on the premises, employees actually get in their cars and drive to the front gate to have a cigarette.

Smoking in the workplace became a safety issue when secondhand tobacco smoke was identified as a life-threatening carcinogen by the Environmental Protection Agency.

Cumulative trauma disorders (CTDs) have been the most common occupational disease. Also referred to as repetitive strain injury (RSI), these injuries are the result of repetitive movements on the job. Although automation has helped improve productivity in many industries, it has meant an increase in repetitive motions—and therefore an increase in the incidence of CTDs. Workers in the meat-packing industry have some of the highest rates of CTDs. Large numbers of employees working with computers have experienced a CTD known as carpal tunnel syndrome, in which the wrist bone and nerves are impacted by the repetitive typing motion.

Many organizations are conducting ergonomic studies of employee workstations to better fit equipment to workers in an effort to reduce the number of repetitive strain injuries. This is the reverse of the historical approach to equipment in which people were fit to equipment on the job. A few of the many measurements taken for the average employee's workstation include the following:

- Amount of knee clearance to the desk
- Angle of the seat back
- Height of the backrest
- Height of the computer screen from the floor
- Height of the keyboard from the floor
- Lower back support provided by the chair
- Positioning of the document holder
- Viewing angle from the eyes to the computer monitor
- Viewing distance from the eyes to the computer monitor

A lack of fresh air and ventilation in newly designed buildings has created more incidents of *sick building syndrome.* As chemicals are emitted from office equipment (such as copy machines) and the fumes from cleaning chemicals build up, the lack of ventilation creates hazards for those working in some of these buildings.

Sick building syndrome has cost organizations billions of dollars, resulting in a loss of productivity, increased medical expenses, lawsuits, and increased numbers of sick days. New building designs and improved air ventilation systems are among the solutions being examined.

Workplace Violence

Violence in the workplace has increased substantially in recent years. The media have even coined the term *going postal* to describe workplace violence at its extreme. Homicide is now the number-two reason for deaths in the workplace.

Workplace violence includes a number of situations. Sabotage and revenge are at the core of much of this violence. Although most people immediately think of homicide and physical attacks, violence encompasses much more negative behavior, including threats, verbal abuse, and harassment as well. The term *office rage* is used to refer

> Sick building syndrome has cost organizations billions of dollars, resulting in a loss of productivity, increased medical expenses, lawsuits, and increased numbers of sick days.

to a range of violent behaviors by the desk set. These behaviors include (but are certainly not limited to) verbal abuse, damage to office equipment, or striking employees.

Work conditions that have been found to contribute to workplace violence include the following:

- Cubicle office design
- Cultures that tolerate violence
- Deadlines
- Dictatorial management styles
- Dysfunctional communication styles
- Hazardous work environments
- High stress levels
- Long hours
- Monotonous work with no challenge
- Office politics
- Unpredictable change
- Unsupportive environments

Some of the warning signs include the following:

- Alcohol abuse
- Drug abuse
- High levels of stress (personal or work)
- Increased conflict (or harassment) with coworkers or managers
- Preoccupation with weapons
- Regular disregard and violation of company policies
- Threats of violence

Employers are responsible for watching for these warning signs and for reducing incidents of workplace violence. The human resource department can take the lead in helping line managers create a safe, healthy environment and develop policies to reduce violence in the workplace. Consider the following:

- Closely observe the behavior of employees; monitor nonwork stressors that may lead to workplace violence

> The human resource department can take the lead in helping line managers create a safe, healthy environment and develop policies to reduce violence in the workplace.

- Honestly communicate guidelines for appropriate and inappropriate behavior
- Refer troubled employees to employee assistance programs
- Investigate claims of inappropriate actions and threats
- Clearly communicate a zero tolerance policy for violence or aggressive behavior
- Develop procedures to be followed in violent situations
- Ensure that managers model appropriate behavior

Stress Strikes Everyone

Stress is the body's reaction to the presence of stressors; it plays a major role in workplace violence. Employers are responsible for monitoring the stress levels of their employees. (See Appendix A, page 307, for a sample workplace violence policy.) It has been estimated that stress costs American businesses more than $300 billion a year.

Know the Stressors

Stress is the physical and emotional reaction to life's wear and tear. Work stressors may include deadlines; poor working conditions; unrealistic expectations; too much work; job insecurity; lack of control over work; poor interaction with peers, subordinates, or bosses; and specific demands of the job. Nonwork stressors may include money problems, marital conflict, single-parent responsibilities, and conflicts with dual-career couples. As employees try to balance their many roles (such as mother, employee, wife, car pool driver, cook, home room mother, coach, etc.), stress arises when all of the role expectations cannot be met simultaneously.

Stress can be positive or negative, depending on the situation and the individual. Positive stress is referred to as *eustress*. This functional stress can actually result in higher levels of enthusiasm and, ultimately, better performance.

Negative stress, however, is the organization's primary concern. This stress, known as *distress*, often is dysfunctional and has negative consequences for both the individual and the organization.

> Stress is the body's reaction to the presence of stressors; it plays a major role in workplace violence.

Signs of stress in the individual may include the following:

- Changes in sleeping patterns (including nightmares)
- Difficulty concentrating
- Emotional or angry outbursts
- Excessive eating, drinking, or smoking
- Extreme, continued fatigue
- Feelings of despair
- General loss of interest in most things
- High anxiety levels
- Increased blood pressure
- Increased boredom
- Loss of general perspective
- Shorter attention span
- Withdrawal from relationships
- Working long hours without accomplishing much

The organization suffers when productivity declines or the person withdraws. Stress can also lead to poor customer service levels and employee violence.

Preventive Management

The focus should be on managing stress. All stress will never be totally eliminated. Stress is a part of life. The key is to focus on managing it. Otherwise, frustration will compound the already high stress levels.

The American culture is preoccupied with time. Time stressors can be addressed with effective time management programs. These programs might include the following tips:

- **Use a to-do list.** It will make you plan, get organized, and set deadlines.
- **Keep things organized.** Avoid wasting time looking for your things. Have a place for everything and keep it in its place.
- **Do urgent things first.** Don't put off the high-priority items. They only get worse.

> The focus should be on managing stress. All stress will never be totally eliminated.

Organizational time management seminars can help employees reduce stress by giving them coping strategies.

- **Do small tasks simultaneously.** For example, try opening the mail, talking on the phone, and booting up your computer to check your e-mail.
- **Use the 80/20 rule.** Twenty percent of what you do accounts for 80 percent of your success. Be sure to pick the right 20 percent!
- **Set aside quiet time each day.** You need time to think, regroup, and refresh yourself.

TIP

Organizational time management seminars can help employees reduce stress by giving them coping strategies.

Health Care Programs

The meaning of a safe and healthy workplace is still evolving. Organizations can take advantage of various opportunities to create this kind of an environment. To more effectively handle stress and general health, organizations should consider providing stress management programs, wellness programs, and employee assistance programs. Stress management programs can run the range from time management to support groups. Wellness programs are designed to promote good health, reduce health care costs (which are now topping $1 trillion a year), and increase awareness of health risks in the workplace. These programs are very cost-effective for the organization. Wellness programs and employee fitness programs have grown in popularity. To be effective, a wellness program must appeal to everyone and must explicitly communicate what the employee gains by participating. In addition, the organization's goals must support the program. For example, the company's on-site cafeteria should support its nutritional wellness program by offering fruit, salad, and other healthy food choices (instead of burgers and fries).

Some wellness programs cover a wide range of health issues, including the following:

- CPR training
- Exercise programs (such as aerobics)

- First-aid training
- Nutrition training
- Risk factor screening (such as high blood pressure or high cholesterol)
- Weight control programs

Privacy Issues: A Special Challenge

U.S. law mandates the right to equal opportunity employment, the right to collectively bargain, and the right to a safe and healthy working environment. The Constitution guarantees each individual the right to privacy. Workers have other rights as well, although the extent of some of these rights is still being hotly debated.

When an employment contract exists between worker and employer, the terms of employment are explicitly itemized. Not every employee has an employment contract, however. Often an implied contract exists with the employee handbook.

There has been a rise in workplace litigation as more employees question alleged violations of their rights—some written, some implied, and some unwritten.

A few of the privacy issues under debate include the extent of e-mail monitoring, voice mail monitoring, and video surveillance. Most employers are exercising their right to monitor both e-mail and voice mail communication. Employers may also search the work areas of employees they believe are violating company policies and procedures. Employees are also monitored as part of regular evaluations of their performance. For example, telemarketing customer service representatives are regularly monitored to track their job performance.

The privacy issue involved centers on the extent of the monitoring and the locations being monitored. For example, video surveillance to monitor for employee theft or ensure employee safety (such as in parking garages) does not seem to be a subject of great concern. Placement of surveillance cameras in private areas, however, has been the subject of substantial debate. Restroom monitoring has also been questioned as employee rights to privacy are pitted against the employer's rights.

> When an employment contract exists between worker and employer, the terms of employment are explicitly itemized.

Employees also have the right to due process. That is, whenever actions are taken against an employee, he or she has the right to explain what happened.

Summary

Safety, health, and privacy issues will continue to evolve. And as they do, organizations will be under increasing pressure to respond to these changes. Although legislation mandates specific issues for organizations to address, these responses appear to be more straightforward. The concern lies more with the appropriate approach to handling issues that are currently considered ethical responsibilities.

> The overwhelming percentage of accidents on the job (over 88 percent) occur when people perform acts that are unsafe—and usually contrary to company policies.

Streetwise Advice

- **Safety committees in organizations have been effective in improving safety records.** A safety committee conducts safety inspections and solicits feedback from employees on possible hazards in the workplace. They then make recommendations for improvement.

- **The overwhelming percentage of accidents on the job (over 88 percent) occur when people perform acts that are unsafe— and usually contrary to company policies.**

- **Do not take OSHA standards lightly.** Punishment for willful violations includes criminal fines and prison sentences. Company managers who have intentionally disregarded OSHA standards have served prison sentences.

- **Power naps are being used on a wider scale today.** Some organizations have even established nap rooms to facilitate these breaks to refresh employees and reduce stress.

- **The Social Readjustment Rating Scale developed by Holmes and Rahe (doctors at the Washington School of Medicine) identifies the number of changes people experience. Weights** are then assigned to these life changes and a stress index is calculated.

- **More firms today are conducting security audits.** These audits analyze an organization's security. The audit might include a review of access to the company's facilities and the appropriate screening of applicants (to identify those with violent tendencies). To conduct these audits, human resource staff members and managers should partner with outside security experts including security consultants and police.

- **Tell employees that they are being monitored.** In fact, take this one step further and have employees sign consent forms that they know they are being monitored on the job. These forms should be retained in the employee personnel file.

- **Establish a peer review panel to provide due process.** A peer review panel is a committee comprised of company employees. Employees seeking due process may appeal disciplinary actions to the panel. This panel is often viewed as a fairer process than having one executive hear the case.

- **Provide incentives as part of wellness programs.** More companies are providing cash bonuses to employees who successfully take part in wellness programs. Some firms have paid employees to stop smoking or to lose weight. The company benefits from the wellness programs with healthier employees who are more productive, take fewer sick days, use fewer medical benefits, and are more energetic on the job.

- **Provide hazardous substance training to all appropriate employees.** This training should include information outlining the dangers of the substance, how to safely handle the substance, a review of the MSDS, an explanation of any warning labels for the substance, and the procedures to be followed in the case of an emergency.

- **Family stressors are not unique to mothers.** Research has determined that fathers are also experiencing high levels of stress today. Well over half of the working fathers indicate that

> A peer review panel is a committee comprised of company employees.

family concerns have impacted their work—especially in their preference to avoid promotions in exchange for more time with their family.

- **Teach and use temporary stress-reduction techniques.** Some techniques for temporary stress-reduction include muscle relaxation (to relieve tension in the whole body), imagery (using mental pictures to visualize relaxing past events or fantasies), deep breathing (to cleanse the mind), and reframing (to frame a situation as less stressful and better able to manage).

- **More organizations are employing safety engineers.** These individuals conduct studies to identify dangerous situations in the workplace and to develop solutions to correct these situations.

- **Workplace violence is closely correlated with substance abuse and a history of violence.**

- **There are nearly 2 million victims of workplace violence each year. The costs to business are as high as $35 billion annually.**

More organizations are employing safety engineers. These individuals conduct studies to identify dangerous situations in the workplace and to develop solutions to correct these situations.

Diversity

D iversity presents wonderful opportunities for the organization. Yet these benefits come with obstacles to be overcome as well. Diversity often requires restructuring organizational cultures to include more opportunities for everyone. The competitive advantages, then, are balanced by the management challenges of diversity.

The multicultural work force is here to stay. Diversity is concerned with the creation of an inclusive environment in which all organizational members contribute their unique talents. It's an environment of cooperation and harmony that celebrates differences.

An inclusive environment welcomes diversity in all employment functions (not just at the point of hire). This environment requires a genuine acceptance of people—just as they are and without trying to fit them into a mold of how they should be. The basic foundation to managing diversity is respecting the differences among all people.

The changing demographics of the work force have contributed in large part to the increasing diversity.

Diversity Defined

Diversity is reflected in the differences among people in the work force today. It's all about celebrating the fact that people are not alike in their gender, ethnic origin, age or religion. Diversity is no longer a question of building on similarities. Now the concern is to recognize those differences and to provide opportunities for each individual to contribute his or her unique talents to the organization.

The changing demographics of the work force have contributed in large part to the increasing diversity. As more women entered the work force, gender differences needed to be addressed. The work force has aged as well. Globalization has also increased diversity. And more people with disabilities are contributing members of the work force than ever before.

A Look at the Demographics

Diversity reflects all the differences in the work force, including age, gender, ethnicity, and disability. The average age of American workers is increasing. The population swell created by the baby boomers is still in the work force, while lower birth rates in the generation after the baby boomers have meant that fewer younger workers are entering the work force. With improved health care, the baby boomers are remaining active employees for longer periods.

The impact of the aging of the work force has been felt in every organization. Older workers are generally viewed as more stable. They are thought to contribute more as a result of their high levels of experience. They also tend to be more loyal and to believe that organizational rewards should be provided for this loyalty and hard work. The cost, however, of more medical benefits has risen as the workers age. Older workers generally look for different benefits than younger workers. Older workers are more concerned with job security and preparation for their retirement.

The proportion of women in the work force has also been steadily increasing. By the year 2006 women will make up nearly half of the work force. This increase has come with new issues; the most publicized of these is the glass ceiling. This invisible barrier to promotion into high-level positions poses challenges for women and minorities.

TIP

John Naisbitt, author and motivational speaker, identified women in leadership as a megatrend in the twenty-first century. The glass ceiling in some larger organizations caused women to start record numbers of businesses during the 1990s. The hope is that these new organizations will be more responsive to the diversity found in today's workplace.

> The number of women in the work force has also caused human resource departments to re-evaluate the benefits offered.

The number of women in the work force has also caused human resource departments to re-evaluate the benefits offered. Working mothers require different benefits than working fathers whose wives are homemakers. Child and elder care are subjects of great concern. Human resource departments are also making efforts to decrease the differences in pay and promotion opportunities offered to women in the work force.

The variety of ethnic groups represented in the work force today has also increased dramatically. The percentage of whites in the work force is declining. By the year 2006, 73 percent of the work force will be white. The Hispanic portion of the work force is expected to rise to almost 12 percent by 2006. The Asian portion is projected to increase to 5 percent of the American work force by 2006.

A wide range of disabilities, both physical and mental, is represented in the work force today. As organizations education themselves, they find it easier to accommodate workers with disabilities and discover an untapped pool of talented individuals who can make valuable contributions.

The percentage of workers with diverse national origins has also increased. The human resource department is responsible for helping employees understand this diversity and the uniqueness of each individual.

The increasing disparity in the quality of education has also impacted the diversity of the work force. The work force is becoming more bipolar, with larger numbers of highly educated people and functionally illiterate workers. More jobs are requiring higher skill levels, which are not necessarily found in workers with lower educational levels.

> The human resource department is responsible for helping employees understand this diversity and the uniqueness of each individual.

Diversity: A Source of Competitive Advantage

Diversity is good for business and it is good business. Capitalizing on the opportunities diversity offers can add to a company's bottom line. An improved competitive position in the marketplace is just one advantage diversity brings.

Managing a diverse work force prepares a manager for dealing with diversity outside the organization. Understanding diversity helps the organization better serve diverse markets. and depict these diverse groups in advertising. Diverse employees provide valuable input into the products and services to be offered, including how to package and advertise these products.

If the firm cannot manage diversity well, productivity is generally lower and turnover rates tend to be higher (as women and minorities leave to join firms that better manage diversity). Effective diversity management, then, pays off on the bottom line. When a company manages diversity well, its reputation spreads and it is more successful in attracting more talented individuals from these diverse groups. The result is better overall talent in the organization if the firm is attracting employees from all the available talent pools.

TIP

A commitment to diversity can also have a positive impact on customers. Diverse consumer groups are often more comfortable buying products and services from an organization that values diversity. On the other hand, a reputation that suggests your firm does not value diversity often results in customers deciding not to support your organization—or perhaps, at the extreme, deciding to boycott your products.

Greater levels of diversity usually lead to greater creativity. The firm avoids one single way of thinking. Instead, a variety of perspectives are presented. More ideas lead to better solutions. The firm can be more flexible in responding to the environment and changing customer preferences.

Managing Diversity Means Valuing Diversity

Managing diversity means providing choices. Organizations must develop flexible policies that enable employees to respond to their unique needs.

Just as many benefits are gained from a diverse work force, some problems occur as well. Diversity presents an increased opportunity for conflict. Questions of unfairness in hiring must be combated, addressing both affirmative action issues and reverse discrimination. Feelings of fear and distrust and misunderstandings often result from increased diversity.

To deal more effectively with diversity on an individual level, everyone must understand that people are not the same and "fair treatment" means understanding these differences. Treating everyone in the same manner disregards diversity.

Employees must also understand the unique perspectives of their coworkers and how they may feel or perceive things. Tolerance is a key component in the management of diversity. Beyond understanding that differences exist, they must be tolerated.

> Diversity presents an increased opportunity for conflict.

And people must be willing to communicate their concerns and issues. Otherwise, they fester and become larger. This communication, however, must be honest and two-way. Offensive behaviors will be repeated if people don't communicate their feelings.

Guidelines to Supporting a Diverse Work Force

Supporting a diverse work force means that the unique preferences and needs of workers must be addressed. To find out what employees really want, organizations should conduct employee surveys, hold staff meetings to discuss needs, and conduct focus groups. By asking what employees want, the organization can ensure personal relevance.

Start at the Top . . .

Diversity in the top management ranks reflects the organization's commitment to diversity. Organizational policies must communicate what behaviors are appropriate and what behaviors are not appropriate. This communication can be accomplished through diversity training. These policies should focus on behavior guidelines as well as on how employees should be treated. Some policies, such as the commitment to equal employment opportunity, impact the diversity of the firm itself. Organizational policies must address how to resolve diversity problems. The consequences of violating these policies also communicate the importance placed on the commitment to diversity.

TIP

Years ago, a well-known company provided progressive diversity training and was held up as an example to other companies. But as soon as the company fell on hard economic times, diversity training was among the first programs cut. In reality, the company didn't place the value on its diversity training that it said it did. Employees, customers, suppliers, and the local community look for these kinds of signals from organizations.

> To find out what employees really want, organizations should conduct employee surveys, hold staff meetings to discuss needs, and conduct focus groups.

Procedures should reflect flexible practices to accommodate diversity and the inherent differences among organizational members. Inclusive and flexible policies (such as flexible benefit plans) communicate a greater commitment to diversity.

An organization's mission statement usually reflects its commitment to diversity. If there is no mention of diversity, it is generally not a high priority. Those organizations that have committed themselves to diversity make their position clear.

. . . And Bring It to the People

Diversity training can communicate a company's commitment to diversity and assist in better meeting the challenges that arise. The primary role of this training is to help employees learn to understand the differences among people in the work force in order to function more effectively.

In part, diversity training must explain how each employee's actions affect his or her coworkers and then how their actions impact other workers, and on and on throughout the organization. Employees must understand the cultures represented in the workplace. Human resources can take the lead by providing insight into ten aspects of culture:

- Beliefs
- Dress
- Food
- Language
- Learning
- Relationships
- Time consciousness
- Use of space
- Values
- Work practices

Beliefs

Religion provides many of the basic values embraced by different cultures. Work schedules should take into account religious holidays,

> An organization's mission statement usually reflects its commitment to diversity.

recognizing the wide variety that exists. Employees also have to be trained to provide input to the decision-making process since some cultures are not as comfortable with this responsibility.

TIP

Organizations must also be careful to accommodate religious beliefs where reasonable. If religious accommodations are not made, the organization must be prepared to demonstrate undue hardship or a business necessity.

Dress

Dress varies significantly from culture to culture. It is one of the most visible differences among cultures. While the American culture has norms for appropriate dress in the workplace, these norms are not applied across other cultures. Hiring a culturally diverse work force means that dress will certainly vary. Organizations must be flexible in their approach to dress, hair, and appearance as a result of these cultural differences.

Although first impressions are created partially on appearances, employees must be reminded to take into account the norms of other cultures. Some employees may need to be taught the appropriate dress of your organization.

Family Relationships

Family relationships in the workplace are considered nepotism in the American culture. For the most part, these relationships are viewed as favoritism and are avoided. Some other cultures, however, place a great deal of emphasis on family and members are responsible for their family.

TIP

Some cultures even value family relationships so highly that it is extended to the business arena. While American businesses often frown on nepotism, it is seen as a family obligation in some cultures to hire family members.

> Family relationships in the workplace are considered nepotism in the American culture.

Employees from different cultures often involve family members in employment decisions; they may require more time for discussion before making a decision. For example, the entire family may come to a college admission interview and the head of the family may decide whether the female student will attend the institution. Managers should also realize that they may be perceived to hold authority positions and may be asked to counsel younger employees from other cultures.

Food

As more business is conducted over meals, the differences in food across cultures must be considered. Many religious groups prohibit the eating of certain foods such as pork, any meats, shellfish, or alcoholic beverages. The way in which food is consumed also varies greatly from burping to picking teeth.

Companies should consider varieties of food or alternatives when preparing food for meetings. Careful consideration should be given to known dietary preferences whenever possible—such as when inviting an individual to a lunch meeting at a restaurant.

Language

Language includes both verbal and nonverbal (or body) communication. Eye contact is an especially important part of the process. But eye contact is interpreted differently across cultures. In the American culture, avoiding eye contact is associated with disinterest or dishonesty. In Latin cultures, however, avoiding eye contact is a sign of respect for authority.

Among multicultural individuals, hand gestures can be especially dangerous. The gestures accepted and understood by Americans communicate very different messages in other cultures. Even nods and smiles can easily be misunderstood. Smiles in some cultures may communicate embarrassment rather than friendliness.

When language barriers exist, employees should assume that they may not be understood. A common error is to assume that you are understood if you are not questioned. The reverse should be assumed, however. When speaking, avoid as much nonverbal communication as possible; you will be much less likely to send mixed messages.

> The gestures accepted and understood by Americans communicate very different messages in other cultures.

Learning

Problem-solving approaches also vary with culture. Americans tend to logically seek the answer to problems and then fix them. Some cultures view any disruptions to the status quo very negatively and react more with intuition (versus rational problem-solving).

Employees should be trained in a wide variety of decision-making techniques to capture the best of both approaches. Rather than just focusing on rational problem-solving, techniques such as brainstorming should also be utilized.

Time Consciousness

Time is also viewed very differently across cultures. Americans, however, must be reminded that their preoccupation with time is not observed in all other cultures.

Variations in time consciousness are rooted in culture, not in manners. It is important to explain the American orientation toward time and why deadlines must be met. Explaining the consequences of missed deadlines can be helpful in teaching others how to make adjustments.

Use of Space

Most Americans consider a circle about three feet around them as personal space. Only those with whom we have more intimate relationships (such as family) are invited into that space.

These norms are not the same for other cultures. The Japanese culture generally maintains greater personal space distances while Middle Eastern cultures enjoy a smaller amount of personal space. These space norms are usually reflected in the general formality of these cultures as well.

To avoid offending members of more formal cultures, use formal introductions for all new employees. Ask people what name they prefer, instead of informally using their first name. Familiarity with employees should be avoided until they give the go-ahead. It is best to read others' cultures and not assume anything.

> Most Americans consider a circle about three feet around them as personal space.

Values

The values of the American culture can be the source of much misunderstanding in the workplace. Americans believe in individuality and competition while many other cultures value conformity and a cooperative environment.

Americans tend to be more open about feelings than some cultures. American employees may discuss family issues and personal problems with their coworkers. Members of other cultures may see this practice as incredibly inappropriate and retain their privacy. The perception of authority is different as well. Americans tend to question authority, but some cultures believe that authority should be blindly accepted.

Work Practices

The Protestant work ethic has guided the American culture for decades. Members of other cultures may await instructions from authority figures, rather than taking the initiative themselves. Americans also think they must be doing something all the time while other cultures place more emphasis on relaxation.

This focus is even seen with the amount of vacation time provided by employers around the world. Americans have some of the shortest vacations. Even the work week and "normal" work hours vary around the globe.

Diversity training can help employees understand some of the differences that are brought to the workplace. Understanding and discussing these differences will help each individual make the greatest contributions he or she can.

Summary

Diversity has become a critical management and human resource management challenge for every organization. Those organizations that fail to respond to increased diversity with more flexible human resource policies and approaches to managing people will find themselves missing valuable opportunities for competitive advantage.

> Diversity training can help employees understand some of the differences that are brought to the workplace.

Streetwise Advice

- **Flexible working hours help accommodate diversity in terms of religious holidays, family situations, and day care.**

- **The glass ceiling is cracking.** Although most large organizations still have a disproportionate number of white males in executive positions (and on boards), more women are occupying middle management positions.

- **Obtain demographic information to paint a picture of the future work force composition.** Demographic information is available from the U.S. Bureau of the Census at *www.census.gov*.

- **Fight ethnocentrism.** Thinking that your culture's way of doing things is the best way is self-defeating. The key is to build learning organizations.

- **Business-education partnerships have become more common.** Businesses are assisting schools with curriculum development to ensure that workers are emerging with the skills required in the marketplace. Educators are also coming into businesses to help provide the remedial training on-site needed to help develop basic skills in reading, writing, and math for a portion of the work force.

- **Make an effort to understand your own work force trends.** Work force trends are available to help plan for the future. Local governments are compiling statistics and colleges and universities are monitoring trends. The Department of Labor provides census figures by state. Professional associations also provide industry information. Understanding the shifts in your local labor market helps you prepare for the future.

- **The best way to understand more about other cultures is to ask.** You may ask employees about their culture or read reference books, or just observe. Then you should discuss and share what you learn with others.

- **Conduct diversity audits.** A diversity audit is an assessment tool to provide insight into how effectively your organization is managing diversity. Questionnaires, interviews, or focus groups can be used to conduct an audit.

> Thinking that your culture's way of doing things is the best way is self-defeating.

- **Use support groups or mentors to help employees from diverse groups advance in the organization.** The commitment to diversity does not end with the hiring process. Support systems must be established to ensure these employees learn more about being successful in the organization. Networks of women have been created in some organizations to help understand how they might get ahead. Providing formal mentors to minority employees has also been an effective tool.

- **Maintaining face is critical in many cultures and it is especially important when providing feedback to employees from other cultures.** Constructive criticism is needed to inform employees of what they are doing wrong and how to improve. It must, however, be handled in such a way as to ensure that the employee does not lose face. Try to ensure that a supportive, respectful relationship has been established before giving criticism. Focus feedback on behaviors, not on personality. Also frame the feedback in terms of the appropriate behavior that should be engaged in (versus statements such as "that's not the way you should do that"). Avoid yelling and emotional outbursts. Be sure to provide the feedback in private and in a calm manner.

- **Log on to *www.shrm.org/diversity* for assistance.** The diversity Web site for the Society of Human Resource Management is a good resource with links to their diversity publication and other helpful resources.

- **Training is crucial to diversity management, but you need more.** You cannot just offer training to manage diversity effectively. You must also change organizational processes to support this new environment. These processes include reward systems, benefits, compensation, training, and career development.

- **More organizations are trying diversity councils.** A company-wide diversity council can be accountable for the effectiveness of managing diversity, including setting training objectives and surveying the work force to read the climate of the organization.

> Constructive criticism is needed to inform employees of what they are doing wrong and how to improve.

Appendices

APPENDIX A HELPFUL HR TIPS AND QUICK REFERENCES **APPENDIX B** SELECTED EXCERPTS FROM MAJOR LEGISLATION IMPACTING HUMAN RESOURCES **APPENDIX C** FORMS AND APPLICATIONS **APPENDIX D** GLOSSARY

Helpful HR Tips and Quick References

Appendix A

This appendix provides a handy reference list of the following key human resource management responsibilities:

- Sample equal employment policy
- Sample sexual harassment policy
- Sample workplace violence policy
- Tips for nonsexist job titles
- Sample table of contents for an employee manual
- Tips on interview questions: legal pitfalls

Sample Equal Employment Policy

[Company name] supports the principle of Equal Employment Opportunity. It is our policy not to discriminate against any applicant for employment or employee because of race, color, religion, age, sex, national origin or ancestry, marital status, veteran's status, or disability in accordance with applicable federal, state, and local law. This policy extends to every phase of the employment process.

We will provide reasonable accommodations for qualified job applicants, staff members, and customers with disabilities, provided such disabilities have been brought to our attention.

Any incident that you believe involves discrimination or harassment should be brought to the immediate attention of your supervisor or the human resource department.

> Any incident that you believe involves discrimination or harassment should be brought to the immediate attention of your supervisor or the human resource department.

Sample Sexual Harassment Policy

It is our policy that there shall be no sexual harassment of any of our employees. *[Company name]* is committed to providing a work environment totally free of harassment.

Harassment demeans individuals and creates unacceptable stress for the entire organization. Significant costs are involved and morale is adversely affected. Work effectiveness declines. Persons harassing others will be dealt with swiftly and vigorously. Any employee who violates this policy is subject to disciplinary action up to and including discharge.

Sexual harassment is behavior of a sexual nature that is unwelcome and personally offensive to its recipients.

Unwelcome sexual advances, requests for sexual favors, and other verbal or physical conduct of a sexual nature constitute "sexual harassment" when submission to such conduct is made explicitly or implicitly a condition of an individual's employment; submission to or rejection of such conduct is used as a basis for an employment decision affecting the employee; or the harassment has the purpose of effect of unreasonably interfering with the employee's work performance or creating an environment that is intimidating, hostile, or offensive to the employee.

> Harassment can occur with a single incident, or through a pattern of behavior where the purpose of effect is to create a hostile, offensive, or intimidating work environment.

Harassment can occur with a single incident, or through a pattern of behavior where the purpose of effect is to create a hostile, offensive, or intimidating work environment.

Any employee who feels that he or she has been sexually harassed should immediately report the matter to his or her supervisor. If that person is unavailable or the employee believes that it would be inappropriate to contact his or her supervisor, the employee should contact the human resource department.

Any supervisor or manager who becomes aware of any possible sexual harassment should immediately advise the human resource department, which will handle such matters in a lawful manner to ensure that such conduct does not continue. All complaints of sexual harassment will be investigated in as discreet and confidential a fashion as possible. No person will be adversely affected in employment as a result of bringing complaints of sexual harassment.

Sample Workplace Violence Policy

It is the policy of *[Company name]* to promote a safe environment for its employees, customers, and visitors. *[Company name]* is committed to working with its employees to maintain a work environment free from violence, threats of violence, harassment, intimidation, and other disruptive behavior.

Violence, threats, harassment, intimidation, and other disruptive behavior in our workplace will not be tolerated. Such behavior can include oral or written statements, gestures, or expressions that communicate a direct or indirect threat of physical harm. Individuals who commit such acts may be removed from the premises and may be subject to disciplinary action, up to and including discharge.

If you observe or experience violent, threatening, harassing, intimidating, or other disruptive behavior by anyone on Company premises, whether he or she is a company employee or not, report it immediately to your supervisor, the human resource department, or some other manager or official of the Company. All reports will be taken seriously and will be dealt with in a timely manner.

> Violence, threats, harassment, intimidation, and other disruptive behavior in our workplace will not be tolerated.

Sample Table of Contents for an Employee Manual

TABLE OF CONTENTS

Tips for Nonsexist Job Titles

Inappropriate	Instead, consider . . .
Businessman	Businessperson
Cameraman	Camera operator
Deliveryman	Delivery clerk
Doorman	Doorkeeper
Draftsman	Drafter
Fireman	Firefighter
Foreman	Supervisor, leader
Lineman	Line installer
Mailman	Letter carrier
Middleman	Liaison, agent
Policeman	Police officer
Pressman	Press operator
Salesman	Salesperson, sales associate
Spokesman	Spokesperson
Stewardess	Flight attendant
Tradesman	Tradespeople
Waiter, waitress	Server
Weatherman	Weather forecaster

Tips on Interview Questions: Legal Pitfalls

1. **Do not ask questions that solicit information concerning the applicant's marital status.** Do not ask a woman what her maiden name was. It is appropriate, however, to ask if the applicant has ever worked under another name.
2. **Do not ask questions about the applicant's age.** It is only appropriate to determine that the applicant is the legal age for employment.
3. **Do not ask questions whose answers will indicate ancestry or national origin.** "Where were you born" is an illegal question. You may not ask the ancestry of the applicant's name. If the job does not require knowledge of a foreign language, do not ask about proficiency in foreign languages.
4. **Avoid questions about physical characteristics.** Do not ask questions about height or weight. Statements about an applicant's attractiveness (or lack thereof) could lead to charges of harassment or discrimination.
5. **Do not ask questions about health and physical condition.** It is more appropriate to simply ask if there is anything that would interfere with job performance. If health is a job requirement, a physical examination may be given.
6. **Do not ask the applicant where she attends church.** You may ask if there are any reasons the applicant cannot work Saturdays if Saturday work is required for the position.
7. **Do not ask if the applicant has ever been arrested.** You may, however, ask questions about criminal convictions
8. **Do not ask questions about the applicant's family.** You may not ask how many children he has.
9. **Avoid asking the applicant about membership in any clubs or organizations.** Professional association memberships may be questioned (such as the IMA or SHRM) since they may be job-related.
10. **Avoid questions about financial status.** You may not ask if the applicant owns her home, where she lives, or if she owns a car. You may, however, ask whether the applicant anticipates any problems getting to work. Limit the interview questions to job-related issues.

> Avoid questions about physical characteristics. Do not ask questions about height or weight.

Selected Excerpts from Major Legislation Impacting Human Resources

Appendix B

Every line manager and human resource professional must be familiar with the federal legislation that governs human resource issues. The following pages include excerpts from the major legislation that is enforced by the Equal Employment Opportunity Commission. These laws include the following:

- The Age Discrimination in Employment Act of 1967
- The Americans with Disabilities Act of 1990
- The Civil Rights Act of 1991
- The Equal Pay Act of 1963
- Title VII of the Civil Rights Act

Complete copies of the legislation may be found on the EEOC's Web site, at *www.eeoc.gov/policy*.

Complete copies of the legislation may be found on the EEOC's Web site, at *www.eeoc.gov/policy*.

Excerpts from the Age Discrimination in Employment Act of 1967

It shall be unlawful for an employer—

> to fail or refuse to hire or to discharge any individual or otherwise discriminate against any individual with respect to his compensation, terms, conditions, or privileges of employment, because of such individual's age;

> to limit, segregate, or classify his employees in any way which would deprive or tend to deprive any individual of employment opportunities or otherwise adversely affect his status as an employee, because of such individual's age; or

> to reduce the wage rate of any employee in order to comply with this chapter.

It shall be unlawful for an employer to reduce the wage rate of any employee in order to comply with this chapter.

Excerpts from the Americans with Disabilities Act of 1990

Disability. —The term "disability'" means, with respect to an individual—

a physical or mental impairment that substantially limits one or more of the major life activities of such individual;

a record of such an impairment; or

being regarded as having such an impairment. . . .

Reasonable accommodation.—The term "reasonable accommodation" may include—

making existing facilities used by employees readily accessible to and usable by individuals with disabilities; and

job restructuring, part-time or modified work schedules, reassignment to a vacant position, acquisition or modification of equipment or devices, appropriate adjustment or modifications of examinations, training materials or policies, the provision of qualified readers or interpreters, and other similar accommodations for individuals with disabilities.

Undue hardship.—

In general. —The term "undue hardship" means an action requiring significant difficulty or expense, when considered in light of the factors set forth in subparagraph (B).

Factors to be considered. —In determining whether an accommodation would impose an undue hardship on a covered entity, factors to be considered include—

the nature and cost of the accommodation needed under this chapter;

the overall financial resources of the facility or facilities involved in the provision of the reasonable accommodation; the number of persons employed at such facility; the effect

> The term "reasonable accommodation" may include making existing facilities used by employees readily accessible to and usable by individuals with disabilities.

on expenses and resources, or the impact otherwise of such accommodation upon the operation of the facility;

the overall financial resources of the covered entity; the overall size of the business of a covered entity with respect to the number of its employees; the number, type, and location of its facilities; and

the type of operation or operations of the covered entity, including the composition, structure, and functions of the workforce of such entity; the geographic separateness, administrative, or fiscal relationship of the facility or facilities in question to the covered entity. . . .

DISCRIMINATION SEC. 12112. *[Section 102]*

General rule. —No covered entity shall discriminate against a qualified individual with a disability because of the disability of such individual in regard to job application procedures, the hiring, advancement, or discharge of employees, employee compensation, job training, and other terms, conditions, and privileges of employment.

Construction. —As used in subsection (a) of this section, the term "discriminate"' includes—

limiting, segregating, or classifying a job applicant or employee in a way that adversely affects the opportunities or status of such applicant or employee because of the disability of such applicant or employee;

participating in a contractual or other arrangement or relationship that has the effect of subjecting a covered entity's qualified applicant or employee with a disability to the discrimination prohibited by this subchapter (such relationship includes a relationship with an employment or referral agency, labor union, an organization providing fringe benefits to an employee of the covered entity, or an organization providing training and apprenticeship programs);

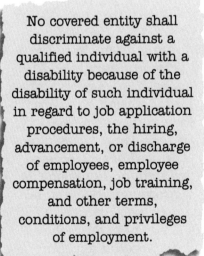

No covered entity shall discriminate against a qualified individual with a disability because of the disability of such individual in regard to job application procedures, the hiring, advancement, or discharge of employees, employee compensation, job training, and other terms, conditions, and privileges of employment.

utilizing standards, criteria, or methods of administration—
have the effect of discrimination on the basis of disability; or

that perpetuate the discrimination of others who are subject to common administrative control;

Including or otherwise denying equal jobs or benefits to a
qualified individual because of the known disability of an
individual with whom the qualified individual is known to
have a relationship or association;

not making reasonable accommodations to the known
physical or mental limitations of an otherwise qualified
individual with a disability who is an applicant or
employee, unless such covered entity can demonstrate
that the accommodation would impose an undue hardship
on the operation of the business of such covered entity; or

denying employment opportunities to a job applicant or
employee who is an otherwise qualified individual with a
disability, if such denial is based on the need of such covered entity to make reasonable accommodation to the physical or mental impairments of the employee or applicant;

using qualification standards, employment tests or other
selection criteria that screen out or tend to screen out an
individual with a disability or a class of individuals with
disabilities unless the standard, test or other selection criteria, as used by the covered entity, is shown to be
job-related for the position in question and is consistent
with business necessity; and

failing to select and administer tests concerning employment in the most effective manner to ensure that, when
such test is administered to a job applicant or employee
who has a disability that impairs sensory, manual, or speaking skills, such test results accurately reflect the skills, aptitude, or whatever other factor of such applicant or
employee that such test purports to measure, rather than
reflecting the impaired sensory, manual, or speaking skills

> Denying employment
> opportunities to a job
> applicant or employee who
> is an otherwise qualified
> individual with a disability,
> if such denial is based on
> the need of such covered
> entity to make reasonable
> accommodation to the
> physical or mental
> impairments of the
> employee or applicant.

of such employee or applicant (except where such skills are the factors that the test purports to measure). . . .

DISCRIMINATION SEC. 12112. *[Section 102]*

General rule. —No covered entity shall discriminate against a qualified individual with a disability because of the disability of such individual in regard to job application procedures, the hiring, advancement, or discharge of employees, employee compensation, job training, and other terms, conditions, and privileges of employment.

Construction. —As used in subsection (a) of this section, the term "discriminate" includes—

limiting, segregating, or classifying a job applicant or employee in a way that adversely affects the opportunities or status of such applicant or employee because of the disability of such applicant or employee;

participating in a contractual or other arrangement or relationship that has the effect of subjecting a covered entity's qualified applicant or employee with a disability to the discrimination prohibited by this subchapter (such relationship includes a relationship with an employment or referral agency, labor union, an organization providing fringe benefits to an employee of the covered entity, or an organization providing training and apprenticeship programs);

utilizing standards, criteria, or methods of administration—

that have the effect of discrimination on the basis of disability; or

that perpetuate the discrimination of others who are subject to common administrative control;

excluding or otherwise denying equal jobs or benefits to a qualified individual because of the known disability of an individual with whom the qualified individual is known to have a relationship or association;

> As used in subsection (a) of this section, the term "discriminate" includes limiting, segregating, or classifying a job applicant or employee in a way that adversely affects the opportunities or status of such applicant or employee because of the disability of such applicant or employee.

not making reasonable accommodations to the known physical or mental limitations of an otherwise qualified individual with a disability who is an applicant or employee, unless such covered entity can demonstrate that the accommodation would impose an undue hardship on the operation of the business of such covered entity; or

denying employment opportunities to a job applicant or employee who is an otherwise qualified individual with a disability, if such denial is based on the need of such covered entity to make reasonable accommodation to the physical or mental impairments of the employee or applicant;

using qualification standards, employment tests or other selection criteria that screen out or tend to screen out an individual with a disability or a class of individuals with disabilities unless the standard, test or other selection criteria, as used by the covered entity, is shown to be job-related for the position in question and is consistent with business necessity; and

failing to select and administer tests concerning employment in the most effective manner to ensure that, when such test is administered to a job applicant or employee who has a disability that impairs sensory, manual, or speaking skills, such test results accurately reflect the skills, aptitude, or whatever other factor of such applicant or employee that such test purports to measure, rather than reflecting the impaired sensory, manual, or speaking skills of such employee or applicant (except where such skills are the factors that the test purports to measure) . . . .

POSTING NOTICES SEC. 12115. *[Section 105]*

Every employer, employment agency, labor organization, or joint labor-management committee covered under this subchapter shall post notices in an accessible format to applicants, employees, and members describing the applicable provisions of this chapter, in the manner prescribed by section 2000e-10 of this title *[section 711 of the Civil Rights Act of 1964].*

> Every employer, employment agency, labor organization, or joint labor-management committee covered under this subchapter shall post notices in an accessible format to applicants, employees, and members describing the applicable provisions of this chapter, in the manner prescribed by section 2000e-10 of this title *[section 711 of the Civil Rights Act of 1964]*.

Excerpts from the Civil Rights Act of 1991

An Act to amend the Civil Rights Act of 1964 to strengthen and improve Federal civil rights laws, to provide for damages in cases of intentional employment discrimination, to clarify provisions regarding disparate impact actions, and for other purposes . . . .

The purposes of this Act are—

to provide appropriate remedies for intentional discrimination and unlawful harassment in the workplace;

to codify the concepts of "business necessity" and "job related" enunciated by the Supreme Court in *Griggs v. Duke Power Co.,* 401 U.S. 424 (1971), and in the other Supreme Court decisions prior to *Wards Cove Packing Co. v. Atonio,* 490 U.S. 642 (1989);

to confirm statutory authority and provide statutory guidelines for the adjudication of disparate impact suits under title VII of the Civil Rights Act of 1964 (42 U.S.C. 2000e et seq.); and

to respond to recent decisions of the Supreme Court by expanding the scope of relevant civil rights statutes in order to provide adequate protection to victims of discrimination.

The purposes of this Act are to provide appropriate remedies for intentional discrimination and unlawful harassment in the workplace.

Excerpts from the Equal Pay Act of 1963

SEC. 206. *[Section 6]*

No employer having employees subject to any provisions of this section shall discriminate, within any establishment in which such employees are employed, between employees on the basis of sex by paying wages to employees in such establishment at a rate less than the rate at which he pays wages to employees of the opposite sex in such establishment for equal work on jobs the performance of which requires equal skill, effort, and responsibility, and which are performed under similar working conditions, except where such payment is made pursuant to

a seniority system;

a merit system;

a system which measures earnings by quantity or quality of production; or

a differential based on any other factor other than sex: *Provided,* That an employer who is paying a wage rate differential in violation of this subsection shall not, in order to comply with the provisions of this subsection, reduce the wage rate of any employee.

No employer having employees subject to any provisions of this section shall discriminate, within any establishment in which such employees are employed, between employees on the basis of sex by paying wages to employees in such establishment at a rate less than the rate at which he pays wages to employees of the opposite sex in such establishment for equal work.

Excerpts from Title VII of the Civil Rights Act: Unlawful Employment Practices

SEC. 2000e-2. *[Section 703]*

It shall be an unlawful employment practice for an employer—

to fail or refuse to hire or to discharge any individual, or otherwise to discriminate against any individual with respect to his compensation, terms, conditions, or privileges of employment, because of such individual's race, color, religion, sex, or national origin; or

to limit, segregate, or classify his employees or applicants for employment in any way which would deprive or tend to deprive any individual of employment opportunities or otherwise adversely affect his status as an employee, because of such individual's race, color, religion, sex, or national origin.

It shall be an unlawful employment practice for an employment agency to fail or refuse to refer for employment, or otherwise to discriminate against, any individual because of his race, color, religion, sex, or national origin, or to classify or refer for employment any individual on the basis of his race, color, religion, sex, or national origin. . . .

Notwithstanding any other provision of this subchapter, it shall not be an unlawful employment practice for an employer to apply different standards of compensation, or different terms, conditions, or privileges of employment pursuant to a bona fide seniority or merit system, or a system which measures earnings by quantity or quality of production or to employees who work in different locations, provided that such differences are not the result of an intention to discriminate because of race, color, religion, sex, or national origin, nor shall it be an unlawful employment practice for an employer to give and to act upon the results of any professionally developed ability test provided that such test, its administration or action upon the results is not designed, intended or used to discriminate because of race, color, religion, sex or national origin. It shall not be an unlawful employment practice under this subchapter for any employer to differentiate upon the basis of sex

It shall be an unlawful employment practice for an employer to limit, segregate, or classify his employees or applicants for employment in any way which would deprive or tend to deprive any individual of employment opportunities or otherwise adversely affect his status as an employee, because of such individual's race, color, religion, sex, or national origin.

in determining the amount of the wages or compensation paid or to be paid to employees of such employer if such differentiation is authorized by the provisions of section 206(d) of title 29 *[section 6(d) of the Fair Labor Standards Act of 1938, as amended]* . . .

An unlawful employment practice based on disparate impact is established under this title only if—

> a complaining party demonstrates that a respondent uses a particular employment practice that causes a disparate impact on the basis of race, color, religion, sex, or national origin and the respondent fails to demonstrate that the challenged practice is job related for the position in question and consistent with business necessity; or

> the complaining party makes the demonstration described in subparagraph (C) with respect to an alternative employment practice and the respondent refuses to adopt such alternative employment practice.

With respect to demonstrating that a particular employment practice causes a disparate impact as described in subparagraph (A)(i), the complaining party shall demonstrate that each particular challenged employment practice causes a disparate impact, except that if the complaining party can demonstrate to the court that the elements of a respondent's decision making process are not capable of separation for analysis, the decision making process may be analyzed as one employment practice.

If the respondent demonstrates that a specific employment practice does not cause the disparate impact, the respondent shall not be required to demonstrate that such practice is required by business necessity.

The demonstration referred to by subparagraph (A)(ii) shall be in accordance with the law as it existed on June 4, 1989, with respect to the concept of "alternative employment practice."

A demonstration that an employment practice is required by business necessity may not be used as a defense against a claim of intentional discrimination under this title.

An unlawful employment practice based on disparate impact is established under this title only if the complaining party makes the demonstration described in subparagraph (C) with respect to an alternative employment practice and the respondent refuses to adopt such alternative employment practice.

Forms and Applications

Appendix C

Several sample forms have been included in this appendix. Although these are samples intended to provide guidance, each organization should customize generic forms to best meet its needs. Furthermore, have your attorney or legal department review all employment documents before your company adopts them. Finally, be sure to conduct a careful review of state and local (as well as federal) laws to ensure that all documents used in any phase of the employment process meet legal standards.

The forms and apllocations provides here:

- Employment evaluation
- Exit interview form and checklist
- Termination checklist
- Performance checklist
- Employment selection checklist
- New employee checklist
- Employee orientation checklist
- Disciplinary form
- Meeting planner
- Project planner
- Staffing calendar
- Weekly organizer
- Authorization to release information
- Employee separation notice
- Employee time sheet
- Employee warning notice
- Employee application
- Personnel record
- Pre-employment reference check letter
- Quarterly payroll record/deductions

> Furthermore, have your attorney or legal department review all employment documents before your company adopts them.

Employment Evaluation

Employee: _____ Title: _____

Department: _____ Employee ID #: _____

Date of Evaluation: _____

Date of Next Scheduled Evaluation: _____

Evaluate the employee's performance as it pertains to the requirements of the job. Use the following scale to rate the employee's performance. Circle the number reflecting the description that best describes the employee's performance.

1	2	3	4	5
Unsatisfactory	Below Average	Average	Above Average	Outstanding

Be sure to add comments to explain the ratings.

Adherence to policy: The degree to which the employee follows company rules and regulations.

1	2	3	4	5
Unsatisfactory	Below Average	Average	Above Average	Outstanding

Comments:

_____

_____

_____

Job knowledge: The degree to which the employee understands the job responsibilities and possesses the appropriate knowledge, skills, and abilities to perform these tasks.

1	2	3	4	5
Unsatisfactory	Below Average	Average	Above Average	Outstanding

Comments:

_____

_____

_____

Creativity: The degree to which the employee demonstrates initiative and provides suggestions for new ideas to improve processes.

1	2	3	4	5
Unsatisfactory	Below Average	Average	Above Average	Outstanding

Comments:

_____

_____

_____

Dependability: The degree to which the employee can be depended on to complete assignments and work with others.

1	2	3	4	5
Unsatisfactory	Below Average	Average	Above Average	Outstanding

Comments:

_____

_____

_____

Teamwork: The degree to which the employee has demonstrated an ability to work well with others and be a contributing member of the team.

1	2	3	4	5
Unsatisfactory	Below Average	Average	Above Average	Outstanding

Comments:

_____

_____

_____

Independence: The degree to which the employee is able to work without close supervision.

1	2	3	4	5
Unsatisfactory	Below Average	Average	Above Average	Outstanding

Comments:

_____

_____

_____

Work quality: The level of quality exhibited in the employee's work including accuracy and appropriateness.

1	2	3	4	5
Unsatisfactory	Below Average	Average	Above Average	Outstanding

Comments:

_____

_____

_____

Areas for Improvement and Goals (Include recommendations for development and training.):

_____

_____

_____

Evaluator's Signature: _____

Employee Signature: _____
(Note: Employee signature denotes receipt of the evaluation but not necessarily agreement with the appraisal.)

Date Scheduled for Follow-up Discussion: _____

Exit Interview Form and Checklist

Employee's Name _____ Job Title _____

Employee Number _____ Department_____

Last Date of Employment_____ Employee's Supervisor _____

Date Notification Was Given_____

Human Resource Interviewer _____

Would you recommend for rehire? ❏ Yes ❏ No

Please explain:_____

_____

_____

_____

Reason for Employee's Departure:

❏ Dismissal (Documentation attached.)

❏ Retirement

❏ Layoff (If temporary, expected date of rehire.)

_____

❏ Resignation

❏ Other (Please provide details.)

_____

_____

_____

Termination Checklist

- ❏ Obtained forwarding address for employee.
- ❏ Obtained new employer information.
- ❏ Obtained reason for leaving company's employ.
- ❏ Conducted exit interview.
- ❏ Discussed vacation and benefit payments.
- ❏ Notified payroll department.
- ❏ Notified insurance company.
- ❏ Sent COBRA letter.
- ❏ Retrieved keys, badges, and ID cards as appropriate.
- ❏ Retrieved all company property as appropriate.

Supervisor's Signature _____

Supervisor's Title _____

HR Interviewer's Signature _____

HR Interviewer's Title _____

Performance Checklist

	Above Average	Average	Below Average
Attendance	❏	❏	❏
Cooperation	❏	❏	❏
Job Knowledge	❏	❏	❏
Productivity	❏	❏	❏
Reliability	❏	❏	❏
Quality of Work	❏	❏	❏
Initiative	❏	❏	❏
Communication Skills	❏	❏	❏
Team Player Skills	❏	❏	❏

Any Additional Comments:

_____

_____

_____

Would you rehire the applicant? ❏ Yes ❏ No
   Explain:

_____

_____

_____

   What was the applicant's reason for leaving?

_____

_____

_____

Completed by: _____

Signature _____

Position _____

Employment Selection Checklist

Applicant's Name: _____

Position Applied For: _____

Checklist:
- ❏ Application Completed . . . . Date: _____
- ❏ Initial Interview Completed in HR . . . Date: _____
- ❏ Employment Testing Completed . . . . Date: _____
- ❏ Reference Checks Completed . . . . . . Date: _____
- ❏ Initial Recommendation by HR . . . . . Date: _____
- ❏ Line Management Interview . . . . Date: _____
- ❏ Medical Examination . . . . Date: _____
- ❏ Drug Test . . . . Date: _____
- ❏ Offer Extended . . . . Date: _____
- ❏ Orientation . . . . Date: _____

New Employee Checklist

- ❏ Obtained completed, signed application
- ❏ Obtained employee data for records:
    - ❏ Full name, address, phone number
    - ❏ Date of birth, social security number
    - ❏ Job title and location
    - ❏ Emergency contact information
- ❏ Employee number and ID/badge
- ❏ Obtained completed enrollment forms
    - ❏ Group life insurance
    - ❏ Disability insurance
    - ❏ Health insurance
    - ❏ Retirement plans
    - ❏ Dental insurance
- ❏ Obtained signed receipt for employee handbook

Completed by: _____ Date _____

Employee Orientation Checklist

❏ Provided a tour of the facilities/department . . . . . . Date _____
❏ Break room. . . . . Date _____
❏ Restrooms. . . . . Date _____
❏ Bulletin boards. . . . . Date _____
❏ Time clock . . . . Date _____
❏ Copy machine. . . . . Date _____
❏ Mail room . . . . Date _____
❏ Human Resource Department. . . . . Date _____
❏ Emergency exits. . . . . Date _____
❏ Introduced to coworkers . . . . Date _____
❏ Reviewed key documents/policy statements . . . . . . Date _____
❏ Telephone directory. . . . . Date _____
❏ Facility layout. . . . . Date _____
❏ Organization charts . . . . Date _____
❏ Department safety rules and equipment. . . . . Date _____
❏ EEO policy statement . . . . Date _____
❏ Sexual harassment policy statement. . . . . Date _____
❏ E-mail policy statement . . . . Date _____
❏ Complaint procedures . . . . Date _____
❏ Training and development opportunities . . . . Date _____
❏ Performance expectations . . . . Date _____

Completed by: _____ Date _____

Disciplinary Form

Employee Name _____ Date _____
Job Title _____
Date of Hire _____ Supervisor _____

Discipline Taken:
❑ Written Warning ❑ Reprimand ❑ Suspension ❑ Discharge
❑ Other (Explain):

_____

_____

Reason (Attach additional sheet, if necessary):

_____

_____

_____

Rule or Policy Violated:

_____

Prior Disciplinary Record:

_____

_____

_____

Signature of Supervisor _____ Date _____
Signature of Human Resource Manager _____ Date _____
Signature of Employee* _____ Date _____

*BY SIGNING THIS DISCIPLINARY FORM, THE EMPLOYEE MERELY
ACKNOWLEDGES THAT HE OR SHE HAS READ IT. SIGNING DOES NOT
IMPLY AGREEMENT WITH ITS CONTENTS.
Summary of Disciplinary Conference (to be completed by supervisor):

_____

_____

Meeting Planner

TIME	SUBJECT	PERSONS ATTENDING	URGENT
6–6:30			
6:30–7			
7–7:30			
7:30–8			
8–8:30			
8:30–9			
9–9:30			
9:30–10			
10–10:30			
10:30–11			
11–11:30			
11:30–12			
12–12:30			
12:30–1			
1–1:30			
1:30–2			
2–2:30			
2:30–3			
3–3:30			
3:30–4			
4–4:30			
4:30–5			
5–5:30			
5:30–6			
6–6:30			
6:30–7			
7–7:30			
7:30–8			
8–8:30			
8:30–9			
9–9:30			
9:30–10			
10–10:30			

Project Planner

Name: _____
Department: _____
For week of: _____

PROJECT NAME	PROJECT NUMBER	MON.	TUES.	WED.	THUR.	FRI.	TOTAL HOURS

Staffing Calendar

Date from: _____

Date to: _____

EMPLOYEE	MONDAY	TUESDAY	WEDNESDAY	THURSDAY	FRIDAY	SATURDAY	SUNDAY

Weekly Organizer

TIME	MONDAY	TUESDAY	WEDNESDAY	THURSDAY	FRIDAY	SATURDAY	SUNDAY
6:00							
:30							
7:00							
:30							
8:00							
:30							
9:00							
:30							
10:00							
:30							
11:00							
:30							
12:00							
:30							
1:00							
:30							
2:00							
:30							
3:00							
:30							
4:00							
:30							
5:00							
:30							
6:00							
:30							
7:00							
:30							
8:00							
:30							
9:00							
:30							
10:00							
:30							
11:00							

Authorization to Release Information

From: _____

_____

_____

To: _____

_____

_____

I have applied for a position with: _____

I have been requested to provide information for their use in reviewing my background and qualifications. Therefore, I authorize the investigation of my past and present works, character, education, military and employment qualifications.

The release in any manner of all information by you is authorized whether such information is of record or not, and I do hereby release all persons, agencies, firms, companies, etc., from any damages resulting from providing such information.

This authorization is valid for 90 days from the date of my signature below. Please keep this copy of my release request for your files. Thank you for your cooperation.

Signature: _____ Date: _____

Witness: _____ Date: _____

Medical information is often protected by state laws and civil codes. Consult your attorney if you wish to seek this information.

Employee Separation Notice

Date: _____

Name: _____

Check Reason	Remarks:
❏ Lack of Work	_____
❏ Sick	_____
❏ Absence	_____
❏ Injury	_____
❏ Death	_____
❏ Retired	_____
❏ Quit	_____
❏ Other	_____
_____	_____
_____	_____
_____	_____

Department: _____

Signature of Supervisor: _____

Official Signature: _____

Employee Time Sheet

From _____ To: _____
Name: _____
Number: _____
Department: _____

| DATE | MORNING | | AFTERNOON | | OFFICE USE ONLY | |
	IN	OUT	IN	OUT	REGULAR HRS	OVERTIME HRS

Signature: _____

Employee Warning Notice

❏ 1st notice   ❏ 2nd notice

Date: _____

Name: _____

Department: _____

Violation	Remarks:
❏ Late Arrival ❏ Early Departure ❏ Absent ❏ Attitude ❏ Safety Violation ❏ Defective Work ❏ Other _____ _____ _____	_____ _____ _____ _____ _____ _____ _____ _____ _____ _____ _____

Signature of Supervisor: _____

Official Signature: _____

Employee Application

Date of application: _____

Position(s) applied for: _____

How did you hear
about this position?
 ❏ Advertisement ❏ Friend ❏ Relative ❏ Walk-in
 ❏ Employment agency ❏ Other_____

Name: _____
    Last   First   Middle

Address: _____
    Number   Street   Apt no.

_____
    City   State   Zip

Telephone: _____

Social Security No: _____

Please check respone

If employed and under 18, can you furnish a work permit?. . . . . ❏ Yes ❏ No

Have you ever applied for work here before? . . . . ❏ Yes ❏ No

If "Yes," give date _____

Have you ever been employed here before? . . . . ❏ Yes ❏ No

If "Yes," give date _____

Are you employed now?. . . . . ❏ Yes ❏ No

May we contact your present employer?. . . . . ❏ Yes ❏ No

Are you prevented from lawfully becoming employed in
this country because of Visa or Immigration Status? . . . . ❏ Yes ❏ No
(Proof of citizenship or immigration status will be required upon employment.)

On what date will you be able to work? _____

Please check the category that best . . . . ❏ Full-time ❏ Part-time
summarizes your available hours . . . . ❏ Shift work ❏ Temporary

Can you travel if the job requires it?. . . . . ❏ Yes ❏ No

Are you on a lay-off and subject to recall? . . . . ❏ Yes ❏ No

Have you ever been convicted of a felony within the last five years? . . . . . ❏ Yes ❏ No

If "Yes," please explain _____

_____

Are you a veteran of the U.S. Military?. . . . . ❏ Yes ❏ No

If "Yes," specify branch _____

Was your discharge other than honorable? . . . . ❏ Yes ❏ No

If "Yes," please explain _____

	HIGH SCHOOL	COLLEGE/UNIVERSITY	GRADUATE/PROFESSIONAL
School name, location			
Years Completed/Degree			
Diploma/Degree			
Describe course of study			
Outline specialized training, apprenticeships, internships, skills, and extracurricular activities			

Honors Received: State any additional information you feel may be helpful to us in considering your application. If necessary, please use a separate sheet of paper.

_____

_____

List professional, trade, business, or civic activities and offices held. (You may exclude memberships that would reveal sex, race, religion, national origin, age, ancestry, or handicap or other protected status.)

_____

_____

Please list the name, address, and daytime telephone number of three references who are not related to you and are not previous employers.

_____

_____

Briefly summarize special skills and qualifications you have acquired from your employment or other experience.

_____

_____

Do you speak a foreign language? If so, note below; please list your ability to read and write in that language.

_____

_____

Employment History

Please give an accurate, complete employment record, filling out all sections. Start with your present or last job. Include military service assignments and volunteer activities. You may exclude organization names that may disclose your race, religion, color, national origin, gender, handicap, or other protected status.

Company name and mailing address		Reason for Leaving	
Phone	Job Title	Employment Dates From: To:	
Work performed		Hourly Rate/Salary Starting: Final:	
		Supervisor	
Company name and mailing address		Reason for Leaving	
Phone	Job Title	Employment Dates From: To:	
Work performed		Hourly Rate/Salary Starting: Final:	
		Supervisor	
Company name and mailing address		Reason for Leaving	
Phone	Job Title	Employment Dates From: To:	
Work performed		Hourly Rate/Salary Starting: Final:	
		Supervisor	

If you need additional space, please continue on a separate sheet of paper.

The information provided in this Employment Application is true, correct, and complete. If employed, any misstatement or omission of fact on this application may result in my dismissal.

I authorize you to engage a consumer reporting agency to investigate my credit and personal history. If a report is obtained you must provide, at my request, the name and address of the agency so I may obtain from them the nature and substance of the report.

I understand that an offer of employment does not create a contractual obligation upon the employer to continue to employ me in the future.

Date	Signature

Personnel Record

Name: _____   Employee # _____

Address: _____

City: _____   State/Zip _____

Phone: _____

Dates of Employment

From: _____   To: _____

Date(s) entered in file:

❏ Application ....   _____

❏ Resume ....   _____

❏ References ....   _____

Required Tax Forms:

_____

_____

_____

❏ Attendance Record ....   _____

❏ Wage Report ....   _____

❏ Advance Request ....   _____

❏ Absentee Report ....   _____

❏ Warning Notice ....   _____

Pre-Employment Reference Check Letter

Applicant: _____ Position: _____

Company contacted: _____ Phone: _____

Name of company representative: _____

Title of company representative: _____

Dates of employment: _____

Salary information:

      Regular pay: _____   Overtime pay: _____

      Bonus: _____   Shift differential: _____

Date of last wage increase: _____

What was your relationship with the applicant? _____

_____

What were the applicant's job title and duties? _____

_____

_____

_____

How long did you supervise this employee? _____

How would you compare this employee to others doing similar work and responsibilities?

_____

_____

   Strong points: _____

_____

_____

_____

Areas for improvement: _____

_____

_____

_____

How would you rate this applicant's ability on a scale of 1 to 5 (5 being the highest) regarding the following:

Attention to detail: _____   Comment: _____

Learn: _____   Comment: _____

Follow directions: _____   Comment: _____

Accept responsibility: _____   Comment: _____

Follow through _____   Comment: _____

Initiate: _____   Comment: _____

Quarterly Payroll Record/Deductions

Quarter number   ❑ 1   Employee name: _____
               ❑ 2   Employee number: _____
               ❑ 3
               ❑ 4

| | DEDUCTIONS | | | | | | | NET PAY | CHECK NUMBER |
| SOCIAL SECURITY | WITHOLDING TAXES | | | INSURANCE | | | | | |
	FEDERAL	STATE	LOCAL						
$	$	$	$	$	$	$	$	$	

Appendix D

Glossary

achievement test: A selection tool used to measure current knowledge or skills.

adverse impact: A method of proving discrimination reflecting an applicant rejection rate for a protected class that is higher than the rate for the unprotected class.

affirmative action: A remedy for past discrimination that increases the numbers of protected classes in the organization's work force.

Americans with Disabilities Act (ADA): Federal legislation making it illegal to discriminate against people with disabilities in employment decisions.

apprenticeship: An on-the-job training technique used in the skilled trades to allow an inexperienced employee to learn the craft from a skilled worker.

aptitude test: A selection tool used to measure the applicant's capacity to learn new skills.

Behaviorally Anchored Rating Scale (BARS): A performance appraisal system that uses scales anchored by descriptions of critical incidents to measure behaviors of employees on the job.

Bona Fide Occupational Qualification (BFOQ): A legal exception to discrimination whereby the employer may specify hiring based on gender, age, religion, sex, or national origin.

broadbanding: A compensation system that collapses several salary grades into a few broader categories.

cognitive ability test: A selection test used to measure mental skills.

comparable worth: The equality of jobs performed by women and men in terms of the value or worth to the company (though the jobs are different).

compensable factors: Factors (such as skills or responsibilities) used in job evaluation to determine the relative worth of jobs to the organization.

compensation: Rewards offered to employees in exchange for their contributions to the organization.

compressed work weeks: Alternative arrangements to complete forty hours of work in a week in less than the traditional five days.

contingent workers: Temporary workers who help the organization even out the cyclical nature of business.

core competencies: Broad knowledge sets required for successful performance that span the entire organization and differentiate it from other organizations.

critical incident: Incidents of exceptionally good or exceptionally poor performance recorded for use in job evaluation.

discipline: Organizational programs used to shape employee performance by administering punishment for inappropriate behaviors.

disparate treatment: Intentional discrimination basing employment decisions on race, color, religion, national origin, age, or disability.

distress: Negative or harmful stress.

diversity: The differences reflected in the members of the work force.

downsizing: A turnaround strategy implemented to reduce costs in the organization usually through eliminating positions.

due process: The employee's right to present his or her side during disciplinary actions.

e-commerce: Conducting business over the Internet.

elder care: Care provided to elderly family members of an employee.

employee assistance programs (EAPs): Services provided to employees to counsel and advise for problems interfering with work performance.

employee involvement groups: Groups of employees who meet to resolve specific problems in the organization.

employee leasing: Hiring employees back through leasing companies to perform their original function.

employment-at-will: The right of an employer and an employee to terminate the employment relationship without reason.

empowerment: Delegating power throughout the organization to encourage employees to make decisions concerning their own work.

Equal Employment Opportunity: The treatment of employees in a fair and impartial way in all aspects of employment.

equity theory: A social comparison motivation theory in which people compare the ratio of their inputs to outputs to the ratio of another person's inputs to outputs.

ergonomics: The study of the design of equipment in the workplace. Equipment is fit to people to reduce the possibility of injuries.

ethics: Individual beliefs concerning right and wrong.

eustress: Positive stress that propels people to higher levels of performance.

expatriate managers: Managers in multinational corporations sent on international assignments from their home country.

expectancy theory: Motivation theory based on the value of the reward being offered, the belief that the person can work at that level, and that the reward will indeed be given if the level of performance is delivered.

factor comparison system: A system of job evaluation that compares jobs factor by factor.

fair employment practices (FEPs): Equal employment opportunity laws on the state and local level.

flexible benefits plan: Cafeteria-type benefits plans that allow employees to select from a list of benefits those that best meet their needs.

flextime: Flexible working hours that enable employees to choose their working hours within core designated hours.

forced distribution: Performance appraisal method in which raters must place a specific percentage of employees into predetermined categories.

four-fifths rule: The test to determine adverse impact in discrimination cases.

functional job analysis: A system of job analysis that examines jobs based on data, people, and things.

glass ceiling: The invisible barrier that prevents women and minorities from moving into the topmost levels of management in some organizations.

globalization: The trend toward more international markets.

graphic rating scale: A method of performance appraisal that uses a scale to rate employees across a variety of characteristics.

groupthink: An agreement in a group situation not to disagree.

hierarchy of needs: Motivation theory developed by Abraham Maslow to explain the needs that drive people's behavior.

hostile environment: Harassment that results from the creation of an offensive work environment.

human relations skills: Interpersonal skills.

human resource management: The set of activities focused on the effective management and development of the organization's work force.

human resource planning (HRP): The process of identifying the future staffing needs of the organization.

human resources: The people of the organization.

Human Resources Information System (HRIS): A computer system designed to aid in the administration and decision-making process of human resource management.

integrity tests: Paper and pencil tests to measure honesty in the selection process.

job analysis: The process of systematically gathering information concerning the tasks and responsibilities of a job.

job characteristics model: An approach to job design that results in increased performance levels and greater worker motivation.

job description: A document that itemizes the tasks and responsibilities of a job.

job design: A method of structuring jobs to improve worker satisfaction and organizational performance.

job enlargement: A job design technique that expands a job by adding tasks that are on the same responsibility level.

job enrichment: A job design technique that adds tasks on a higher responsibility level to increase job satisfaction.

job evaluation: A process of systematically determining the worth of jobs in an organization.

job posting: A method of internal recruiting to notify employees of an opening within an organization.

job ranking: A job evaluation technique that determines the relative worth of jobs by simplistic rank ordering.

job specification: A document generated in the job analysis process that lists the qualification of employees to effectively perform the job.

KSA: Knowledge, skills, and abilities.

law of effect: Thorndike's law of reinforcement proposing that those behaviors that are met with a positive consequence are more likely to be repeated.

learning organization: An organization that constantly seeks new information and then uses that information to make internal changes.

leniency error: A performance appraisal error that occurs when raters rank everyone leniently.

Markov analysis: A technique used in human resource planning to track the movement of people through jobs in the organization.

material safety data sheets (MSDSs): Documents listing vital information concerning hazardous materials.

GLOSSARY

needs analysis: The assessment of an organization's training needs to ensure that budgets are spent in the most effective way.

nondirective interview: An unstructured interview in which the applicant is given freedom to determine the direction of the interview.

Occupational Safety and Health Act of 1970: Federal legislation requiring employers to ensure that the workplace is safe and healthy for the work force.

on-the-job training: Training provided in a hands-on approach.

orientation: The socialization process that is used to acquaint employees with the organization.

outplacement: Services offered to help employees who have been terminated find new employment.

outsourcing: Contracting with outside firms to perform nonessential functions for the organization.

part-time employees: Those employees who work fewer than forty hours a week.

pay equity: The perception of employees that their compensation is equal to the worth of their work.

pay secrecy: The extent to which an organization keeps individual pay rates a secret.

peer appraisal: Performance appraisals performed by coworkers.

performance appraisal: The formal evaluation of an employee's work on the job.

point system: A quantitative job evaluation system that uses specific elements of jobs to rate their worth to the organization.

progressive discipline: The method of discipline that uses a system of progressively more serious punishments for violations.

protected classes: Women, people with disabilities, minority races, and older people in the work force.

punishment: Unpleasant consequences resulting from specific behaviors.

quid pro quo harassment: Harassment that occurs with an exchange of sexual favors for employment decisions.

realistic job preview (RJP): A realistic portrayal of a job that includes both its negative and positive aspects.

reasonable accommodation: Adjustments made in the workplace to accommodate people with disabilities.

recruitment: The process of attracting applicants to the organization.

re-engineering: The radical redesign of organizational processes.

referral: The recruitment process whereby individuals apply for positions through informal, word-of-mouth contact with current employees.

repetitive motion injuries: Inflammatory injuries that occur as a result of repeated motions performed on the job.

replacement charts: Listings for each organizational job of potential candidates to fill openings.

reverse discrimination: Showing preference to protected classes in hiring to the extent that unprotected classes feel discriminated against.

safety engineers: Experts in the study of workplace safety.

scientific management: The study of jobs to determine the one best way to perform the job in order to maximize efficiency.

selection: The process of identifying the best individuals to hire from a pool of applicants.

sexual harassment: Unwelcome sexual advances in the workplace.

skill-based pay: Pay based on the skills, knowledge, and abilities acquired by an employee.

skills inventories: Skills banks used to track the knowledge, skills, and abilities of employees.

social security: A benefit required by federal legislation to provide income to retired workers.

stress: The emotional and physical wear and tear of life.

structured interview: An interview conducted with job applicants using prepared questions.

succession planning: The process of identifying and tracking potential management candidates.

telecommuting: The use of computer technology to work from home or satellite offices via electronic links to the office.

temporary employees: Workers who are employed for specific periods and who are not permanent employees of the firm.

Title VII of the Civil Rights Act: Federal legislation that prohibits discrimination in all employment decisions based on race, religion, color, sex, or national origin.

transfer of training: The application of training material to job performance.

trend analysis: A quantitative forecasting technique used to identify the demand for labor.

unemployment insurance: A required benefit that provides income to employees who are out of work.

vestible training: Simulation training that mirrors actual job conditions.

virtual team: A team that works together from different geographic locations using electronic links.

wellness programs: Organizational programs that emphasize keeping workers healthy.

workers' compensation insurance: Insurance payments made to employees who suffer illnesses or injuries on the job.

yield ratio: A calculation of the percentage of job candidates from a specific recruitment source who make it to the next stage of the selection process.

OTHER TITLES IN THE STREETWISE® SERIES:

Streetwise® Achieving Wealth Through Franchising

Streetwise® Business Letters

Streetwise® Business Valuation

Streetwise® Complete Business Plan

Streetwise® Complete Business Plan with Software

Streetwise® Complete Publicity Plans

Streetwise® Crash Course MBA

Streetwise® Customer-Focused Selling

Streetwise® Do-It-Yourself Advertising

Streetwise® Finance & Accounting

Streetwise® Financing the Small Business

Streetwise® Human Resources Management

Streetwise® Independent Consulting

Streetwise® Landlording & Property Management

Streetwise® Low-Cost Marketing

Streetwise® Low-Cost Web Site Promotion

Streetwise® Managing a Nonprofit

Streetwise® Managing People

Streetwise® Marketing Plan

Streetwise® Maximize Web Site Traffic

Streetwise® Motivating and Rewarding Employees

Streetwise® Project Management

Streetwise® Restaurant Management

Streetwise® Retirement Planning

Streetwise® Sales Letters with CD-ROM

Streetwise® Selling Your Business

Streetwise® Small Business Start-Up

Streetwise® Start Your Own Business Workbook

Streetwise® Structuring Your Business

Streetwise® Time Management